THE TRIUMPH OF EVIL

unbound

With special thanks to Gerry Ford

THE TRIUMPH OF EVIL

Genocide in Rwanda and the Fight for Justice

Charles Petrie

with Spike Zephaniah Stephenson

unbound

First published in 2021

Unbound
TC Group, Level 1, Devonshire House, One Mayfair Place, London W1J 8AJ
www.unbound.com
All rights reserved

Text design by PDQ Digital Media Solutions Ltd.

A CIP record for this book is available from the British Library

ISBN 978-1-78352-928-5 (hardback)
ISBN 978-1-78352-929-2 (ebook)

Printed in Great Britain by CPI Group (UK)

1 3 5 7 9 8 6 4 2

'Well, my friend, they can't accuse us
of not having tried.'

Dedicated to the memory of my best friend
(and the only person who ever called me Chuck),
Gregory 'Gromo' Alex (1954–2013)

'All that is necessary for the triumph of evil is that good men do nothing.'

Edmund Burke, Irish political philosopher (1729–1797)

Essential Consideration

Many of those presumed to have participated in this brutal period of Rwanda's history have yet to account in front of a court of law for their alleged actions. Until they have done so, acts such as those contained in this book cannot be used to confirm guilt.

One of the key tenets of the justice system I was brought up with is that individuals are presumed innocent until proven guilty. But the doubts that are allowed to persist in cases such as the one described in this book are as unbearable for the victims as they are for any falsely accused individual. Thus, it has to be hoped that the case currently being prepared in French courts will be exhaustive and result in a definitive ruling.

The story of the UN's inaction, not only as regards pursuing the case as in honouring its obligation towards its own staff killed, is another matter altogether. There is little that still needs to be proven. Corrective action is all that is now demanded.[*]

---

[*]   As detailed in my letter to the current UN secretary-general dated 25 March 2019.

CONTENTS

Author's Note

Kamana Rumbashi steps out into the surprisingly mild April air. It is a beautiful evening, a perfect end to a night of celebration. He revels in his acquittal. True, it took time. As did his release from jail. But what a stunning triumph! He laughs aloud. To have had his indictment reversed – a first in the history of the International Criminal Court.

He smiles as he remembers the prosecutor's face. That moment in the packed courtroom when the prosecuting team was forced to acknowledge the inadequacy of their work, the looks of shock on their faces. Ah, the immense satisfaction that moment had brought.

It's almost uncanny, he reflects, his ability to emerge victorious from desperate legal battles. First there was the case in Kosovo accusing him of acts of genocide. Dismissed. Then he sued the UN for unlawful dismissal, and won. Better still, he netted double the initial compensation on appeal. Now, finally, this historic release from the ICC. Kamana's thin smile widens. Fortune truly does favour the bold.

He breathes in the sweet scent of a promising spring. The streets of Paris are empty. Only murmurs and occasional peals of laughter from the café behind him disturb the peaceful night. Somewhat unsteadily, he strolls down the path leading to Chateau d'Eau, the nearest metro station. It is the very early hours of a new day. With each step he feels the thrill of newfound freedom.

It is a moonless night and the dim glow of the street lamps guides him from one illuminated patch to the next. As he approaches the intersection with the Boulevard de Strasbourg, he senses rather than hears behind him the movement of someone in a hurry. He turns. A figure approaches rapidly and draws a long object from the pocket of a coat. With a flick of a wrist, the object doubles in length, its sharp metallic tip catching a spark of light from the street lamp. The person accelerates, comes near and with a quick jerk of the head looks skyward. Puzzled, Kamana does the same. A strange pressure slides across his throat. Something warm pulses out, and Kamana collapses into darkness.

The killer turns and walks on, not looking back, towards the Commissariat de Police of the 10ème arrondissement. The light of the police station silhouettes the blood-spattered figure as it mounts the steps and opens the door. Inside, still clutching the barber's razor, the killer stops and stands immobile as the duty officer stares in shock.

*

I am Charles Petrie. After having tried for so long and in so many different ways to bring Kamana Rumbashi,* a UN colleague, to account for his actions – the alleged involvement in the murder of thirty-two men, women and children – this is how I sometimes envisaged an ending to the story. But, of course, in reality, Kamana doesn't die. The truth is that he lives comfortably somewhere in France. And I have yet to come to terms with this profound injustice.

*   Not his real name.

What follows has taken me years to write. The story itself was excruciatingly painful to live through, and it is difficult still to recount. At points along the way I sank into complete despair, even contemplated checking out. I just couldn't, and still can't, accept that the United Nations, an institution charged to act as the guarantor of the Convention on the Prevention and Punishment of the Crime of Genocide,* would be unwilling to investigate one of its own who is alleged to have committed this crime. Worse still, that it would refuse to seek justice for those of its own – Florence Ngirumpatse and other UN colleagues – whom Kamana Rumbashi is said to have been involved in killing.

How could an institution created to serve a higher ideal be effective if it did not itself uphold, or defend, its basic values? I couldn't fathom what it was that made the institution so blind to the consequences and significance of its inaction. I questioned myself. Had I not done enough to explain the situation clearly? Why was there even a need to do so? Wasn't the case itself sufficiently self-explanatory?

Of course, I realize that a failure of this kind and on this scale is not unique to the United Nations. This tale could just as easily have been set in the Vatican, as it tried to hide the emerging scandal of paedophile priests, or in a Bush administration trying to deny the evidence of torture

---

* The Convention on the Prevention and Punishment of the Crime of Genocide was unanimously adopted by the United Nations General Assembly on 9 December 1948 (GA Resolution 260). It came about as a result of the unrelenting efforts of Raphael Lemkin, a lawyer of Polish-Jewish descent. Genocide is defined as acts with the intent to destroy, in whole or in part, a national, ethnical, racial or religious group. Such acts include, (i) killing members of the group; (ii) causing serious bodily or mental harm to members of the group; (iii) deliberately inflicting on the group conditions of life calculated to bring about its physical destruction in whole or in part; (iv) imposing measures intended to prevent births within the group; and (v) forcibly transferring children of the group to another group. Most importantly, the Convention establishes the obligation on all 'State Parties' to take measures to prevent and to punish the crime of genocide. The obligation is binding on all States, whether or not they have ratified the Genocide Convention.

in Abu Ghraib. This is a story about systems and bureaucracies failing those whom they have been set up to serve. It is about individuals in these organizations abrogating their responsibility to uphold the very tenets of the institution.

But ultimately this is a story about injustice and the insidious way in which evil triumphs. Time allows evil to triumph, by diminishing the significance of acts to the point where they seem almost banal. When individuals are eventually confronted by evil, it is often cloaked in such a mantle of ordinariness or apparent irrelevance that, instead of acting, they retreat into the comfort of doing nothing.

Confronting the UN's refusal to address this injustice initially seemed to be an obvious course of action, but, with the repeated failures to get the institution to act, it turned into an obsession that has defined much of my life. Yet through it all, I never lost my admiration for, and my total commitment to, the values and principles that the UN embodies. Today, more than ever, an institution created to confront the scourge of war and to serve the peoples of the world has a vitally important role to play. Lest we forget, it is an institution born from the horrors of two world wars, created by an inspired group of world leaders who at the time understood that unchecked nationalistic self-interest could not guarantee long-term peace.

True, it is an institution that can be no more effective than its membership of 193 countries allows it to be. *How many times have I heard this refrain – almost an excuse.* But it is also an institution that has not always been served well by those entrusted with the responsibility to lead it. It is an institution peopled by individuals who believe in its principles, and who strive to promote and uphold them, but with leaders who tend to put politics above principles, and in an organizational culture too often defined by entitlement, intimidation and even fear.

You may well wonder why I feel compelled to reiterate the details of a period of history so appalling, of a project in which I so conspicuously fail, and why I continue to do so at a time when recounting them might only serve the interests of those intent on dismantling such an institution. An institution that, however flawed, is still vitally needed. Many times, I have asked myself the same question. What's the point of telling this story? Who cares any more? A quarter of a century has passed and, except for the surviving members of the victims' families, who continue to live daily with the traumatic absence of loved ones, the crimes committed have become part of history. A history of a country that is determined to move on. And the UN's inaction? These events? Now nothing more than a blip on the radar of an institution's failures.

And then I remembered Father Vjeko Curic's advice given to me in June 1994, when it seemed as if the killings in Rwanda would never stop. Father Vjeko was a man of extraordinary principle, who saved thousands of his parishioners during the atrocities. I was exhausted. Those days were so unnaturally long. Impressed by the dogged determination of Father Vjeko, I asked what kept him going. This is what he said:

'If you believe in something, in something that you hold to be profoundly true, and yet feel you are failing in your purpose, don't give up! You never know – you could be the person who holds the torch in the middle of the darkness that will guide someone else to achieve what you wanted to accomplish.'

This story wishes to be one such guiding light in a world that I have discovered to be in places profoundly dark.

Florence Ngirumpatse

PART ONE

BEGINNINGS

Who am I? I was born into a comfortable life. My father was a British diplomat committed to the European project, a position possibly nurtured by my mother, a French art restorer of mixed European lineage. As a result, I grew up feeling neither particularly British nor French. I guess I was what one would call a global kid, one without any clear attachments to a single country.

I have always been subject to intense passions, and my first, from the moment at age nine when I discovered his writings, was Saint Francis of Assisi. I was convinced that my calling was to be a Franciscan missionary. So, while others of my age were struggling to deal with the mental and physical confusion of their early adolescence, I floated over those same years living moments of elation and rapture that accompanied the dream of what I was convinced would be my future.

Midway through my adolescence, when visiting the Abbaye des Hommes in Caen with my mother, I approached a young priest and asked him to guide me on the path to priesthood. We talked and corresponded for almost two years. Finally, one day, it was agreed that I would be interviewed by the former rector of a Franciscan seminary, an interview that was expected to launch me onto the path of acceptance into that order.

To my utter dismay, I was rejected. The elderly priest, with little patience for immature adolescents, asked one simple question: Why had I come? Unable to express the fervour that had led me to this moment, I panicked. My mind went completely blank. I felt abandoned. And whatever chance there could have been was lost.

From that moment I began a long and frustrating search for a commitment that would give meaning to my life. I felt bereft. All my certitudes were gone. I tried to reignite the passion that I had been unable to draw on during that fateful interview, travelling to Jerusalem to witness Easter, and undertaking a lone pilgrimage to Lourdes, tracing part of the route to Santiago de Compostela, having late night discussions with priests in old abbeys along the way. I worked alongside religious groups who aimed to assist juvenile delinquents in the suburbs of Paris. All to no avail.

My search for meaning continued at university, and after. Even more unsure than my peers of who I was or what I wanted, I allowed myself to be distracted. I entered university when I was sixteen, and it took me almost six years to finish my undergraduate studies in international relations and art history. In between those years, I undertook military service as an officer in a French infantry regiment. I went off to India for six months to teach English and maths in a leper colony. On graduation, I took up a job with an investment bank in Paris, preparing credit arrangements to finance government-subsidized contracts to poorer countries in Africa. It wasn't particularly exciting work, but it had the merit of involving me in a continent that already then had captured my imagination. The part of the job I really liked was the commute. My 500 cc trail bike with its front fender well above the wheel, and its gas tank painted with the logo of the Paris–Dakar Rally, represented escape from drudgery. It represented adventure. If I wanted, I told myself, I could ride on it to the ends of the earth.

It was in this phase of my life that I met France, a woman whose traditional upbringing echoed my own. After a period of time, we married. My naïve hope was that making the commitment would give purpose to my life. The fact that it didn't made me feel even more adrift.*

I stuck it out in the bank for three years in order to get into a good business school, INSEAD. I thought that doing so would launch me

---

* As regards my personal trajectory, and specifically the part involving my ex-wife and our three sons, I have attempted to be as respectful for the feelings of those I have hurt as possible. Actions of mine that have caused anguish and pain have been purposefully truncated to ensure that they do not detract from the core of the story, i.e. Rumbashi's alleged involvement in killings and the UN's inaction. Thus, for those I love and have hurt, who will be seeking answers to questions they have, I fear they will not find them in the pages that follow.

professionally, and that I would be able to provide a comfortable life for my wife and children, but I found the subject-matters taught there very uninspiring. A friend said to me, 'You don't go to business school to be inspired, Charles, you go to learn to make money.' I understood the point he was making, but the longing to commit myself to something more meaningful didn't go away.

I vividly remember a morning when bright sunlight struck through the window of the bathroom. I was shaving before heading off to INSEAD for a statistics exam for which I had done little to prepare. Getting married and attending a top business school was meant to have set me up for life, I thought. I should feel satisfied – maybe not overjoyed, given my lack of preparation for the test, but at least content. But I wasn't. Life had no flavour, and it wasn't anybody's fault but my own.

All of a sudden, I was struck by a solution – the only solution, it seemed to me. At the age of forty-two I would commit suicide. Why forty-two? I don't know. At that time, I hadn't read *The Hitchhiker's Guide to the Galaxy*. But forty-two it was, and this decision brought relief. I only needed to hang on in there for eighteen more years and it would all be over.

I finished shaving. In much better spirits, I dashed off to take an exam that I masterfully failed.

*

On graduating from INSEAD, my yearning for travel and adventure, and my deep wish to be part of something meaningful, drove me to seek work with a humanitarian organization in Africa. I contacted a number of aid organizations, but my business school credentials held no sway with the personnel officers of the NGOs. Instead I found work in a management-consulting firm based in London offering support to African countries struggling to reform their civil service. The work allowed me to travel to Africa, but it still gave me no real sense of purpose. I had almost given up on the aid world when fate intervened and, almost by accident, I acquired my first United Nations posting.

It was 1989. I was in Khartoum, seconded to the Ministry of Finance to work on a less-than-effective World Bank project, when General al-Bashir overthrew the elected government, and the World Bank closed its programme down. I had developed a constructive and pleasant working relationship with my Sudanese colleagues in the Ministry of Finance, and was surprised by how unaffected they were by the sudden political change. One of my colleagues mentioned that the 'democratic' government the military had overthrown had not necessarily been that great for the people. Rather, it had allowed corruption and political in-fighting to paralyze the country. I wanted to stay on to see how much of a fundamental change the coup d'etat would provoke, so I spoke to the head of the International Monetary Fund (IMF) in Khartoum. He had nothing to offer me, but he mentioned me to the UN Representative in Sudan who, fortuitously, needed a deputy leader for the newly established UN Emergency Unit. After some financial juggling in which the French Embassy was involved, I was offered the position.

Though the UN Emergency Unit was responsible for providing support to UN relief operations throughout the country, the core of its activity was actually focused on government-controlled garrison towns in southern Sudan. The Khartoum authorities held a few isolated pockets in the south, while different factions of the Sudan People's Liberation Army (SPLA) controlled the rest.*

---

*   The humanitarian needs in the rebel-held portions of the country were being served by a UN-led operation called Lifeline Sudan based in Lokichokio, in northern Kenya.

Six months after my appointment, the first Gulf War began. Many of the UN international staff were evacuated back to their home countries. The Emergency Unit on the other hand was considered essential, and all the staff were asked to stay.

For those of us who remained in Khartoum, the impact of the Gulf War was limited to hostile gestures directed at us as we drove through the city. But the unit chief, my immediate boss, was a US national who was on his Christmas break when the war started. It was considered prudent for him to extend his absence, and by the time he was able to return, he had been re-assigned to New York. Per Janvid, who was the UN Representative in Sudan, then asked me to take on the post of Chief of the UN Emergency Unit.

Thus, at the age of thirty-one I found myself in the midst of a crisis with overall responsibility for support of the UN presence in eight besieged government-held towns in southern Sudan and the management of two planes. I was also charged with obtaining Sudanese government authorization for the relief flights from Kenya into the rebel-controlled south.

My life all of a sudden had purpose. My blue UN laissez-passer represented a direct link with an organization born out of massive tragedy, and an obligation to play a part in ending human suffering.

PART TWO

SUDAN AND SOMALIA

The core of this story is Rwanda, the horrific events of 1994, and my battles with the UN afterwards. I have hesitated to include my prior experiences with the United Nations in Sudan and Somalia, fearing that it would confuse the core narrative. But my experiences there do provide essential context for an understanding of the workings of the UN bureaucracy, and will to some extent help to explain the almost obsessive nature of my 'quest for justice' following the horrors of Rwanda.

Most importantly, Sudan presents the 'before', as much as Somalia does the 'after', of the UN's approach to addressing human tragedy. In the Sudan a national government could deny any of its violations and get away with it. The fall of the Berlin Wall, the symbolic end to the Cold War, separates the two periods. The protection that the paralysis of the East–West divide offered was to be no more, and a new world order based on respect for universal principles seemed achievable. Somalia was the first such attempt, and the international community failed. Rwanda paid the price of this failure. One cannot understand the international community's inaction in Rwanda without taking into account what happened in Somalia.

1

Sudan: *Embarking upon the Steep UN Learning Curve*

If I had to pinpoint the moment in time when my career with the UN really took off, it would be the morning of 22 December 1990. I was having a late leisurely breakfast, when I was suddenly summoned by Per Janvid, the UN representative, to accompany him on an unexpected trip outside Khartoum.

That is how I found myself sitting next to Colonel Osman Nuri, a senior officer from Sudan's state security, in the third car of a four-car convoy driving through the desert. In the car in front were seated Per Janvid and Sharaf Bannaga, the Sudanese minister of housing and urban planning. The minister was taking us to a desolate site one hour out of Khartoum – a place where more than one and a half million displaced southerners were destined to be dumped. The location was thought to be close enough for the international community to provide assistance, but far enough away to

9

make it difficult for the internally displaced to return to the capital. It was the government's rather drastic response to an anticipated threat.

Since 1984, because of fighting and famine in southern and western Sudan, almost two and a half million people, mostly Christians or animists, had moved to Khartoum. Fleeing violence and starvation, they had come to the capital to find work. A vast majority lived in squalid settlements scattered throughout the city or close to the garbage dumps on the margins. Khartoum was big enough to accommodate the numbers. Though the international aid community gave some relief, the southern operation was the priority, not the Khartoum displaced, who received the bulk of their support from local charity organizations. Many of the displaced people had jobs of sorts and access to some food and water. They were integrated and for a long time didn't really seem to represent a problem.

But everything changed in the very early hours of that morning of 22 December, when suddenly vast numbers of these impoverished people were uprooted and driven into the desert, their squalid settlements dismantled, the precarious lives they'd forged for themselves in Khartoum shattered. As our convoy drove out of the city, we passed through immense empty places that bore testimony to the thorough destruction of their homes.

When the convoy stopped, it stopped in the middle of nowhere. We were surrounded by an ocean of sand. Small clusters of impoverished people, with their worldly possessions dumped unceremoniously on the ground, dotted the vast expanse of nothingness. Sharaf Bannaga, the Sudanese minister, gestured with pride at the scene that lay before us. Here, he insisted, was the beginning of an ambitious urban renewal plan.

Per Janvid and I were appalled. What urban renewal plan? The area was completely desolate. Water to meet the needs of (in the first instance) fifty thousand people would have to be trucked in, at least until the distant day that boreholes to a depth of seventy metres could be dug. To Bannaga, this was a 'minor technicality' that he expected the United Nations to resolve. Hence the purpose of our visit.

In reality, rather than an urban plan, the project was nothing more than a strategy to pre-empt a political crisis. As soon as it took power, the military government of Omar al-Bashir had implemented drastic economic reforms. The Sudanese currency was devalued overnight. It was done once, and then again, and again, and again. The cost of the war in the south kept increasing, and the government printed more and more money to pay off its national debt. Inflation ran rampant. Food prices skyrocketed. The survival of the poor was threatened and their anger at the regime was growing. The government of Omar al-Bashir knew full well that the popular unrest in 1985 that had led to the fall of a former president had started in the squalid squatter camps of Khartoum. They were determined not to let the pattern be repeated.

On the drive back to Khartoum, I shared a car with Per Janvid. He was furious at this enforced movement of people into barren desert. It was totally inhuman, he said. It had to be stopped. He instructed me to draft a confidential cable to New York explaining what we had seen and requesting immediate support from the highest levels of the UN to get the government to suspend the project until the new areas were equipped with minimal conditions.

I prepared the draft, to which Per Janvid made a few amendments, and it was sent off that very evening. A few days later a call was scheduled to discuss our report with New York.

For me, this was an exhilarating moment. The UN was going to intervene in a desperate situation to prevent further suffering, and I was going to play a central part.

After some initial difficulty, contact was made with the Secretariat of the Under-Secretary-General for Political Questions, Regional Cooperation,

Decolonization and Trusteeship. The under-secretary-general had to be called out of a meeting. After preliminary exchanges, Per Janvid launched into an explanation of why it was imperative that the UN should pressure the Sudanese government to stop its action. But within a minute or two, he was abruptly cut off. New York had questions: what was the position of the US? Of various European countries? Of the European Commission? And so on. Per Janvid mouthed the questions to me, and lifted his hand, inviting a response. I didn't know.

I saw Per Janvid's confidence evaporate. *I don't know*, he responded. *It was complicated*, he agreed. Of course, he understood: if the UN were not going to pay to keep the internally displaced where they were, then we couldn't tell the government to stop its operations.

Per Janvid offered to call back once he had answers to the questions that had been raised. His offer was rejected. Send a cable instead, he was told. End of story.

I was devastated. In my enthusiasm, I had naïvely pinned everything on this one discussion. From it would flow a UN response that would make a crucial difference. From it would be unleashed the forces of good. But instead, the whole thing had just fizzled. There had been no interest from New York.

Ultimately, the failure of the UN to deal with the plight of the Khartoum displaced would turn out to be for me nothing more than part of a very steep learning curve, the first of many reality checks, and unfortunately there would be so many more.

*

The rain had stopped, but massive clouds still blackened the sky, as I emerged from a Sudanese Red Crescent briefing on a situation that could only be described as a screw-up. An incredible story: tens of thousands of people from the Nuba Mountains, mainly animists and Christians, fleeing into the hands of the Muslim Arabs of the north – supposedly seeking protection from SPLA attacks.

As I understood the situation, in late 1991 a faction of the SPLA had had temporary success with an offensive against government troops in southern Darfur. But when the better-equipped government forces started to push them back, and they lost ground, they encouraged the armed elements of the Nuba to open a second front. This proved to be disastrous for the Nuba people, who had inferior equipment and far less training. Their attacks on government positions provided an excuse for the government to declare a 'jihad' and launch its forces into the Nuba Mountains, whose people it had wanted to subjugate for decades.

The fighting caused massive displacement. Populations fled from the fighting to urban centres, which were under government control. They hoped for humanitarian assistance, but the local administrations couldn't cope with the numbers.

Expecting the mission to trigger international donor support, the government asked the UN Emergency Unit to undertake an assessment of the needs in southern Kordofan, the northernmost point of the Nuba Mountains, where large numbers of the displaced had gathered. I formed a small team and went to Kadugli.

It was quickly apparent that the displaced, who had been temporarily parked in makeshift buildings, had been provided with very little in terms of assistance. It was early evening when we walked through the camp, and some of the women were cooking. Peering into the pots, I saw only sorry mixtures of grass and water. A light grey haze from the fires hung over the courtyard. Two things struck me as we walked around. First, that everything was eerily quiet; even the children were silent. Second, that throughout the entire day, we had seen only women and children. 'Where are the men?' I asked our guide. The response – 'In the fields' – came swiftly and automatically. *During the rains?* I thought. *Highly unlikely.*

After spending the night in Kadugli, our team flew to the capital of the province in the north, El-Obeid, to meet the Governor of Kordofan, Lieutenant General al-Hussein. We went through the standard niceties, and then I got to the point. Why was it, I asked, that the temporary shelters housed large numbers of women and children, but no men? With a broad smile, the governor trotted out his surreal story. Insurgents were attacking the people of the Nuba Mountains, he said, and they had fled for protection into the welcoming arms of their Arab brothers. 'And the men?' I pressed again. The displaced were very proud people, he explained. The women insisted on repaying the kindness of their hosts by working in the houses of the families who had received them, and the men by volunteering to work in the large government-run agricultural schemes in south Kordofan.

I returned to Khartoum, shocked by the clear indications that large numbers of people were being forced into servitude. I set down what I had seen, heard and concluded in a lengthy report. Per Janvid was horrified by the implications and immediately sent my report to New York.

2

Sudan: *The Reality Check*

The report on the effective enslavement of the Nuba people proved to be timely. It coincided with pressure mounting within the UN to do something about the 'Khartoum Displaced', as they were now officially called. New York was now provoked into action, and the secretary-general dispatched a special envoy to Khartoum.

I guess I could have foreseen the failure of the mission from the very beginning. I presented the programme of government meetings arranged for the visit, explaining that the most significant were with the minister of relief and rehabilitation at the beginning of the mission and again at the very end. The head of state had consistently refused to meet any non-Muslim dignitaries, and the minister was, effectively, the highest official that the special envoy could hope for.

The special envoy appeared satisfied with these arrangements. This mission, he emphasized, was a very important one and that was why the UN secretary-general, Boutros Boutros-Ghali, had entrusted it to him. He then launched into an elaborate exposé of the intrigues and goings-on in New York. It puzzled me that he wasn't asking questions about the issues in the briefing, but I supposed that he was already fully in control of his files.

Things went downhill from the moment of the first meeting. Very astutely, the minister explained that, time permitting, he would try to arrange for the special envoy to be received by the head of state. The special envoy could barely contain his excitement at what he saw as a major bureaucratic coup. He assured the minister that the secretary-general himself would see this as an extraordinary sign of goodwill.

The minister then went on to address the issues that the envoy had raised. On the relocation of the populations from Khartoum, the minister offered to arrange a tour of the new sites. He was certain that the special envoy would be impressed by how much had been accomplished with minimum support, and with the government's commitment to cleaning up the city. People were being moved from unhealthy areas rife with criminality to clean areas with open spaces, fresh air and security. Of course, there were some people who were not happy. But that was always the case when a government with limited means attempted to implement a farsighted urban development plan. The situation would get better quickly, as they were in discussions with the World Bank to finance this plan.

The special envoy was caught off guard. He regarded World Bank funding as a clear sign of the international community's confidence in the government's plans. For my part, I had heard nothing of any such funding, and thought the minister was bluffing.

The minister then turned to the question of the Nuba Mountains. He said he was embarrassed, even confused, as he didn't know to what the special envoy was referring. The special envoy explained that he understood that large numbers of people were fleeing ongoing confrontations and being channelled to the north of Kordofan. The UN secretary-general had received a report that these were mostly women and children, and that the men were being kept in the south to work on government agricultural schemes. The minister professed astonishment. Who had told the special envoy this? This was the first time he had heard of it. Who had sent the secretary-general the report? Surely, if it had been true, the minister himself would have known.

Confused, the special envoy pointed to Per Janvid and said that the report came from him. Per Janvid, caught totally off guard, started to mutter a few words as he tried to collect his thoughts. The Sudanese minister, not giving him the time he needed to respond, quickly stated that it was clear that there had been disinformation. Everything was quiet in the Nuba Mountains. No movement of population, no fighting and, most certainly, no enforced work. He added that the Sudanese government had full confidence in Per Janvid. However, he felt that some UN personnel did not demonstrate the appropriate level of objectivity, and he hoped that the special envoy would deal with the matter.

*

A few days later, Per Janvid, the special envoy and I sat down together to prepare the final communiqué of the mission. Save for the meeting with the head of state, I had accompanied the special envoy to all of his encounters, and all had echoed the disappointing telephone conversation of many months before. Worse, perhaps, because this time I was seeing the most senior levels of the UN at work. But, however acute my discomfort, the special envoy was beaming with satisfaction. 'Am I really the only non-Muslim person to have been granted an audience with the head of state?'

he asked. Assured that it was so, he crowed with delight. How jealous people in New York would be at the news.

We then began work on the communiqué. The special envoy invited me to present the draft I had prepared. With significant apprehension, and already a sense of impending defeat, I began with the question of the Khartoum displaced. It was brushed aside. Since there was World Bank involvement, the special envoy insisted, there was little he could say about it. I reminded him that it wasn't at all clear that any such discussions were actually underway. 'All the more reason to say nothing,' he answered.

I then turned to the issue of the Nuba Mountains. 'And what was it that needed to be said?' he asked. Just what had been reported to him, I offered. The special envoy was annoyed. But nothing was happening, the head of state had assured him that everything was calm. In any case, he continued, the mission that I had led into the Nuba Mountains, and which was the basis for the report to New York, was not what the UN would call an in-depth investigation. I pointed out that the representatives of the various aid organizations working in the area had also provided details of recurrent atrocities; couldn't the special envoy just pass this information on? Compelling as these details were, the special envoy acknowledged, they came from non-UN sources. He couldn't take a position on something that the UN itself had not investigated fully.

It was at that the moment that I really triggered the special envoy's irritation. 'Surely,' I asked, 'the UN can't ignore a case of potential genocide?' It was a step too far. 'You have no right to use that word!' the special envoy answered back angrily. Genocide was a contentious term that carried explicit obligations. To date, the Genocide Convention had never been triggered. And I, as a UN official, had absolutely no right to invoke it. I was told that I was young, naïve and still had a lot to learn.

Shaken by the strength of the special envoy's response, I still found the courage to ask if he dismissed outright the possibility that something untoward was going on in the Nuba Mountains. 'All I know,' he replied, 'is that nothing can be done about it as long as a UN member state denies a situation, whatever it is. The issue of sovereignty is sacrosanct, which means there is nothing we can say or do.'

'And what about the new world order after the collapse of the Berlin Wall that you talked about on the first night of your mission? The new international commitment to enforce universal principles and the rule of law?' I asked in complete despair. The response I got was that the only places where the new world order would be tested were the two failed states of Somalia and the former Yugoslavia, states without functioning sovereign governments.

Wishing to put an end to the discussion, the special envoy instructed me to focus the communiqué on what he had done during the visit: 'Say where I went and whom I saw. Mention that I raised a variety of humanitarian concerns, but above all, highlight the fact that I was granted an entirely exceptional audience with the head of state.'

The next morning, at Khartoum airport, when the special envoy thanked me for the hard work the team had put into the visit, I asked if I could be sent to Somalia. It was a spontaneous request that came out of a fretful night trying to come to terms with the failure of the special envoy's mission. The request took him by surprise. But after a short reflection he admitted that the mission there needed people.

3

Somalia: *Setting the Stage for Inaction in Rwanda*

That is how, in early September 1992, I found myself in Somalia. The Mogadishu I flew into was a city of noises: the persistent sound of generators, the arming of automatics, the click of safeties off, individual shots or those rapidly repeated, and then the sharp clack of unspent chambered rounds being ejected before the click of the safeties back on. It was only later that the thwacking of helicopter rotor-blades came to define the madness that was Somalia – a madness that I was immersed in for more than eighteen months.

When I arrived, the civil war was well into its second year. Somaliland in the north had already decided to go its own way. The centre of the country, anchored around Galkayo, was thinking of doing likewise. It was only in the south that two principal contenders were fighting it out to fill the vacuum left by the ousting of former dictator Siad Barre.

Mayor Ali Mahdi and General Mohamed Farah Aideed were the nominal representatives of two of the noble clans, the Darod and the Hawiye. Between them, they were in the process of destroying southern Somalia. Lesser warlords, such as Omar Jesse and Morgan, took advantage of the chaos to strip bare whatever part of the country they could. Digging up pipes and ripping out the copper wires from telephone lines to sell as scrap metal was the norm. The Somali state was in meltdown.

On arriving in Mogadishu, I joined a small UN presence that had been set up in support of the new UN envoy, Ambassador Mohamed Sahnoun, the former Algerian minister of foreign affairs. In fact, I arrived on the same day as five hundred Pakistani soldiers, who were to constitute the military force of a mission that went under the acronym UNOSOM (United Nations Operation Somalia). My arrival also coincided with General Aideed's capture of the key town of Baidoa from the forces of Ali Mahdi. Aideed had now gained the upper hand throughout most of southern Somalia. It was hoped that he would impose some semblance of order, at least enough to permit relief operations to run smoothly.

The fighting that had gone on for the preceding two years in the south had completely disrupted local agriculture. People's survival, uncertain even at the best of times, was rendered more precarious by the onset of a drought. Very quickly, populations started moving, fleeing the violence and the famine. Camps sprung up around and within most of the main towns of the south. The camps around Mogadishu were bad, but far worse was the situation in Baidoa.

Though most of the south was in the hands of General Aideed, Mogadishu remained a special case. The confrontations in the city had stabilized around a 'green line' which had nothing green about it: members of a clan from one side would not survive even a few minutes on the other. And while General Aideed controlled much of the city, Ali

Mahdi had a grip on the port and was denying the relief ships access to the harbour.

*

Baidoa was the epicentre of the warlord-induced famine and reputed, at the time, to be the closest a person could get to hell on earth. Within a few days of joining the UN mission, I was dispatched to meet with the NGOs operating there. A UN World Food Programme relief convoy had been attacked the day before and all its food looted. Ambassador Sahnoun wanted me to learn what had happened, and to work out how the five hundred newly arrived Pakistani peacekeepers could best be used.

Before going to meet the NGOs, I decided I needed to see one of the camps. It was still early when I arrived in the main camp on the outskirts of town, but the heat of the day was starting to make itself felt. The ground was dry, with only a few tufts of grass here and there. Huts, made for the most part from twigs covered with cardboard or burlap sacks, were spread out over the vast expanse.

It was extraordinarily quiet, and when I asked one of the Médecins Sans Frontières (MSF) aid workers why, she told me that all the men and many of the women were out gathering wood or looking for work. Only young children remained. As I walked through the camp, I saw many of them just sitting there, doing nothing, their grimy cheeks streaked with tears. They looked at us with blank *what's happening?* stares.

The aid worker accompanying me explained that it was becoming more and more difficult for MSF to support these camps. As soon as they provided assistance, the warlords sent their militia to confiscate the supplies. This theft was becoming more and more blatant. She motioned towards a group of fighters lounging near a vehicle. 'They used to wait to start looting until well after the aid had been delivered,' she said. 'Now they hover around like vultures. They swoop in and take what they want the minute the aid vehicles leave. We are reduced to making what we provide less appealing. To cutting holes in the blankets. Putting less sugar in the gruel.'

The feeding centre was located on higher ground to the left of the camp. As early as it was, a line of children had formed in front of a wall of prickly bushes. There was no need for the NGO guard to impose discipline. Everyone was silent. Everyone was still.

At the back of the feeding centre, I spotted a field of newly dug graves. The aid worker followed the direction of my glance. Many of the children didn't make it, she explained: 'What with the lootings and the attacks on aid convoys, there just aren't enough supplies.' She hesitated. 'What is wrong?' I asked. She raised her chin and added, 'It is us, the MSF staff – young nurses and doctors – who have to decide every single day who will get the food and who will be left to die. Can you imagine how difficult it is? The responsibility we will carry forever and ever?'

*

As soon as I returned to Mogadishu, I went to brief Ambassador Sahnoun. The famine was so dire in Baidoa, I reported, and the looting so relentless, that aid workers believed the only way to tackle the starvation was to immediately flood the area with food – to get so much in that the smaller amounts needed for the feeding centres would inevitably trickle through. Having the Pakistani troops to protect the convoys would help (at least until the militia developed the courage to confront them), and the rains, only six or seven weeks away, would bring a reprieve. The real bottleneck was the inability of relief ships to dock in Mogadishu port.

Ambassador Sahnoun listened attentively. Once I had finished, he announced that he had a meeting scheduled that very day with Ali Mahdi. 'You'll accompany me,' he instructed. 'Share what you saw in Baidoa.' This would, he hoped, convince the mayor of the compelling need to allow access to the port for ships delivering aid. Only the day before, the *Milos L*, a ship loaded with a thousand tons of grain for the World Food Programme, had been shelled when it attempted to enter the port.

*

The meeting didn't go well. Ali Mahdi remained intransigent. On his return to UN headquarters, Ambassador Sahnoun was forced to inform the secretary-general that all efforts to reopen the port had failed. The decision was taken in New York to identify an alternative port. One was found, but with reduced capacity, to the north of Mogadishu. Although the quantities unloaded in the new location were significantly less, sufficient amounts nevertheless reached Baidoa. These shipments, combined with the onset of the rains, meant that by early November the rates of malnourishment began to level out. However, the more regular movement of food also meant that the aid convoys were attacked with greater frequency and the demand on the five hundred Pakistani troops quickly became intolerable.

Somalia continued to be a site of tragedy. And the international community continued to turn its face away. It was only when Ambassador Sahnoun openly expressed his contempt for the Security Council's indifference to Africa, and handed in his resignation, that serious thought was given to the plight of the region. In many ways the timing of the ambassador's outburst suited the US. They were trying to find a way to demonstrate their commitment to tackling suffering and injustice in the post-Cold War world, and engagement with Somalia would shift attention away from the implosion of Yugoslavia, a complicated conflict that the US did not want to be part of. Thus, President George H. W. Bush offered to contribute between twenty to thirty thousand troops to be deployed in a UN operation in Somalia.

On the evening of 4 December 1992, the US president informed the American people that troops would be sent to Somalia in a mission to be called Operation Restore Hope. On the evening of the 7th, I received a call from New York. I was to inform all the NGOs that, in order to avoid any mishaps, from the following evening they were to stay in their bases for twenty-four hours.

4

Somalia: *Operation Restore Hope*

Early on the morning of 9 December, I stepped onto the roof of the house I was staying in and looked out over the sea. A US warship was gliding silently through the water. As dawn broke, the rest of an armada poised well off shore became visible on the horizon. The city was calm, quiet, expectant. The crackling of my radio broke the spell; I was convened to a meeting at UN headquarters.

When I arrived, I found a room filled with uniformed and non-uniformed US officials – the architects of the new world order's first attempt to make the planet a better place. In the middle of the group stood Phil Johnson, former head of the American relief organization CARE International and now newly appointed UN Humanitarian Coordinator. Others I recognized as senior government officials from Washington. What was striking was how supremely confident they looked.

The meeting began with the clip-like efficiency to be expected of any professional military gathering. The colonel in charge of reporting on the deployment explained that no major difficulties had been encountered during the landing on the beaches. There could have been a nasty incident at the port, when troops coming over the line of containers were disoriented by photographers' flashbulbs, but the soldiers held their fire. At the airport, a number of Somalis who had not heeded the call to stay away had been arrested. 'Smooth operation, nothing else to report,' was his summation.

The discussion then turned to what Phil Johnson regarded as the crucial matter of timing: how quickly could the positive impact of the intervention be tracked? President Bush was handing the White House over to President-elect Bill Clinton on 20 January, and by then things had to be wrapped up. This timetable may have been taken for granted by everyone else in the room, but it was news – and shocking news – to me. How could anybody think that Somalia could be 'saved' by 20 January?

One of those present suggested that progress could be demonstrated by tracking mortality rates. Timidly, given the authority of the people present, I dared point out a problem: with the start of the rains, and with the aid that had been brought in since November, mortality rates had already stabilized, and perhaps even gone down. A more accurate indicator of progress in restoring stability to the region would be the number of technicals* that had been dismantled.

The colonel fixed me with a stony stare. 'Sorry, no can do,' he said. The 'technicals' were a by-product of the intra-Somali fight, in which Operation Restore Hope could not get involved. The meeting agreed on the use of mortality rates as a measure of progress, and I was silent from then on.

---

*   Technicals were decapitated heavily armed Toyota Land Cruiser pickups. These chariots were equipped with a variety of armaments, ranging from the long tubes of recoilless guns, to .50 calibre heavy machine guns, and even the honeycombed face of a helicopter gunship pod. They derived their name from the budget line to which international aid organizations allocated the payments they were forced to make for protection.

It seemed to me that during the discussions that followed, which were purely logistical in nature, there was an absence of reflection on the real issues. It was as if this huge international force wanted at all costs to avoid getting involved in politics – specifically, to avoid confronting the warlords. Ultimately, to accomplish nothing more than what the small Pakistani force of five hundred soldiers had been tasked to do four months before. Towards the end of the meeting, it was announced that the next deployment was to be to Kismayo. Phil Johnson instructed me to go down to Kismayo that very afternoon to help prepare the ground.

As I walked back to the house to pack for the trip, I crossed paths with a foot patrol of the 13th Demi-Brigade of the French Foreign Legion, made up of a mixture of races and nationalities. They stretched in a long line from the airport to the K4 roundabout. All carried enormous packs, automatic weapons held firmly in their hands, the officer leading the troops with his radio operator behind him. I looked over at the airfield and saw a French military transport plane. They must have just landed and were moving on foot to their position. As the unit marched up the hill, it was overtaken by a line of massively armoured vehicles. It was strange to see a military unit doing it the old way, marching rather than riding into the city. The unit was adhering to its age-old motto: March or Die. Little did I realize how soon I would come across them again.

*

As the weeks slipped by, it became increasingly clear that a secure environment would not be established by the January deadline. The departure date for the US-led force slipped. In early March, bending to a demand from President Clinton that the US should no longer carry full responsibility for the intervention, the secretary-general recommended the transition of the US-led intervention to a UN-led operation.

The new UN-led mission, to be known as UNOSOM II, was to complete the task begun by the US forces. However, the objective had changed in a significant way. More emphasis was to be placed on the restoration of peace and stability – a tall order, since there was still no effective functioning government or local security force in Somalia. UNOSOM II would be given a mandate 'to assist the Somali people in rebuilding their economic, political and social life, through achieving national reconciliation so as to recreate a democratic Somali State'. In other words, the goal of state-building in Somalia was officially decreed.

*

The transition went relatively smoothly, in part because most of the command infrastructure remained staffed by the same US officers. Admiral Jonathan Howe, a US national, was named as the secretary-general's special representative. Admiral Howe had made his name as commander of a nuclear submarine, and had later served as Deputy National Security Advisor to President Bush.

Everybody seemed happy with the arrangements for UNOSOM II – everybody, that is, except General Aideed. The months leading up to the intervention, when he had held control of southeastern Somalia, and then the initial months of the international presence, had – with hindsight – demonstrated his inability to govern. While the general was able to direct the forces under his command towards targets of destruction, he seemed unable to rein them in. But he had had the intelligence to be the first to cooperate with the US command when Operation Restore Hope had been launched. He had allowed his equipment to be cantoned and had participated in early attempts to set up some form of transitional administration. But he had not shown any inclination to reach out and reconcile with others in order to govern. The arrogance he demonstrated in the National Reconciliation Conference held in Addis Ababa in March did little to lift his credibility in the eyes of the Western ministers present.

So Aideed had demonstrated his inability to control his forces and missed his opportunity to govern the country. And though Ali Mahdi's influence was still felt in some areas of southeastern Somalia, once he had lost out to Aideed he had retreated into voluntary exile in Nairobi. So, Somalia still had no effective leader.

In the early days of UNOSOM II, there were almost daily incidents of sub-sub-clan on sub-sub-clan violence, which the troops were unable to contain. In hindsight, however, those initial months of the intervention seemed incredibly smooth compared to what came after.

In June, the situation exploded.

*

On 5 June 1993, a Pakistani force, now integrated into the new UN mission, was sent to inspect an arms depot that belonged to General Aideed, which was located near a radio station under his control. When the Pakistani force arrived at the site, they were greeted by angry Somali protesters. The Pakistani soldiers attempted to move past the mob. Someone triggered something, and the crowd turned on the soldiers. The motive remains unclear. Could it have been linked to a fear that the radio was going to be shut down? Whatever the cause, at a feeding centre not far away, another Pakistani unit, protecting distributions, was also attacked. All in all, twenty-four Pakistani soldiers were killed on that day – horrifically torn apart – and fifty-four more were wounded.

I was alerted to the attack on the Pakistani soldiers by the sound of gunfire. A short time later came instructions, which I relayed to my NGO contacts, for all international staff to remain where they were. The firing continued all day.

Late in the evening I received word from New York that the secretary-general was seeking full authority to bring those responsible for the attacks to account. The proposal, which included consideration of military options, amounted to a declaration of war on Aideed and his militia. I was advised to contact the NGO community again and now encourage them to leave Mogadishu.

On 12 June 1993, American troops started attacking targets in Mogadishu in hopes of finding Aideed. Spectre gunships were used, massive C-130 aircraft with the ability to fire thousands of heavy calibre rounds into an area half the size of a football field. Driving around Mogadishu checking on my NGO contacts, I saw for myself how contained the firing of the Spectre gunships could be. I would drive by a compound that had been obliterated and yet see scarcely any impact on the adjacent walls.

Admiral Jonathan Howe issued a 25,000 USD bounty for any information leading to the arrest of Aideed.[*] To most Somalis it seemed like a ridiculously small amount, given the fortunes that were being made by the warlords from looting. Aideed retaliated by issuing notice of a reward of one million USD for the capture of 'Animal Howe'.

*

It was mid-afternoon of 3 October and I was sitting deep in thought on the roof of the guesthouse when a sizeable number of Blackhawk helicopters flew over. They were protected by heavily armed Apache helicopters and

---

[*] The amount of 25,000 USD was the financial authorization level given at the time to the head of a UN mission.

accompanied by Little Birds, each with special forces operatives perched on the door ledge, feet dangling or resting on the skids. The volume of the chatter on the secure handheld radio confirmed that something big was going on.

From my vantage point, I saw the helicopters hover over the Bakara market, a gathering place for Aideed fighters in the middle of the city. For a while the activity seemed to attract little attention. Then, all of a sudden, the sound of gunfire blasted from every direction. This was the beginning of the final battle for Mogadishu. The fighting lasted well into the night, the shattering sound of gunfire ebbing and flowing. There would be moments of calm. Seconds later, an isolated shot would break the silence, and then, as if in response to the impudence of that solitary shot, I'd hear multiple detonations. By the next morning the scale of the tragedy started to be known: eighteen US soldiers killed and seventy-three wounded. Casualties on the Somali side were many times greater, in all probability well into the thousands.

When over the next days news outlets around the world broadcast again and again the image of a dead US soldier being dragged through the streets of Mogadishu, I understood that the first post-Cold War intervention was over. The US had not really wanted to get involved in this war in the first place. The initial short timeline of January 1993, the limited ambition, and, more importantly, the refusal to disarm the warlords had already been clear indications of the fact. But now, after such a humiliating defeat, they wouldn't have the stomach to continue.

*

A few days after the battle, Hugh Chalmondeley, Phil Johnson's successor, asked me to join the team preparing a very high-level donor conference to be held in Addis Ababa at the end of the year. The team was being formed in Nairobi.

The conference was intended by UN headquarters in New York to give visibility to the 'success' of the UN intervention and to mobilize financial support from major Western donors. Was this an attempt to camouflage the West's tactical withdrawal from Somalia after the humiliation of 3 October? I wondered.

Hugh Chalmondeley was a remarkable individual – a loyal international civil servant, and a former disc jockey and political commentator in Guyana with an impressively resonant voice. Unfortunately, our relationship got off on a very bad footing. A few months before, I had published under a pseudonym an op-ed in the French paper *Libération* confirming the UN's failings in the Sudan. I had been invited to write the piece by a journalist who explained that his colleague in Khartoum had been told that the points that a number of us had made had been fabricated. Did I want to respond? And I did, believing that the truth needed to be heard. I would have gotten away with the pseudonym had I not learned that UN headquarters believed that someone else on my team in Khartoum was the author.

I immediately wrote to the under-secretary general for humanitarian affairs claiming responsibility for the piece. Given the lack of volunteers for Somalia, they were reluctant to fire me; instead, Hugh was tasked to get my commitment that I would never again write such an article. He argued that using a pseudonym had been cowardly. I acknowledged the point, but I told him that I couldn't make the promise he was asking for. Were the circumstances to be exactly the same, I would probably act in a similar way again. For three days, Hugh tried to get my commitment, but then finally told New York he would act as guarantor for my actions.[*]

---

[*]   The really funny part of this story is that my father, who never reads *Libération*, found himself on a plane that had no papers aside from that one. He saw through the pseudonym and was amused to read what I had written. He didn't necessarily think it would help my future career prospects with the UN, but admitted to me later that it made him chuckle.

Hugh quickly realized the disconnect between New York's beliefs about Somalia and the reality on the ground. He saw too that the overly optimistic views being channelled to New York by the mission in Mogadishu were leading to the development of strategies underpinned by false premises – strategies that were alienating the populations and ensuring the failure of the intervention. The UN leadership simply did not know how thin their support was in Somalia. Admiral Howe had repeatedly stressed that parts of the Somali population were strongly vocal in support of the UN. But he had failed to explain that much of the apparent support actually came from factions who hoped that the UN would defeat their arch-rival, Aideed. The moment they realized that the UN could not or would not vanquish Aideed, their support would evaporate. Hugh came to the conclusion that the prerequisite to success in the upcoming conference was a change of UN leadership on the ground.

Hugh was determined to have Admiral Howe replaced as the secretary-general's special representative for Somalia. From then on, the preparations for the conference were directed towards an official objective – the mobilization of international support – and a hidden one: the ousting of Admiral Howe. As with most conferences, preparation revolved around the writing of papers. Different positions were articulated, supporting arguments researched and developed. New York attached great importance to the conference. The secretary-general and a number of heads of state would be participating. The stakes were high.

A few days before the conference, Hugh sent to New York our confidential briefing note that called for the replacement of Admiral Howe. The note argued that the UN mission, though not yet through its first year, was very close to collapsing. The UN had lost the support of the broader Somali community. One of the turning points was the attack of 5 June on the Pakistani soldiers, but a US-led UN-mandated attack on 12 July was more significant still. As a result of faulty information, the UN/US military had attacked a clandestine meeting of elders while they were trying to agree on a way of isolating Aideed – that is, on a way of bringing a peaceful end to the conflict. The attack killed seventy-two moderate elders of Aideed's clan. The lynching that same afternoon of four journalists by an angry mob in front of the bombed-out house demonstrated the anger that had been triggered.

The note went on to question the way the fighting was conducted. Did it uphold the standards of the UN Charter?* Was the use of non-point-specific weapons, such as mortars, which inevitably led to indiscriminate collateral damage, appropriate? There was room for such weapons in time of war, but shouldn't peace operations be held to higher standards? How could UNOSOM justify the claim that it had the right to retaliate wherever it chose, when it was known that women and children were mingled among the combatants? The paper concluded with a note of caution regarding the consequences if the UN operation in Somalia failed: who would pay the price? The only way forward now was a radical change in the leadership and the objectives of the mission.

Hugh had planned to distribute a sanitized version of the note to the participants of the conference, and I had primed a number of journalists for a major scoop.

*

The night before the conference, a very subdued Hugh invited me into his hotel room. He had just been up to meet with the under-secretary-general

---

* The UN Charter is the founding document of the organization. It is a commitment by the international community 'to save succeeding generations from the scourge of war ... reaffirm faith in fundamental human rights ... to establish conditions of justice and respect for international law ... and to promote social progress and better standards of life in larger freedom'.

coordinating the preparations of the conference, and I could see from his face that the news was bad. Hugh had been told in no uncertain terms that the UN leadership did not agree with his assessment of the situation in Somalia. The call to replace Admiral Howe was totally unacceptable.

'And?' I urged.

'And? If I push the points made in our note, I will be fired,' Hugh said. There was a pause. 'Charles, do you know what that would mean?'

I could guess, but I waited for him to spell it out. It would mean that once he left the UN, his children's education grant would cease. He had struggled to get a university education himself, but now, thanks to the UN he had three daughters in top American universities. If he lost his UN job, they would have to withdraw.

I didn't know what to say. I was saddened and shocked. I could see that Hugh was trapped in a golden cage, and the door was locked. The pain that he was going through was evident, and I respected him for it. The reform that we were pushing for was necessary and right, but it was now clearly destined to fail – and, if we persisted, Hugh and his children would bear the cost of our efforts.

The conference went smoothly. It was extremely well attended. The focus of most of the many speeches that were made was on the need for the Somalis to assume more responsibility. A justification for a future disengagement? That's exactly what it sounded like to me.

5

Somalia: *Flirting with Self-destruction*

My overwhelming disappointment at the failure of the UNOSOM mission made me reckless. I can see that now. I requested a transfer to Galkayo, in the heart of Aideed's territory. I decided that I had to visit every one of Aideed's sub-clans. To explain to each of them that although the UN mission had been a failure – of that there was no doubt – it hadn't been wrong to attempt to bring peace and stability to the war-torn country of Somalia. It hadn't been wicked, nor mad, nor malicious. Though the means turned out to be inappropriate and the approach self-defeating, the intention had been a worthy one.

With the wisdom of hindsight, I'm not really sure what I was actually trying to accomplish. Witnessing the failure of Somalia after the frustrations of the Sudan was just too much for me to handle. I guess this was the only way I could think of to make my experience seem even a tiny bit worthwhile, to have any meaning.

Before I set off, Admiral Howe's military chief of staff, Colonel Jim Abely, summoned me to his office. 'Do you really understand what a transfer to Galkayo will involve?' the colonel asked. There was a minimal UN presence there, and the US was drawing down its involvement in Somalia. Once there, I could expect no support, no backup, from the mission. 'For your own good, Charles, I want you to take back your request,' the colonel said.

Instead I told him that the imminent withdrawal of US troops made me even more determined. In my distraught state, it seemed important to me – important in a way that over-rode even the dictates of common sense and concern for safety – to make the Somalis understand the opportunity that had been lost. I told the colonel that if the UN mission was to close, if Somalia was to be abandoned, then I wanted to make all of Aideed's sub-clans aware of their shared responsibility in the failure of what had been an honourable enterprise.

'You're nuts,' the colonel said. But he said it with a smile. He took something out of his pocket – a handmade Emerson CQC-6 – and passed it to me. The knife had always brought him luck, he said, and he wanted me to have it.

A few days later my plane touched down on a Russian-built landing strip outside of Galkayo. From the air, Galkayo itself had looked like an open-air display of swimming pools. The coloured squares – electric blues, yellows, pinks and reds – were actually roofless houses that attested to years of fighting. By contrast, the landscape round about the town was perfectly flat and colourless – perhaps the ugliest I had ever seen. I was nervous, but also excited, at the thought of becoming the first UN official to enter the home territory of General Aideed and visit everyone of his sub-clans.

I had a speech prepared in my head whenever I met a group of elders. I'd begin by expressing sadness for the grief UNOSOM had brought to all – by acknowledging the tragic cost of the intervention on the Somalis, the suffering it had brought to mothers and fathers, brothers and sisters, wives and husbands and friends. But then the speech went on to point out how other families – in Malaysia, Pakistan, France, Nigeria, the US and Zimbabwe – had also suffered. All this from an intervention that was meant to bring peace, to give the Somali people the chance to enjoy security and freedom. Eventually I raised the question of how to salvage whatever could possibly be salvaged of the intervention.

Each time I sat down with a group of elders, I would ensure that the UN logo on the patch stitched onto my backpack was clearly visible. When I explained that I was from UNOSOM, rather than a UN agency such as the Children's Fund UNICEF, the reaction was surprise and sometimes hostility. The community leader in Dusa Mareb, for example, exclaimed that if he had known, he would have killed me on my entry to the village. But now that I was among them he was willing to listen.

Generally, the speech was well received, but however much I tried to appear upbeat, and the more I gave it, I felt deflated. I knew that the attempt at establishing a 'new world order' – that experiment that was to have been the intervention in Somalia – had failed, and I had an intuition that the consequences of this failure would be catastrophic. When the US-led, UN-hatted troops finally departed, Somalia would no longer have the world's attention. The UN had had a critical rendezvous with history, an opportunity to redefine international politics, and it had been missed. Nevertheless, I continued stubbornly with my goal of visiting every one of the sub-clans.

By early March, there was only one remaining – a clan located in the Geriban district. The place chosen for the meeting with the elders was a small port town. I was warned that the trip would be a complicated one; parts of the road were thought to be mined. I was given a hand-drawn map. We left very early in the morning. We tried to by-pass the mined portions of the main track but found that the rocky alternative path made for exceptionally slow going. After six hours, at less than ten kilometres an hour, we finally returned to the main track, only to find that we had rejoined it a kilometre too soon. When I was told that the necessary detour would involve another bone-jarring three-hour ride, and I saw that aside from a small, restricted portion of a few hundred metres, the track ran through open country, I asked the guards if they would be willing to walk in front of the vehicle, prodding the earth, while I drove slowly behind them. They agreed, and once we had reached the open range, we set off through the bush.

I was exhausted when I met the elders. They presented me with an extraordinary list of demands, and told me that I was expected to deliver, no discussion. I responded by asking them why they acted like spoiled children rather than men. 'A man is willing to hear the truth,' I said, 'but a child hides from it.'

There was a menacing silence. The elders did not like my words. The situation tensed, and then by some miracle our discussion continued.

*

Two days later, in the middle of the night, I woke up in a cold sweat, gripped by fear. I finally realized how foolish I had been. I had gone too far. The trip along the mined portion of the road had been madness. The provocation of the elders was even more perilous. If I continued like this, I thought, I would be lucky to survive another six months.

Through a long and painful night, I faced the fact that this journey was not the only aspect of my life in which I had lost my bearings. I realized I had to get out of my current reckless mindset, before my dream descended into nightmare. I wrote the next morning to Hugh, who was now in New York. I asked him if he could help me find a more traditional UN assignment.

Hugh responded that after the *Libération* article and the attempt to use the conference to oust Admiral Howe, my reputation as a troublemaker had been firmly established. It would take time before he could convince someone to take me.

The month of March passed. I thought I was going to go mad.

And then, on 10 April, a few days after the president's plane was shot down in Rwanda, I was notified that I would be transferred to Rwanda to beef up the UN humanitarian presence there. I refused. I knew that Rwanda would be a disaster. I didn't know anything about the country, and even less its recent history. But it was so clear to me that there would be a heavy price to pay for the UN's failure in Somalia, and that Rwanda would pay it. I didn't want to be part of it.

I pleaded with Hugh. He repeated that my reputation in New York as a troublemaker was so strong that nothing else would be offered. I had only two options.

Hugh didn't mince his words. 'To be blunt, Charles, either you agree to go to Rwanda. Or you leave the UN.'

PART THREE

RWANDA, KAMANA RUMBASHI AND THE BACKGROUND TO THE 1994 GENOCIDE

In October 2014, I was invited to the Central European University in Budapest to speak at a seminar on the 1994 genocide in Rwanda. Travelling there by motorcycle, I visited Auschwitz and Birkenau on the way.

I found Auschwitz and Birkenau at the same time horrific and disturbing. The horror came from knowing of the things that had happened in those two sites. The disturbance came from the realization that the stones and walls of the structures were unable to convey the enormity of the suffering that was inflicted within. Auschwitz resembled a regimental barracks in a small garrison town, which indeed it had been in the past. Birkenau was now little more than a scattering of huts, naked poles and broken-down buildings scattered over a vast open field. The gas chambers had been reduced to slabs of concrete. Against this unremarkable background, the few photographs that had been placed here and there offered a fleeting look into what had been an antechamber of hell. These images drew me back to memories of Rwanda, where bleached skulls had provided spiritless reminders of the horrors that had occurred. Evil will have triumphed, when the real significance of the history it begat is no longer remembered.

I learned that very few of those in charge at Auschwitz were ever brought to justice. Most continued afterwards to live mundane and respectable lives. In fact, one of the leading doctors involved in experiments on the forced sterilization of women had a practice in town during the Nazi era and after. He was considered a very good doctor and an amiable man.

Over the years, I have heard similar pleasantries about Kamana Rumbashi. *He is a good man. He is efficient. He is likable.* Looking at the pictures of him as an adult, he is pudgy but well groomed, with a neatly trimmed goatee, scholarly glasses and a disarming smile. He does appear to be genuinely affable. It is very difficult for me to reconcile this image with the ruthless commander of a genocidal militia. Nevertheless, I have to try.

44

6

A Troubled Independence

It took me years to get to grips with the events that led up to the 1994 genocide. It became commonplace during and after the genocide to attribute the violence to a spontaneous outburst of long-standing ethnic tensions between the Hutus and the Tutsis. I came to understand that, though this view was energetically promoted by certain political interests, it amounted to an oversimplification of the stormy history of Rwanda.

For centuries, in the territories of Rwanda and its neighbor Burundi, the designations 'Hutu' and 'Tutsi' referred to flexible groupings based on wealth and social standing, rather than to categories such as 'race', which are assumed to be fixed and biologically based. Tutsis were the wealthy nobility; Hutus were disenfranchised and relatively poor. However, these labels were not permanent. A Hutu who managed to build up a substantial stock of land and cows could acquire the status of Tutsi.

Tutsis and Hutus are not, as is sometimes imagined, biologically or physiologically distinct. Tutsis are said to be taller and have finer features than Hutus – but for the most part, whether a person is Hutu or Tutsi cannot be decided on the basis of appearance. (That said, when I first arrived in Rwanda I didn't really have a hard time distinguishing between the two groups. Those dead were principally Tutsis. Those alive and out in the open – not in hiding – were almost exclusively Hutu.)

After the First World War, when the territories of Burundi and Rwanda passed from German into Belgian control, the new colonial authorities found it inconvenient that they couldn't easily tell Tutsis and Hutus apart. So, in 1935, the Belgian authorities issued identity cards which fixed people's ethnic designation for life. Anyone with ten or more cattle was designated a Tutsi – one of the ruling minority. Those with fewer cows were known as Hutus. In an instant, a centuries-old tradition of social mobility was eradicated. Tutsis and Hutus came to be treated as immutable categories, and the dominance of the Tutsis was set in stone.

Until the mid- to late 1950s, the Catholic Church, prominent in Rwanda, was an energetic supporter of this hierarchy that accorded dominance to Tutsis. Then as the winds of political change throughout Africa became more strongly felt, the Belgian colonial powers realized they had to allow the Hutu population – who were after all the majority – to have a greater voice. Catholic missionaries in Rwanda were charged with bringing down the arrogant Tutsi elite and empowering the dispossessed Hutus. This facilitated the emergence of a Hutu clergy and a sizeable educated Hutu elite. Once independence was gained, and the Hutu majority attained democratic control, the empowerment of Hutus was seen as a bulwark against any attempt to re-establish the Tutsis-on-top political order that the Church had in the past so energetically supported. Faith can move mountains.

Years later, during and just after the genocide, I would walk through churches filled with the bodies of murdered Tutsis and wonder how the

Church could have been so unconcerned by the policies of exclusion and hate adopted by succeeding Hutu administrations. The two leading papers in Rwanda, both Catholic publications, openly and unashamedly gave their full support to the government. After the genocide, I was told that senior church officials had been shameless in their efforts to be as close as possible to those in power. An archbishop of the Catholic Church was even an influential member of the president's political party. Faith might move mountains, but in this case a fog seemed to have settled on their summits.

In the years before independence, as the great wave of decolonization was building momentum throughout Africa, relations between the Tutsi and Hutu populations in Rwanda became increasingly strained. In Rwanda, the new Hutu political movement started to claim rights, while the Tutsi establishment resisted a democratization process that would strip them of their historic privileges. In 1959, there was an assassination attempt by Tutsi supporters on a prominent member of the Hutu political movement. This triggered a Hutu uprising, in which hundreds of Tutsis were killed and thousands forced to flee to neighbouring states. By the time Rwanda gained independence in 1962, over two hundred thousand people, mainly Tutsis, had already fled over the borders.

In 1963, Tutsi exiles based in Burundi launched an attack on Rwanda, which provoked a savage backlash. More than fourteen thousand Tutsis living in southern Rwanda were killed in retribution. The attack strengthened the hand of Rwanda's first elected president, Gregoire Kayibanda. Anti-Tutsi policies were enacted: mixed marriages were discouraged; quotas were introduced to increase the number of Hutus in education and in the civil service; and the policy of requiring people to carry identity cards stipulating their ethnicity was reinforced.

Burundi and Rwanda are literally mirror images of each other. The colonial past of the two countries were very similar, and yet after independence, sharply different. After independence in Rwanda, it was the Hutu majority who oppressed the Tutsi minority; in Burundi, the Tutsi minority ruthlessly retained the upper hand. As a result, what happened in one country over the course of post-colonial history served to fuel the paranoia of the other.

One such defining event occurred in 1972, when Hutu militia attacked Tutsi populations in Burundi, committing appalling atrocities. Civilian and military authorities were brutally killed, armouries ransacked, weapons stolen. The insurgents killed not only every Tutsi they encountered, but also any Hutu who refused to join them. A pattern was set for the region.

The Tutsi president of Burundi immediately declared martial law. The army moved into the countryside and unleashed unprecedented violence. In the following six months, an estimated 300,000 Hutus were killed and a further 300,000 forced to flee to neighboring countries. The killings, far from being random, systematically targeted the educated. By the end, virtually every schooled Hutu in Burundi, down to secondary level, was either dead or in flight.

A little less than a year after the violence in Burundi, the Rwandan president was overthrown in a coup led by his minister of defence. The new president, General Juvenal Habyarimana, a Hutu, suspended the constitution, dissolved the national assembly and imposed a strict ban on all political activity. He insisted to the international community that he was a unifier rather than a divider. But Habyarimana also launched a new political party, the Mouvement Révolutionaire National pour le Développement (MRND), which, even in its origin, was underpinned by notions of Hutu supremacy. Habyarimana then changed the constitution so that Rwanda became a one-party state.

During a decade of economic prosperity based on strong international demand for Rwandan exports (basically coffee and tea), the influence of President Habyarimana's wife grew. Agathe Habyarimana was from the Hutu elite of northwest Rwanda. She was socially superior to her husband and she made certain he knew it. It is said that she fed her husband's fears of unseen enemies, and the continued repression of Hutus in Burundi gave credence to those fears. The president's wife was able to use this paranoia to position her supporters in prominent places within the government.

Agathe Habyarimana created a secret organization, the Akazu, that was a crucial source of the ideology that came to be called Hutu Power. Its members were driven by a determination never to share power with Tutsis or moderate Hutus.

Towards the end of the 1980s, as a result of drought, corruption, nepotism and, most importantly, falling prices of coffee on the world markets, the Rwandan economy took a turn for the worse. The regime tried to divert the popular unrest in Rwanda that was triggered by the economic downturn onto the Tutsi minority.

*

This increasingly palpable tension between the Tutsis and the Hutus during the 1980s is exemplified by the experiences of a rebel Tutsi officer, Fiacre Mboki, whom I eventually got to know well.

Fiacre had a fairly unexceptional childhood, was good at school and graduated from the Teachers College of the University of Butare. After graduation, he was offered a job in a primary school.

The school had been established by an affluent businessman, Theogene Kanamugir, who had been inspired by President Habyarimana's early promises of a unified country. He wanted a school dedicated to celebrating the richness of the common Rwandan heritage, to teaching the meaninglessness of the Hutu–Tutsi divide, and to instilling within its pupils a truly cross-ethnic sense of national pride. Fiacre found this vision for the school inspiring and he accepted the post.

The first pupils in the school came, for the most part, from Tutsi families in the neighbouring hills, but it was hoped that, with a growing reputation for quality education, the school would also attract increasing numbers of children from Hutu families. Theogene put his own money into the venture, but the spirit of tolerance also attracted financial support from, among others, UNICEF.

From the first day, Fiacre enjoyed the work. He spent more and more time with his students, organizing school outings and weekend sporting events. It was in the course of one of these events that he met the director of the neighbouring parish school, Father Vjeko Curic. Father Vjeko was an avid football enthusiast, and a series of football matches between the schools became the prelude to a growing friendship between the two men.

After the genocide, many recollected the 1980s as years of relative tolerance and security. But it would be more correct to describe them as years of subtly growing intolerance and insecurity. Building on fears of a Tutsi invasion from Burundi, the Habyarimana government increased its control over everyday life. Inspection of identity cards became increasingly frequent at checkpoints. Moving residency from one place to another required a special authorization that was difficult to obtain, and exponentially so for Tutsis. The reach of the administration went down to units of ten houses in each 'colline' or village, and any guest who came to stay from outside the immediate area had to be announced to the head of the administrative unit. Every time Fiacre went to visit his parents, he had to be declared.

It slowly dawned on Fiacre that the restrictions being imposed, far from being arbitrary, were targeted against Tutsis. The road to Murambi, near where his parents lived, passed through Kigali. At the entrance to the capital, Fiacre found himself more and more often being taken off the matatu, the public minibus, for document checks. Nine times out of ten, the inspection took so long that the bus driver dumped Fiacre's bags and left without him.

Fiacre started to notice other signs of oppression. Early on in his tenure, President Habyarimana had introduced monthly collective labour days as part of a development scheme. For two days a month, all of the population were ordered to contribute to a public works project. It seemed an admirable idea and international donors loved it. But the works were selectively targeted: school maintenance was considered a communal service, but Theogene's establishment was not eligible. He tried to rectify what he thought was a simple misunderstanding. But after repeated rebuffs from the administration, it became clear that this was also an aspect of government policy that was used to isolate the Tutsis.

UNICEF supplies to the school then started to become irregular, with the local administration introducing complicated bureaucratic procedures that delayed their arrival. Finally, parents of the few remaining Hutu students came to see Theogene to announce that their children would not be returning for the next school year. They were sorry, but their children were being targeted as Tutsi sympathizers, and they could no longer resist the pressure. Theogene was devastated, but determined to go ahead with preparations for the following term.

In August 1988, as Fiacre returned to the school to launch the new term, he saw a battered pickup belonging to the gendarmerie parked in the schoolyard. The gendarme standing next to it, carrying an old action bolt rifle, was slovenly, his shirt hanging out of his trousers. The gendarme told Fiacre to follow him. There had been a robbery, he explained, as they stepped inside the classroom.

The air was black with flies, and the sound of their buzzing filled the room. A body, partially hidden by desks and chairs, lay at the back. Fiacre hesitated a minute and then moved forward. The sight of Theogene's body made him gag. 'What do you mean a robbery?' Fiacre demanded. 'This man has been hacked to death. You can clearly see that he was tortured and killed.'

'That's not the way I see it,' the gendarme answered. In his view, the victim had surprised the robbers and they had killed him before fleeing. 'Just bad luck,' he said. And that is the way Theogene Kanamugir's murder was registered – merely *bad luck. A robbery gone bad.*

That night Fiacre left for Uganda. He had heard from friends a few months before that a movement of Tutsi exiles had been formed. It was called the Rwandan Patriotic Front (RPF). It had been founded as a political and military movement with three stated aims: the peaceful return of Rwandan exiles; the reform of the Rwandan government; and the introduction of political power sharing.

7

A Regime Rescued

The Habyarimana regime entered the 1990s with the fear of popular discontent as a result of deteriorating economic conditions and the awareness of a new and powerful force emerging arraigned against them. But in an ironic twist of fate, it was this force, the Tutsi-dominated RPF, that saved the collapsing Habyarimana regime.* On 1 October 1990, the rebels invaded Rwanda.

The first wave of the RPF force that attacked Rwanda was composed of rebel soldiers who had survived the hardships of refugee life. They were tough, and they were determined. Many of the fighters were too young to have known their country of origin, but all had been nurtured with the

---

* The RPF originated in Uganda. Many of its elements were originally part of Museveni's rebel army that overthrew first General Idi Amin and then President Milton Obote. Over time a number of these Rwandan fighters were promoted to senior positions by Museveni. But once Museveni had installed himself as the new president of Uganda, the foreign fighters became an embarrassment. Museveni offered to help them reclaim their country.

desire to return to reclaim their land. The official Rwandan military were taken by surprise at the attack, which came not from the south, as they had expected, but from the north. The rebel force penetrated close to fifty kilometres into Rwanda on the very first day of the offensive.

Having joined the rebels a year before, Fiacre Mboki had been fast-tracked on account of his university education to the position of 2nd Lieutenant. On the day of the RPF attack, his unit had come in behind the first wave.

Many years later, Fiacre came to visit me in New York where I was being briefed for a new assignment. Over a glass of wine and a huge steak at Smith and Wollensky, he gave me a vivid description of what it was like to take part in the RPF attack.

His platoon had been given the order to advance late in the evening and had progressed through much of the night. By the morning of the second day, they were well into the country. They had had to march swiftly in pitch darkness through hostile territory and to remain alert to the possibility of rearguard actions by marauding Rwandan government forces. By first light, when Fiacre received the instruction to halt, his men were exhausted.

In the afternoon, believing that the advance would soon resume, Fiacre readied his men. But no order came. He instructed his men to reinforce their positions. He waited all of the second night for orders that never arrived. The morning after, he learned the reason for the delay: the rebel commander, General Fred Rwigyema, had been killed. General Paul Kagame was recalled precipitously from military training he was undergoing at Fort Leavenworth, Kansas, and after a brief respite, the offensive continued.

The pause in the rebel advance provided President Habyarimana with the short reprieve he needed. He called upon outside forces to counter the RPF attack. Belgium, France and Zaire (now called the Democratic Republic of Congo – DRC) sent a combined force of over one thousand men. While the Belgian forces remained in reserve, the Zairian troops immediately went into battle. The French were also meant to stay in reserve, but the French parachutists, who could never resist a good fight, quickly followed the Zairians. Once the foreign troops were fully deployed, they stopped the rebel advance.

The RPF held their ground for days. And then all of a sudden, at the end of October, General Kagame ordered his men to disperse into the volcanic Virunga National Park of northwest Rwanda. Seemingly victorious, the Rwandan government and its allies saw this as a rout.

Feeling that they had accomplished what they'd come to do, the Zairian and Belgian troops withdrew to their respective countries. However, the French military stayed on. For Paris, the fact that the offensive had been launched from Uganda, within the Anglo-Saxon sphere of influence, allowed the government of President Mitterrand to frame the RPF advance as little more than a Ugandan and US-backed attempt to oust French influence in Central Africa. France reinforced its presence, and the Habyarimana regime happily militarized.

Fiacre's RPF unit, having moved deeply into the national park, awaited new instructions. The park consists of dense forest covering the flanks of a chain of steep volcanoes. The terrain is extremely rough, the conditions cold and wet. Fiacre and his troops had to scramble through thick vegetation.

Fiacre had no idea how long it would take to get new orders. The daily attempt at radio contact, where reception was bad, was an exercise in itself. It entailed waking up well before dawn and climbing through thick undergrowth to the clearing near the summit of the volcano. All he got in return for this cold and exhausting climb was an occasional order to wait. He would then return to his encampment and face another day of lying low to avoid helicopter patrols. Waiting, Fiacre admitted, was worse than fighting.

Every day Fiacre sent out foraging parties to find food – to catch wild animals or to collect vegetation that they hoped would be safe to eat. Every few nights the platoon moved to new positions, undertaking a tactical transfer in the dead of night from one position to the next. Fiacre and his men, who couldn't light fires because the smoke might reveal their positions, were constantly cold and wet.

Ten days into this expedition, Fiacre finally received instructions. He was to leave his platoon in charge of his second-in-command and immediately proceed to a point much deeper in the park. The rendezvous was just on the Rwandan side of the border with Uganda, and Fiacre was given little time to get there. The journey was extraordinarily difficult. He used the small paths made by animals living in the forest, walking gingerly past a gorilla and his family, and hearing the grunt of a wild animal that sounded like an elephant. He walked and walked and he made it to the destination in time – only to learn that he had been selected to undergo a hellish officer retraining.

Fiacre explained to me, over our dinner in New York, that the retraining programme was part of General Kagame's plan to reinvigorate the rebel movement. The selection course was conducted in extreme climatic conditions, at a height of more than four thousand metres in the volcanic park, where food was scarce and the cold was excruciating. Sleep was a luxury. Every week their numbers got smaller. Some broke limbs; others died of exhaustion.

A draconian disciplinary code was enforced – the same regime that Fiacre would be expected to enforce on his men. The importance of upholding the highest standards of conduct among local populations was drummed into them. When they encountered villagers, the soldiers were expected to pay for whatever goods they received. There was a total ban on alcohol and drugs – not that they had access to either – and it was inculcated in them that the punishment for offences such as murder, rape and desertion was immediate execution. The final phase of the selection involved one hundred straight hours of operations. Towards the end, Fiacre started to hallucinate. But he was part of a small band – forty out of the original one hundred candidates – who succeeded.

*

If for Fiacre the RPF's October 1990 invasion of Rwanda played out as an extraordinarily difficult ordeal, for President Habyarimana and his party, the MRND, it provided a completely unexpected stroke of good luck. Still reeling from the popular unrest that had followed the downturn in the Rwandan economy and threatened to unseat the government, the invasion gave Habyarimana an excuse to suppress all opposition. Martial law was introduced, and the country was placed on a war footing. Almost from the first day of the invasion, large numbers of opponents of the government were arrested in Kigali and other major towns.

The Habyarimana government took steps to further fuel a state of panic among the population. In mid-October, it staged a false attack on Kigali. In the middle of the night, the sustained cadence of automatic weapons was heard on the outskirts of the capital, even though the rebels were nowhere close. The minister of defence called on all citizens to track down and apprehend the 'infiltrators'.

In the capital, those arrested were placed in the national stadium. Prisoners, for the most part either belonging to the political opposition or Tutsi, were kept in densely crowded conditions, subjected to beatings, thefts and rapes, and denied food and water for days on end.

According to human rights groups, opponents of the government were executed.

This situation lasted for months. Fearing a massacre like the ones that had occurred in Burundi, diplomats and foreign governments mobilized to compel the president to release those being held prisoner in Kigali. Initially he feigned ignorance of the situation, but was forced in December 1990 to open the gates of the national stadium. By then, though, the tone for the future had been set; a list was kept with the names of those who had been detained.

On 23 January 1991, rebel General Paul Kagame launched another attack. This time it was on the northern town of Ruhengeri, in the homeland of the president and his wife, and her powerful clan. Having infiltrated the town the night before, the RPF attacked at dawn, taking Rwandan government forces completely by surprise. By midday the town was fully in the hands of the rebels. Fiacre Mboki was part of the attacking force. He and his men were told to move swiftly to take the prison before the fleeing government forces could massacre its inmates. A sizeable number of the freed prisoners joined General Kagame and his men when they moved on.

This surprise attack dealt a great psychological blow to the Habyarimana government, and more importantly to the president's wife and her entourage. What had been until then just hyped-up talk of an 'impending invasion' had turned into grim reality. And it was a reality that their forces seemed unable to repel.

The realization that, even with French military support, government forces could not stand up to a rebel attack must have come as an alarming wake-up call. Could it have been this recognition that triggered the genocide? Did the Habyarimana regime come to believe that, if they wanted to stay in power, they had no option but to follow the example of the Burundian military eighteen years before, and kill all of the (in this case Tutsi) leadership and intellectuals? It was at this moment in 1991 that the Akazu, Agathe Habyarimana's inner circle, was formed.

Whatever the case, as of that moment a plan seems to have been put in motion – a plan that was a prelude to genocide.* Over the months that followed, senior members of the government made visits to different parts of the country to ascertain the readiness of local officials to use murderous means to 'protect the nation'. If local officials resisted, and if counter-arguments did not do the trick, the reluctant officials were at first transferred. Later, they were simply eliminated.

Then the action began. Local officials were instructed to have their constituencies undertake 'their patriotic duty'. Initially this duty involved relatively innocuous activities, such as building twig fences to stop Tutsi-owned cows gaining access to community fields. But in areas where an RPF incursion had recently occurred, the populations were tasked with chasing down and killing RPF 'accomplices'. The people named as accomplices were likely to be their Tutsi neighbours. As an added incentive, it was announced that the assets of the people murdered could be claimed by those who had killed them.

After the genocide, I became fascinated by the ease with which the wider population, particularly the farmers, were drawn into this plan. Was it the historic acceptance of authority by the populations of the Great Lakes region of Africa, inherited from the colonial period, that made collusion easier? I suppose that the harsh realities of daily life could help to make some levels of violence seem like an everyday matter. But what was most insidious was the use of euphemisms to cloak the brutal actions.

---

*   This said, some have argued that genocidal sentiments existed long before. Gregoire Kayibanda, first elected president of Rwanda, is reported to have declared: 'They (Tutsis) cannot attack us, we have one million hostages.'

There was never any question of killing Tutsis. Instead, the instructions to the farmers were more elliptical. *Clear the ground*, they were told. *Cut down the grass.*

The mobilization of the population to this deadly project was helped by the establishment of Radio Télévision Libre des Mille Collines (RTLMC) in 1993. Set up by the businessman Felicien Kabuga, the station very quickly became popular. Kabuga ensured that the station excited the animosities and prejudices that existed among many young Hutus, and an effective mix was found between hate-filled rhetoric, humour and contemporary Zairian music. Renowned professors expounded on air the historic injustices that had been inflicted by Tutsis on the Hutus, and the station took the use of euphemisms to new levels. It popularized the use of the term 'cockroaches' to describe the Tutsis, and called for the extermination of these pests. Quickly the idea took hold.

The RTLMC played a lead role in the progressive dehumanization of the Tutsis, and was key in preparing the populations for violence on a mass scale. Initially I couldn't understand how anybody would buy some of the nonsense that I was told was broadcast over the airwaves. It was said, for example, that the Tutsis had tails that were hidden by means of specially tailored trousers. But much later I read how the clergy of the Catholic Church had promulgated similar stories about Jews in the 1920s and '30s during Europe's interwar years.

Of course, lack of education made it easier for the masses to accept such myths, but even more enabling was the shocking involvement of many Catholic clergy, and the silence of others, as regards the killings. The hear-no-evil, see-no-evil approach to the mounting violence from the Church amounted to tacit collusion. But not everyone was silent. Take, for example, Antonia Locatelli, an Italian nun living and working in northern Rwanda, who was loved by the people she served. In early 1994, on Radio

France International, Locatelli refuted the official version of the violence. She explained that the killings, far from reflecting a spontaneous outburst of long-standing animosities, were actually the result of carefully prepared and orchestrated assaults. A few days later the sister was assassinated. The astounding thing is that there was no public reaction from her superiors.

8

The Killings Continue

After the RPF's initial attack on Ruhengeri, low intensity fighting dragged on for almost two and a half years. Foreign countries sponsored numerous attempts at ceasefires. Most of the time they achieved little and the fighting continued. But with each failed attempt, the international community ratcheted up the economic and political pressure on both sides to negotiate. In July 1992, finally, a ceasefire was signed in Arusha, Tanzania, in an agreement that became known as the Arusha Accords. In September, political talks began. They were intended to lead to a peace agreement and a government in which power would be shared between representatives of the existing Rwandan government and those from the rebel movement.

The Akazu, the secret organization centred around the president's wife, realized that an end to the fighting would also mean an end to their preeminence. They adamantly opposed the Arusha Accords. The president's wife was heard to say that she had no intention of allowing her husband to be held to the outcome of the talks. And in November 1992, midway through the latest round of talks, Habyarimana publicly dismissed the Arusha Accords. 'Mere pieces of paper,' he declared.

Over the course of 1992, negotiations about power sharing continued without any serious breakthrough. Tension on both sides mounted and, at the same time, there were greater numbers of killings on the ground. In more and more areas, the Akazu tested ways of mobilizing local people to undertake targeted killings, which further strained the fragile peace. In late January 1993, after the massacre of more than three hundred Tutsis in southern Rwanda, the RPF launched a major new offensive and the ceasefire broke.

Once again, the government forces were caught off guard and were pushed back in disarray. The RPF quickly recaptured Ruhengeri, and then began to advance on the capital. Panic spread all the way to Paris. How could the French-trained Rwandan troops have once again melted away so quickly? President Mitterrand dispatched several hundred additional French troops to Kigali with the clear implication that, should the RPF advance on the capital, they would find themselves fighting French paratroopers as well as Rwandan government soldiers. By then, the RPF troops were already within thirty kilometres of Kigali. Recognizing that the balance of forces had shifted, on 20 February the RPF declared a unilateral ceasefire. For the population it wasn't too soon. Over one and a half million civilians, mostly Hutu, had already fled their homes.

Fiacre later wondered whether the RPF may have miscalculated the local reaction to its 1993 incursion into Rwanda. Their objective was to pressure the Rwandan government into stopping the killings of Rwandan Tutsis, but the invasion had served to further instigate anti-Tutsi sentiment. The Akazu were able to argue that the invasion was one more attempt by the RPF to re-impose Tutsi domination. Radio broadcasts urged the Hutu population to oppose the invasion and rally around the president.

Under strong international pressure, an uneasy peace was once again entered into. It didn't remain untested for long. In Burundi, on 21 October 1993, Tutsi extremist officers assassinated the elected president. The mob violence that followed in Burundi left five thousand dead. A new wave of Burundian Hutus fled to Rwanda, bringing with them even greater hate and fear.

But the international political context as regards Rwanda had changed in two important ways which restrained the Akazu from fanning the flames of violence. The first was that the United Nations Security Council had passed a resolution establishing UNAMIR – the United Nations Assistance Mission for Rwanda – which was charged with supervising the implementation of the Arusha Accords; it included the deployment to Rwanda of over 2,500 military personnel, among them Belgian paratroopers. The second and more important change was Rwanda's accession to a two-year rotating seat on the UN Security Council. The Rwandan government was now in a strong position to shape discussions in the Security Council on Rwanda. These changes must have convinced the Akazu that the time was not right for another 'spontaneous' expression of 'popular discontent'.

9

The Indoctrination into a Genocidal Ideology

While the dramatic and complicated history of Rwanda in the lead-up to the genocide is clear to me, I continue to be puzzled by the individual whom I call for the purposes of this story Kamana Rumbashi.

There are few hard facts known about Rumbashi's early years. He was born towards the middle of 1963, in Rwanda, the small nation in the heart of Africa also known as the Land of a Thousand Hills. He gained a university place sometime in the late 1970s, graduating in the early to mid-1980s.* In 1992, he was recruited to a coveted post as an IT specialist within the United Nations Development Programme (UNDP) in Kigali.

---

*   As with much else concerning him, it has been difficult to discover where exactly Rumbashi attended university. There are some indications he may have started at the University of Butare and then was offered the possibility of getting a software engineering diploma from an 'Algerian university', though which one is not known.

A confidential internal investigation of his employment history (in 2004) was unable to identify whether his initial contractual affiliation with UNDP was a short-term consultancy or a longer-term commitment, since the records were found to be 'incomplete and widely dispersed'.*

Like in all other countries in which it operates, the UN in Rwanda was made up of a series of specialized agencies. The welfare of children was managed by UNICEF; matters related to health by the World Health Organization (WHO); agriculture by the Food and Agricultural Organization (FAO); refugees by the United Nations High Commissioner for Refugees (UNHCR); emergency food aid by the World Food Programme (WFP); and development by UNDP. In theory each had its own area of work, but in practice there was a lot of overlap and much fighting over turf. Not only did the UNDP representative coordinate the UN's overall response, but the communications system of the UN also fell under his office. On his appointment to the UN, Rumbashi entered directly the inner sanctum. He had access to the traffic of confidential telexes and cables between the UN system in Rwanda and headquarters in New York.

From a witness statement written against Rumbashi after the genocide, it seems that, while employed by the UN, he was training an Interahamwe militia. The Interahamwe (meaning 'Those Who Attack Together') was the armed element of the Mouvement Révolutionnaire National pour le Développement (MRND), the party of President Habyarimana. It began life as a soccer fan club sponsored by the party but, once trained and equipped by the Rwandan army, the club was transformed into a militia, and rapidly evolved into a killing machine.

---

*   This internal investigation was undertaken in November of that year following an article in the *New York Times* in which I accused the UN of a 'don't tell me, I don't want to know' form of bureaucratic cover up concerning Kamana Rumbashi's misdeeds.

By 1992, Rumbashi had multiple commitments: working with the UN during weekdays, possibly representing the MRND in his local community or quartier, and training with the militia.* In December 1993, according to witness statements, Rumbashi was presented in an MRND rally as the party leader of his quartier, Nyamirambo. If the witness accounts are accurate, did Rumbashi not realize that the goals of the Interahamwe and the principles of the United Nations were incompatible? Did he know but not care, interested only in using the UN to further Hutu power? Or could it be possible that he did believe in the UN ideals but saw Tutsis as not human enough to be worthy of the protections afforded by the Universal Declaration of Human Rights?

Whatever the case, at a December 1993 MRND rally, well into his UNDP career, a witness records Kamana Rumbashi delivering a speech in which he declared that Hutus should help him to achieve his goal of no Tutsis left in Nyarambo.

This speech, if confirmed, would have displayed a measure of the strength of Rumbashi's anti-Tutsi feeling. But what is clear** is that he is known to have shown great hostility towards the more prominent of his UN Tutsi colleagues. His rage was particularly targeted towards Florence Ngirumpatse, the head of personnel within UNDP.

Florence was popular with all the UN staff. Efficient and just in her professional dealings, she was also known to be attentive and almost motherly with staff who had personal difficulties. Florence suspected that Rumbashi was part of the Interahamwe, and will have distrusted –

---

*   In a 24 July 2015 AP interview (available on YouTube *Rebel leader accused of genocide lives in Paris*) Rumbashi emphatically denied the accusation, stating that he had 'never been in touch with any militia, I was not a militia, I didn't have any relationship with militia, I have never been with any militia in any house of anybody.'
**   Told to me by numerous sources, including Gromo Alex.

possibly even feared – him. Rumbashi is alleged to have played a role in Florence's murder.

Florence tried repeatedly to raise concerns about Rumbashi with her bosses. But her complaints were written off as the product of professional jealousy. The only one who did take Florence's concerns seriously was Gromo Alex, who was to become my best friend and is the person who told me this part of the story.

Gromo and I had gotten to know each other over the years leading up to 1994 through the various UN seminars and conferences we both attended. Before being transferred to Rwanda in January 1994, he had headed the UN's Emergency Prevention and Preparedness Group in Addis Ababa, Ethiopia. I took an immediate liking to this bear-like character. Gromo was the archetype of the rough, exuberant and generous American. When he saw me twitch on first being called Chuck, he decided that from then on that would be how I would be known to him.

Gromo had been sent to Rwanda to help coordinate the UN's support to the refugees from Burundi. He worked closely with Florence, whom he quickly got to appreciate and respect, and with Rumbashi, about whom he, too, developed serious doubts.

*

This much about Kamana Rumbashi I believe to be more or less accurate.[*] What I have not been able to establish is how Rumbashi developed such a powerful antipathy for Tutsis, to the point of allegedly leading his fellows into murder. What brought him to this point? There is little to go on.

---

[*] Through official documents, ICTR witness statements, conversations with survivors and friends.

Rumbashi is a Hutu, that is certain. In his early schooling, he would almost certainly have been steeped in a particular view of history that pitted Hutus and Tutsis against one another. He would have been told that the Hutus had been in Rwanda well before the Tutsis. That the Tutsis had come as foreign invaders from Abyssinia. That in any case, the Tutsis, who represented only 15 per cent of the population, had no right whatsoever to dominate political life. But although the Catholic Church may have tried to nurture a sense of the Tutsis as 'other', there is no evidence as to the impact these sentiments had on Rumbashi. Schools in the countryside were not sharply segregated, and it is probable that Rumbashi attended alongside Tutsi children who lived nearby. It would be convenient if there was evidence about a specific incident that could have triggered Rumbashi's extreme antipathy to Tutsis – bullying by a Tutsi schoolmate, say, or a rebuff by a Tutsi girl – but there is not. And even if there were, it would be a disappointingly trite explanation for the dramatic events that followed.

Perhaps university was the site of Rumbashi's political awakening? Though no records exist to confirm this, it is quite possible that Rumbashi attended the University of Butare. Were it the case, many of his fellow students there would have been Hutus who had fled persecution in Burundi. They would have talked freely of their experience of assassination and harassment at the hands of Burundian Tutsis. Moreover, some professors, such as Nahimana Ferdinand (currently serving thirty years after being sentenced by the International Criminal Tribunal for Rwanda), would have further stoked outrage, by harping on the horrors of the purges conducted by the Tutsi military in Burundi.

But the University of Butare was far from an unambiguous bastion of extremism. There would have been moderating influences, of which Rumbashi would have been no doubt aware. When, in the early 1970s,

Hutu students mobilized to throw out their Tutsi counterparts, the rector at the time, Dr Sylvestre Nsanzimana, put a stop to this action. One of the university's most distinguished alumni, Jean-Baptiste Habyalimana, became the 'Prefet' of Butare, who when the mass killings started in April 1994 fiercely resisted the orders from his superiors in Kigali to trigger violence in his area. He held out, resisted and resisted, until they killed him.

10

The Aftermath of the Failed Somali Experiment

While members of the international community who were present in Rwanda were more or less aware of the gravity of unfolding events, the attention in their capitals was focused on Somalia. The US-dominated UN Somalia intervention actually lasted less than twelve months, but it absorbed the full attention of the international community. Unlike Rwanda, Somalia was a failed state – a state in the throes of anarchy, not dissimilar to the Europe of the Dark Ages. This anarchic environment was not the result of confrontation between ethnically or ideologically competing forces seeking to control the institutions of the state. It was an environment defined by profiteers, warlords and their drugged-up hordes.

The dead body of a US special forces soldier dragged through the streets of Mogadishu had marked the end of the Somali experiment, and for almost a decade to come, that image destroyed the appetite of the international community for any more ambitious post-Cold War form of intervention. It is impossible to understand Rwanda without appreciating the significance of the debacle in Somalia. Eight hundred and fifty thousand Rwandans paid a monstrous price for that failure.

The international community was not unconcerned by what it saw happening in Rwanda. However, the Rwandan situation, when compared to the anarchy of Somalia, seemed controllable. Rwandan violence was framed within a narrative of traditional tribal hostilities, an interpretation fuelled by the regime.

France's presence in Rwanda also provided a level of comfort to the international community. The Habyarimana regime was seen as a French client with whom it was possible to work, unlike the various Somali warlords. The dance – whereby the US and UK demanded that a negotiated settlement with the RPF be found, while the Habyarimana government, with the support of the French, resisted – seemed a much more manageable one.

How wrong they all were.

11

The United Nations Assistance Mission for Rwanda (UNAMIR)

On 28 December 1993, the RPF marched into Kigali. It must have infuriated Rumbashi to see the rebel fighters entering his capital. The hundreds of rebels marched in formation, providing a protective cordon around the newly designated RPF ministers who were due to join the power-sharing government.

The whole of Kigali came out to watch the arrival of the rebels. Not a sound came from the crowd. Spectators were too shocked. The fighters filed calmly on either side of the vehicles containing the new ministers. They looked the part of a rebel force: worn combat fatigues, black berets and rubber wellington boots. Some carried AK-47s loosely in their hands, others .50 calibre M2 machine guns and RPG-7 rocket launchers. Many of the people I talked to after the genocide, who had been in Kigali at the time, recalled being struck by how much the fighters exuded confidence.

In spite of the long ordeal they'd been through, they appeared alert and disciplined. No orders came from the officers walking at their side, and none appeared to be needed.

I was told later by Fiacre that each of these soldiers had been handpicked for the task. All were the rank of sergeant or above. If the situation turned bad, if the peace process collapsed, the rebel fighters would be able to operate in small autonomous units.

Initially it appeared as if the rebels had entered Kigali without any other protection than the armament they carried. It was not the case. Discreetly to the sides of their advance were positioned Ferret tanks containing Belgian UN parachutists.

Rumbashi, and other supporters of the Habyarimana regime, must have realized on that day the inadequacy of their own forces. As the lengthy procession moved along, I am told that the crowd slowly began to clap. Soon there was cheering. Rumbashi might have assumed that the celebrants were Tutsis or Tutsi sympathizers. He wouldn't have understood that a large part of the population only wanted peace.

*

Up until this point, President Habyarimana had found excuse after excuse to avoid convening the new power-sharing government. With the arrival of the RPF contingent, he ran out of excuses. Ministers from the region and from the West flew into Kigali to convince the president to honour the agreement he had signed. He still refused. And when he was finally called to Arusha, Tanzania, to a meeting of heads of state from the region, the Akazu members knew that this was the end of their hopes. There was no way that President Habyarimana could resist the pressure from his regional peers. Even the president's wife must have realized that the game was over.

The president's departure for Arusha was unexpectedly delayed. The army chief of staff, an Akazu member who was meant to accompany the delegation, couldn't be found. He was finally brought to the airport, protesting that he had important commitments in Kigali that kept him from boarding. But the president insisted. With visible reluctance, the chief of staff climbed into the presidential plane.

The delegation arrived in Arusha on 5 April. Under tremendous pressure the following morning, the president finally succumbed and signed an agreement committing to the immediate establishment of a transitional government. Late that afternoon, as they prepared to return to Rwanda, the army chief of staff again arrived late at the airport and again argued vociferously against boarding.

But the president insisted that the chief of staff accompany him. The president also offered a seat in his plane to the newly instated Burundian president. Accepting the offer turned out to be a very bad call.

PART FOUR

THE GENOCIDE: *EIGHT HUNDRED AND FIFTY THOUSAND DEAD IN ONE HUNDRED DAYS*

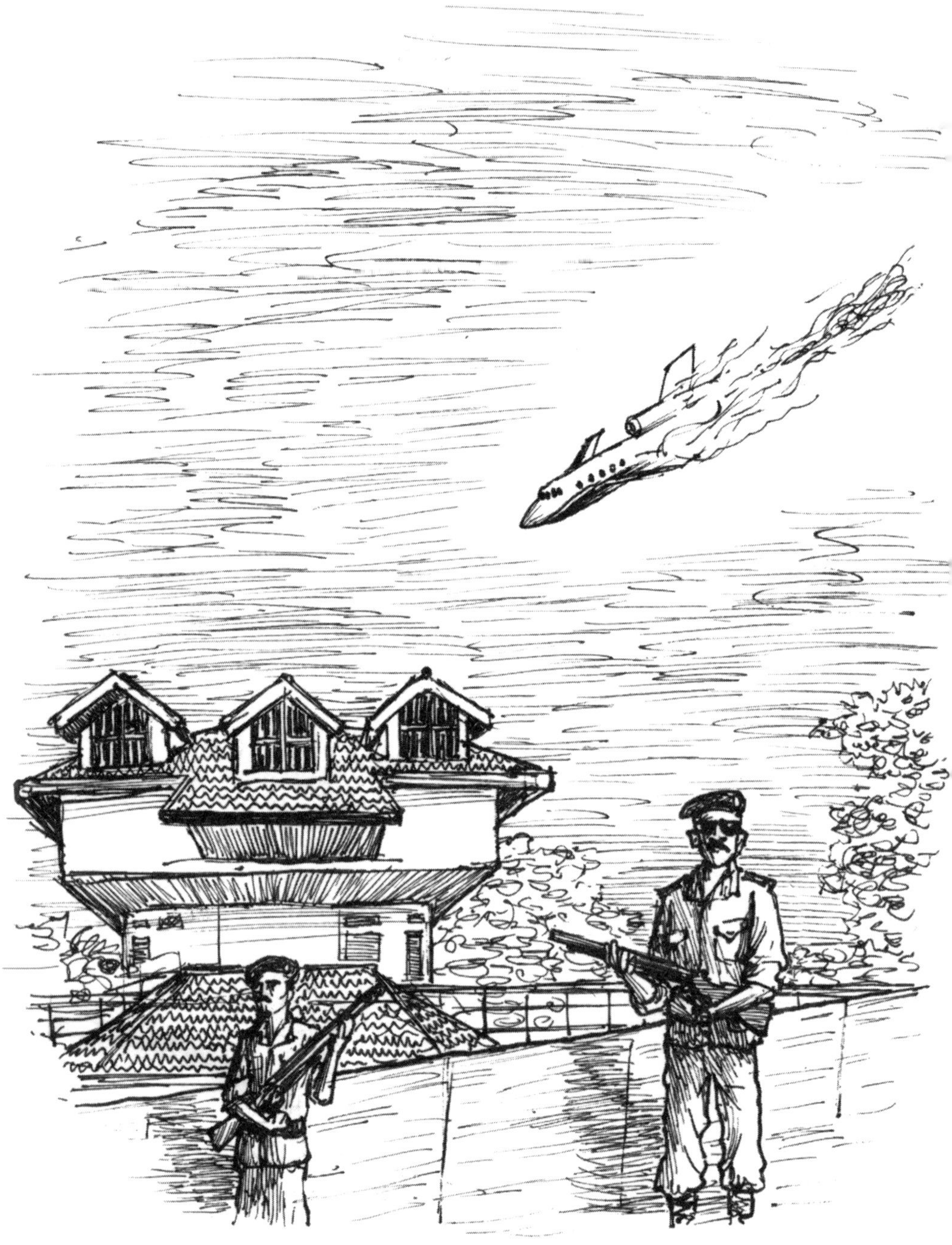

The event that triggered the Rwandan genocide occurred between 20h00 and 21h00 local time on the evening of 6 April 1994. A Dassault Falcon plane carrying the presidents of Rwanda and Burundi was struck just as it was making its final approach onto the runway of Kigali airport. The first surface-to-air missile tore off a wing. The second missile hit the tail. The plane burst into flames and exploded on impact in the garden of the presidential palace.

Controversy still rages over the question of who shot down the plane. Some contend that it was forces loyal to General Paul Kagame. General Kagame wasn't satisfied with the outcome of the peace talks being held in Arusha, they suggest. He shot down the plane knowing full well that it would trigger reprisals against Tutsis in Rwanda and enable him to take control of the country. If this is true, then Kagame was complicit in the genocide of his own people.

Others, however, point to the flaws in this argument. Peace talks looked set to give the RPF, who represented only some 15 per cent of the population, more than they could have hoped for: a 40 per cent representation in the army and a coalition government in which they would play a prominent role. Moreover, the two missiles that shot down the presidential plane were launched from the barracks housing the Presidential Guard and other units known as loyal to the existing regime.

What is irrefutable is that the plane's destruction signalled the start of the bloodiest mass slaughter since the end of the Second World War. In Rwanda, in a period of only one hundred days, approximately eight hundred thousand Tutsis and fifty thousand Hutus were murdered.[1] At times, there were per day more killings in Rwanda than in the three industrialized Nazi death camps – Belzec, Sobibor and Treblinka – combined.

I arrived in Rwanda as the deputy UN humanitarian coordinator about a month into the killings. Gromo Alex had gone to great lengths to persuade me to join him. What was going on in Rwanda was, he insisted, beyond anything that I could imagine. Most of the UN had decamped to Nairobi, and he needed support.

This section of the story draws on what I experienced, on witness statements and other legal documents, on conversations I had during and after the genocide, and on my own research. Most of the prominent witnesses I've introduced before. These include Gromo Alex, the UN humanitarian who never hesitated to speak his mind; the teacher turned rebel Lt Fiacre Mboki of the Rwandan Patriotic Front; and Father Vjeko Curic, the Franciscan priest of Bosnian origin who ran a parish school near Kabgayi. An additional and very significant witness is Josette Umutoniwase, the only one among this group who was a victim and is a survivor of the genocide.

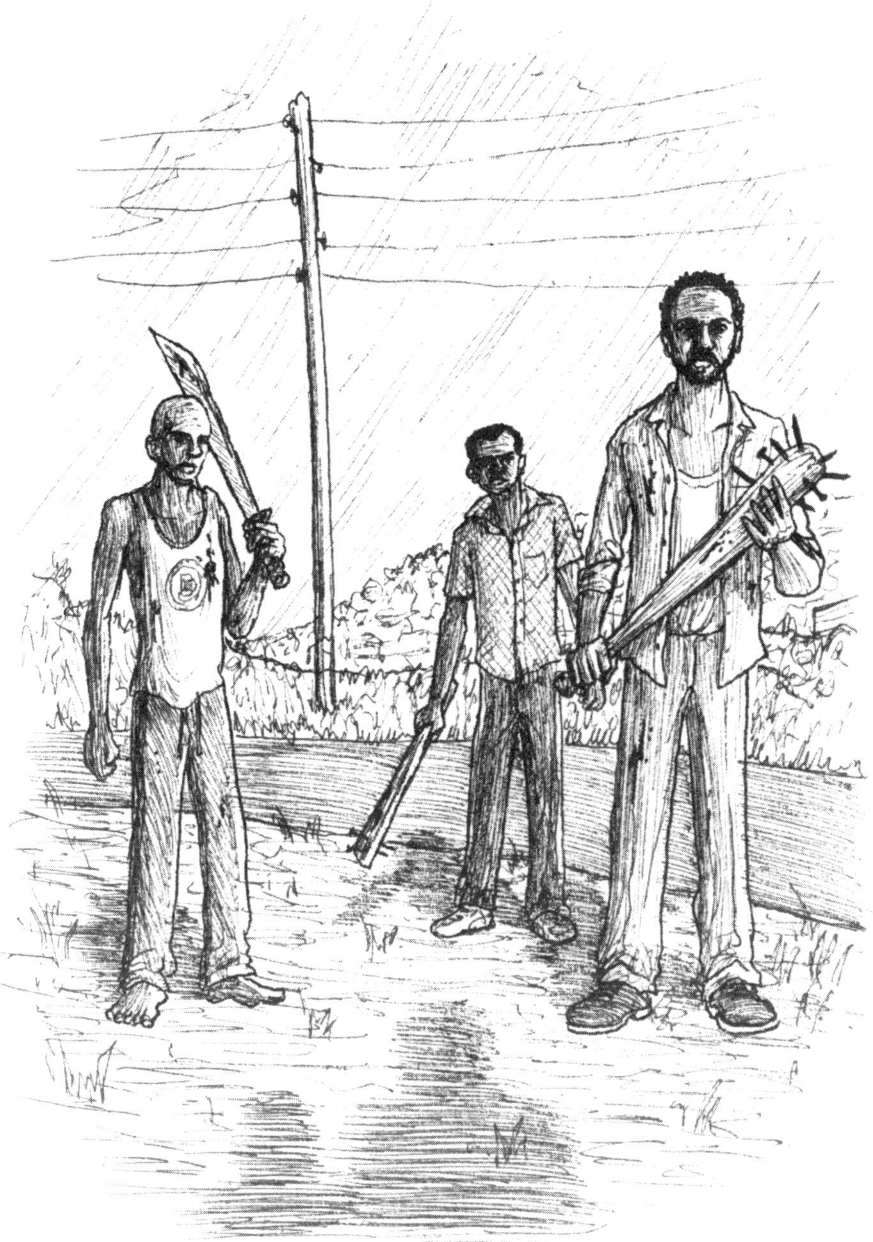

12

The Genocide Begins

Within thirty minutes of the downing of the presidential plane, roadblocks were established throughout Kigali. All who approached the barriers were ordered to show their identity cards. Those who turned out to be Tutsis, or who didn't have such papers, were held at the side of the road. Government troops and Interahamwe began murdering 'enemies' and 'accomplices'.

Kamana Rumbashi*

A number of witnesses identified Rumbashi as managing at least three roadblocks, one of which was conveniently located in front of his own

---

*   It is essential to repeat that many of those presumed to have participated in this brutal period of Rwanda's history have yet to account in front of a court of law for their alleged actions. Until they have done so, acts such as those that follow cannot be used to confirm guilt. This having been said, a list of the allegations made against him were sent to 'Kamana Rumbashi's' lawyer for onward transimission. No response was received.

house. Rumbashi, for his part, emphatically denies these and all the other allegations. The city of Kigali, situated at the heart of the country, is built on eleven ridges with valleys in between. The supposed Rumbashi roadblocks were positioned on a hill or 'colline' known as Nyamirambo. This hill was also the site of the UN offices, of the Sisters of Charity orphanage, and of the Hôtel des Mille Collines.

Gromo Alex

As soon as Gromo heard the explosions, he contacted the UN civilian radio room. They had no news to give him. He then contacted the UN military mission, commanded by the remarkable Canadian General Dallaire. Dallaire's military assistant confirmed that something serious had happened at the airport, and that a UN military patrol had been sent to investigate. The military assistant promised Gromo that he would call back as soon as there was news. Gromo then called each of his staff individually and instructed them to stay home, not to move around the city. By the time he had finished, UN security was issuing similar instructions over the radio network.

At around 22h00, General Dallaire's military assistant called back and told Gromo that the UN military patrol had been turned back at the entrance to the airport. On the way back to the UN base they had seen checkpoints being established by military and the Interahamwe, and elements of the Presidential Guard moving from house to house.

Gromo then shared the information he'd received with the UN representative. His boss seemed nervous. Gromo, an experienced aid worker who had gone through his own baptism of fire many years earlier in Chad, understood how disorienting the initial stages of an emergency could be. He just hoped that the UN representative would be in better shape the next morning.

Lieutenant Fiacre Mboki of the Rwandan Patriotic Front

At around 22h00, Fiacre received instructions from his commander to stand ready to deploy his platoon at a moment's notice. It was only by listening to a bulletin on the BBC World Service that he learned of the uproar in Kigali. Fiacre instructed his platoon to sleep fully equipped.

Father Vjeko Curic

Father Vjeko, an avid listener to Radio France Internationale, heard about the crash when the programme he was listening to was interrupted by a news flash announcing it. He tried to get more information from the archbishopric, but they too were in the dark. He went to the church to say a prayer for the departed soul of those killed, and for peace in the country.

Josette Umutoniwase

Josette had just turned sixteen. She was reading a story to her little sister, ten-year-old Esther, when the explosions from the presidential plane shook the quartier. Shooting followed almost immediately. Later came heavy pounding on the front gate. Augustin Ntashamaje, her father, who worked for the UN World Food Programme (WFP), found himself confronting a group of soldiers from the Presidential Guard. When he showed them his UN identity card, they moved on.

That night, Josette and her family huddled in the living room. They listened to the chatter on the UN radio, but there was little in the way of solid information. It was only by tuning into Radio Télévision Libre des Mille Collines (RTLMC), the hate-filled station sponsored by the government, that the family learned that the president's plane had been shot down. The announcer reported that government troops and the Interahamwe were searching Kigali for the 'enemy and their accomplices'.

13

Days 1–10: Killings in Kigali

Between day one and day ten of the genocide, the killers concentrated their energies in Kigali, targeting opposition members and people of influence who were seen as threats to the Habyarimana regime. The vast majority of the killings were carried out by the Presidential Guard and the Interahamwe militia.

Kamana Rumbashi*

In the first few days after the downing of the presidential plane, Rumbashi, like the other UN staff, was instructed by his superiors to stay at home. This forced absence seems to have served him well.

Witness statements collected by the investigators of the International Criminal Tribunal for Rwanda (ICTR) some seven years later place

---

*   All that is presented in terms of the alleged actions of Kamana Rumbashi come from among the twelve ICTR (International Criminal Tribunal for Rwanda) witness statements collected in 2001. Only a fraction of the allegations have been included in the manuscript.

Kamana Rumbashi in the killings from the earliest days of the genocide. Though the statements are not always consistent with one another, and some are possibly more credible than others, Rumbashi is mentioned in a significant number of the statements as being seen with men carrying machetes, clubs and AK-47 automatic weapons, and he himself is said to have carried a 9 mm semi-automatic pistol, at times even wearing parts of a military uniform. According to several witnesses, he was seen to travel from house to house in order to kill the occupants within. Was he operating on his own initiative? Or was he obeying orders? Given his alleged connections with prominent members of the Interahamwe and the supposed affiliation to the president's political party that a number of witnesses have attributed to Rumbashi, one would imagine the latter being a possibility – at least, in the beginning. Later, at the time when he is alleged to have participated in the murder of his UN colleagues, he may have continued on his own initiative.

In a written statement released by his attorneys some ten years later, 'Kamana Rumbashi' confirmed that during the genocide, he lived with his family in Nyamirambo in the location identified in a number of the ICTR witness depositions. However, he rejected allegations that he was involved in killings in Nyamirambo as 'untrue and improperly motivated'. He added that he, too, was victimized by government soldiers, and braved dozens of militia roadblocks in order to report to work at the UNDP compound.

Whatever the case, a man called Sebujisho and his whole family were among the first to be killed. It is alleged in a witness statement that Rumbashi arrived at the house, located near the Baobab Hotel on an adjacent colline to Nyamirambo, wearing military trousers and a civilian shirt, and carrying a rifle. He was accompanied by a number of Interahamwe. He is alleged to have explained that Sebujisho was a Tutsi rebel sympathizer and that the whole family had to die. He is reported to have instructed the militia accompanying him to eliminate them entirely, and waited outside. Were the statement to be correct, then the men were reported to have gone in and an initial series of shots were heard, followed by a long sequence of multiple shots. Sebujisho, his wife and their four children were dead.

From there the group moved to the nearby home of Gaspard. On the way there, Rumbashi is alleged, in the same witness statement, to have told the men that Gaspard was a Hutu businessman who collaborated with Tutsi spies. He and his family must die. One of the men of the group knocked on the door of the kiosk in front of the house. When Gaspard's wife came out, Rumbashi is reported, by the same witness, to have ordered her to fetch her husband. Rumbashi is then said to have squared up to the husband and demanded to know who had killed the president. Gaspard replied that he did not know; he didn't work for the cockroaches. 'You're lying,' Rumbashi supposedly insisted. The husband and wife were shot.

From there, and according to two witness statements, the group walked to Ignace Mujyarugamba's house. Mujyarugamba too was a cockroach who worked for the UN, Rumbashi is reported to have said. When Rumbashi knocked on Mujyarugamba's door, a child of about eight answered. The child saw blood on some of the men accompanying Rumbashi and ran screaming into the house, with Rumbashi and the rest of the group following close behind. They forced Mujyarugamba out into the open area of the compound. Rumbashi is said to have stood him up against the wall and to have announced that he had come to kill him. Mujyarugamba is reported to have smiled back. This was not the first time that Rumbashi had wanted to kill him, he apparently retorted. Mujyarugamba was shot first in the head, and then in the chest. Allegedly on Rumbashi's orders, the rest of the family were murdered.

From there, according to one witness statement, the group moved on to a house behind Muyarugamba's house.* They walked straight into the compound. Two children and a house girl were in the compound. Rumbashi reportedly asked the house girl where the others were and was told in the house. It is alleged that he then took two of the militia and went into the house with them. There were shots inside and Rumbashi came out. The militia then shot the two children as they left.

What was meant to be the last house of the day was located on the other side of the hill, and belonged to a man called Ntare, a person who frequented the same bar as the men moving towards his house. Though Rumbashi maintained in an interview with the Australian Broadcasting Corporation journalist Ginny Stein that he did not know Ntare,** it is alleged in a witness statement that he told the group accompanying him that no one in the household should be left alive. After multiple shots were heard, the men came back out. They brought the household guard with them, supposedly pointing out to Rumbashi that he was not a family member. 'Kill him anyway,' Rumbashi is alleged to have said. This sparked a small rebellion. They were tired; Rumbashi should do it, said one of his men. According to one of the witnesses who participated in the killings, Rumbashi obliged.

It is again claimed in one witness statement that Rumbashi then explained that there was another family nearby who he wanted killed. The group moved to the house next to Ntare's. When they arrived, Rumbashi

---

*   The witness could not recall the house owner's name.
**   21 February 2007, ABC *Dateline*, *Rwanda – Questions of Murder*. Reporter: 'Do you remember the Ntare family?' Response: 'Ntare family? Yes, I don't know. I don't know that family.' Reporter: 'I spoke to someone who said that they saw you walk into the house and shoot dead the head of the family, and then shoot his wife as she ran down the corridor.' Response: 'Listen, whatever they said is not true. I have not done anything wrong. I have never been involved in any kind of crimes in Rwanda.'

is alleged to have instructed two of the men to go into the house and kill the occupants. They went in, shots were fired, and they came back out. The witness, who provided the statement to the ICTR, then went into the house. He counted eleven bodies, a lady whom he assumed to be the owner* of the house, four children under the age of twelve, two men in their twenties, a house girl and two or three other girls.

*

In those early days of the genocide, it couldn't have been a simple matter for the men with Rumbashi to kill. Most of them were now city dwellers, and few would have had the opportunity to participate in killings back in their villages. Rumbashi has been alleged, in a number of witness statements, to have been their leader, and as such would have had to keep a close eye on them to ensure that they complied. But he would have been helped in doing so by the tension engendered by the operations of other Interahamwe groups roaming nearby, by the shrill sound of their whistles as they chased down escaping victims. Rumbashi and the men with him would not have been alone. The whole of Kigali was in the throes of mass murder.

Still, there must have been one or two reluctant killers. It was once explained to me that each recalcitrant would be taken aside and, while sharing a bottle of Primus, the importance and necessity of the actions explained to them. The way to deal with a reluctant killer, I was told, was to provide more beer, select a Tutsi, and order that Tutsi be killed. Generally, my informant said, this did the trick. And if there was one insubordinate who still held back? One who would unfailingly shuffle to

---

*   Name not provided in the witness statement.

the side when the killings happened? Such a person, it was explained to me, was dangerous to the cohesion of the group and should be used as an example. After consuming large quantities of beer, all the men would have been taken to an open area and told to form a circle. The recalcitrant would be placed in the middle of this circle, along with a young Tutsi girl. He would be taunted and pushed back into the centre each time he tried to get out. The girl would kneel on the ground, crunched up into a ball, her cries drowned by increasingly angry shouts of 'Kill! Kill!' from the men around her. If he continued to resist, then one of the men would enter the circle, machete in hand. He would dispatch the girl with one swift blow and then, with a mighty swing, decapitate the recalcitrant.

In the first few days...

...he was instructed to stay home.

This served him well.

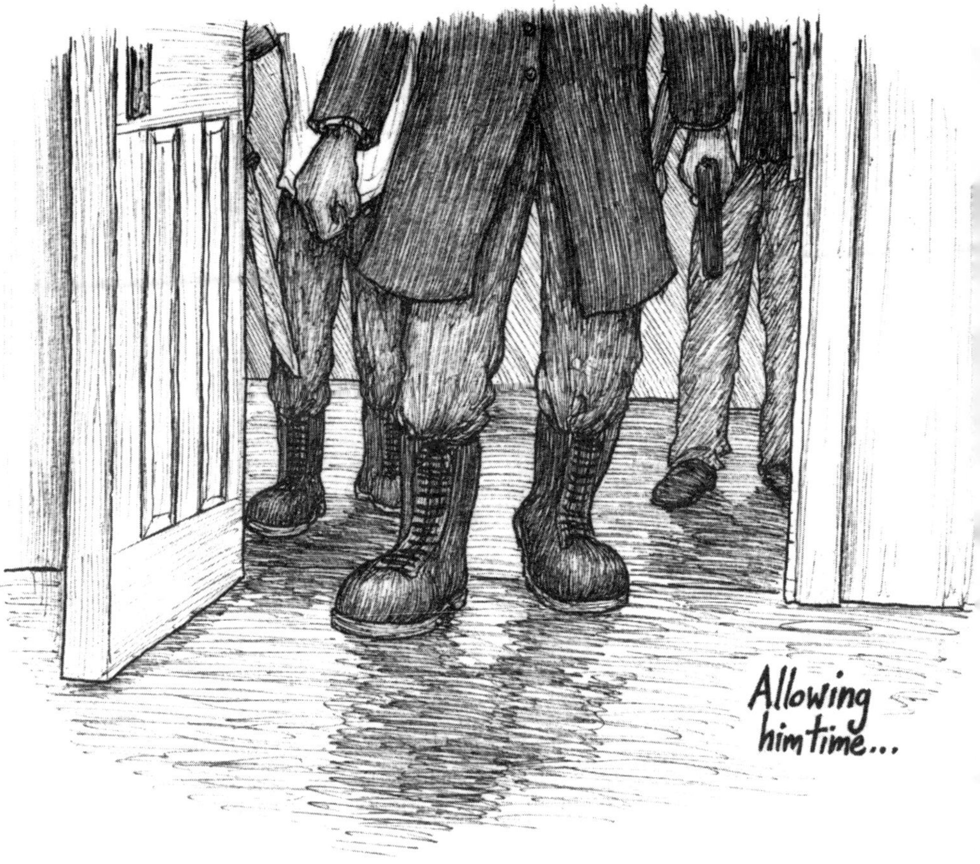
Allowing him time...

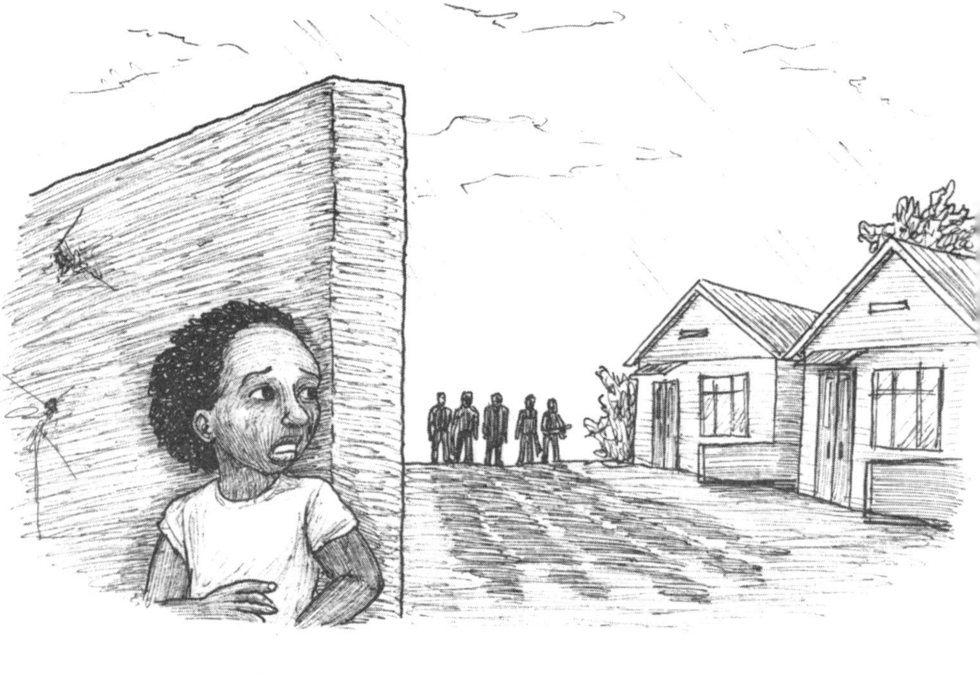

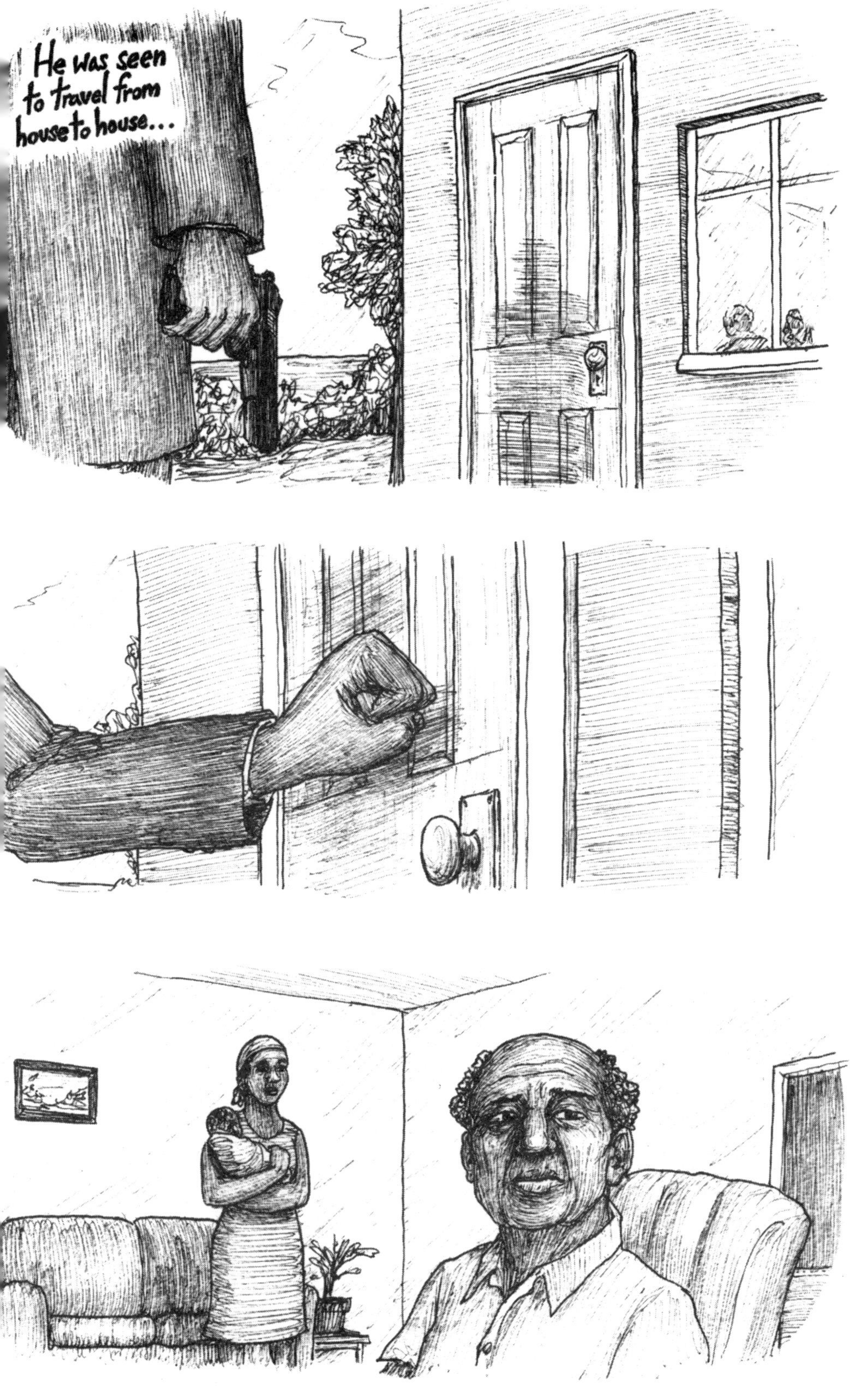
He was seen to travel from house to house...

Was he operating on his own initiative...

... or obeying orders?

Jean Sebujisho...

...was among the first to be killed.

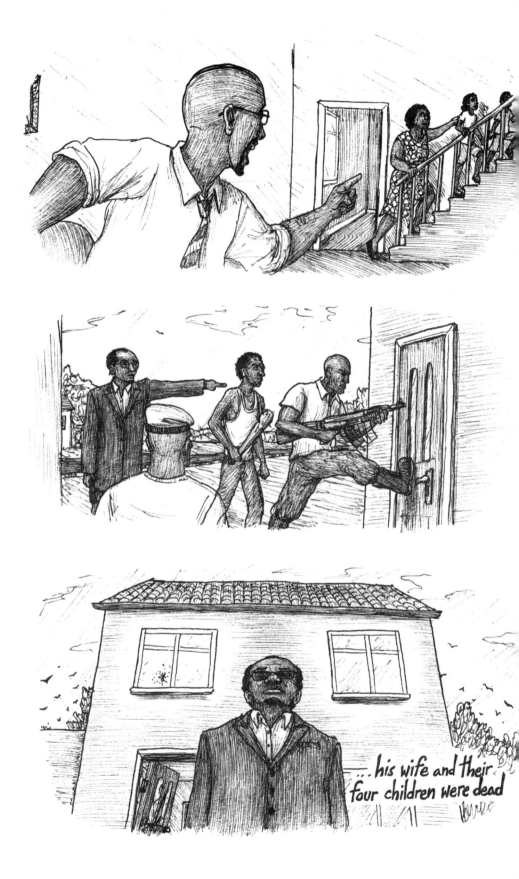

...his wife and their four children were dead

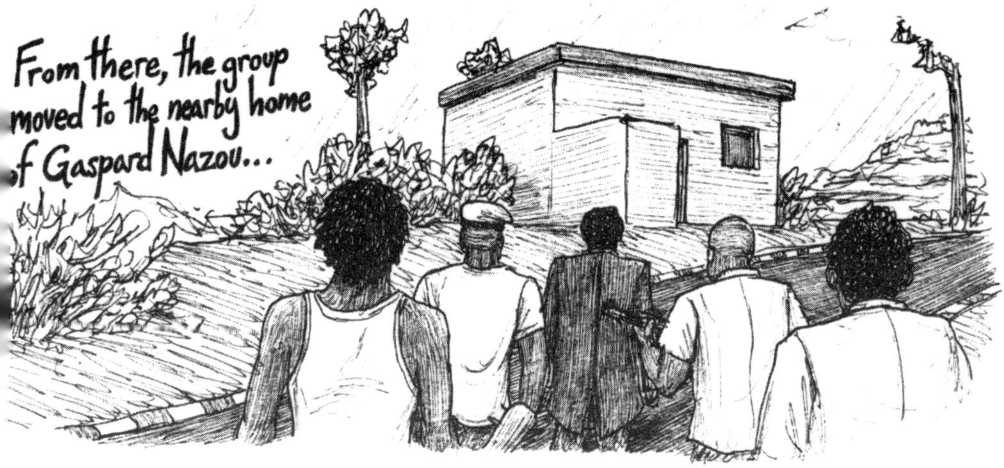
From there, the group moved to the nearby home of Gaspard Nazou...

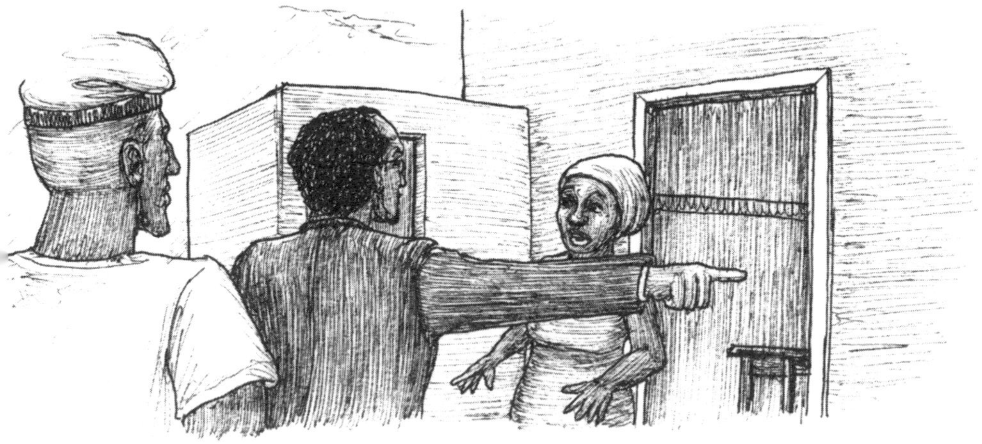

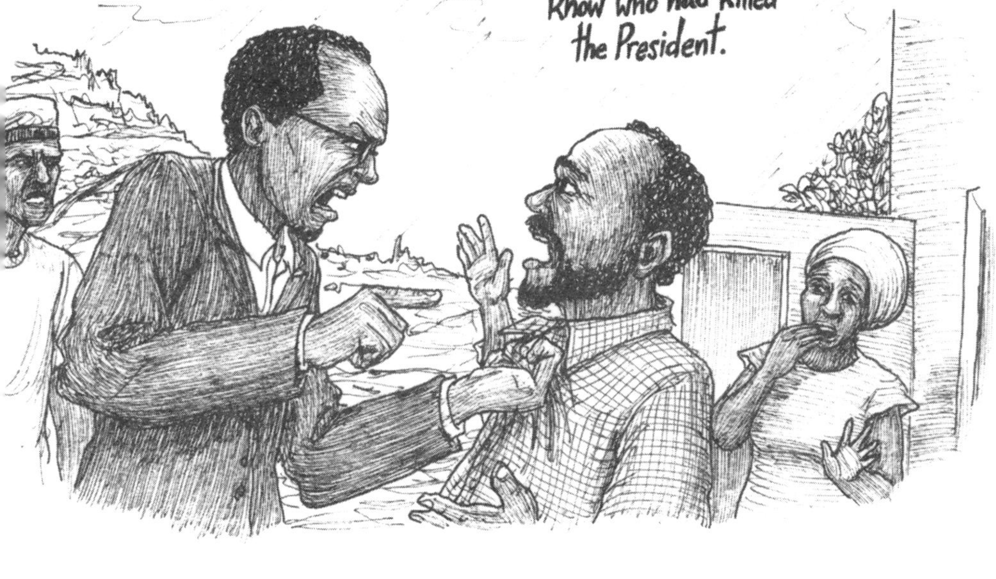
...and demanded to know who had killed the President.

The husband died immediately,
but the wife lay moaning…

Celestin too was a cockroach, he said...

...a very senior one, a high-level government official.

This was not the first time that
he had wanted to kill him...

On the other side of the hill...

...a man named Paul Ntare.

His men knew Paul.

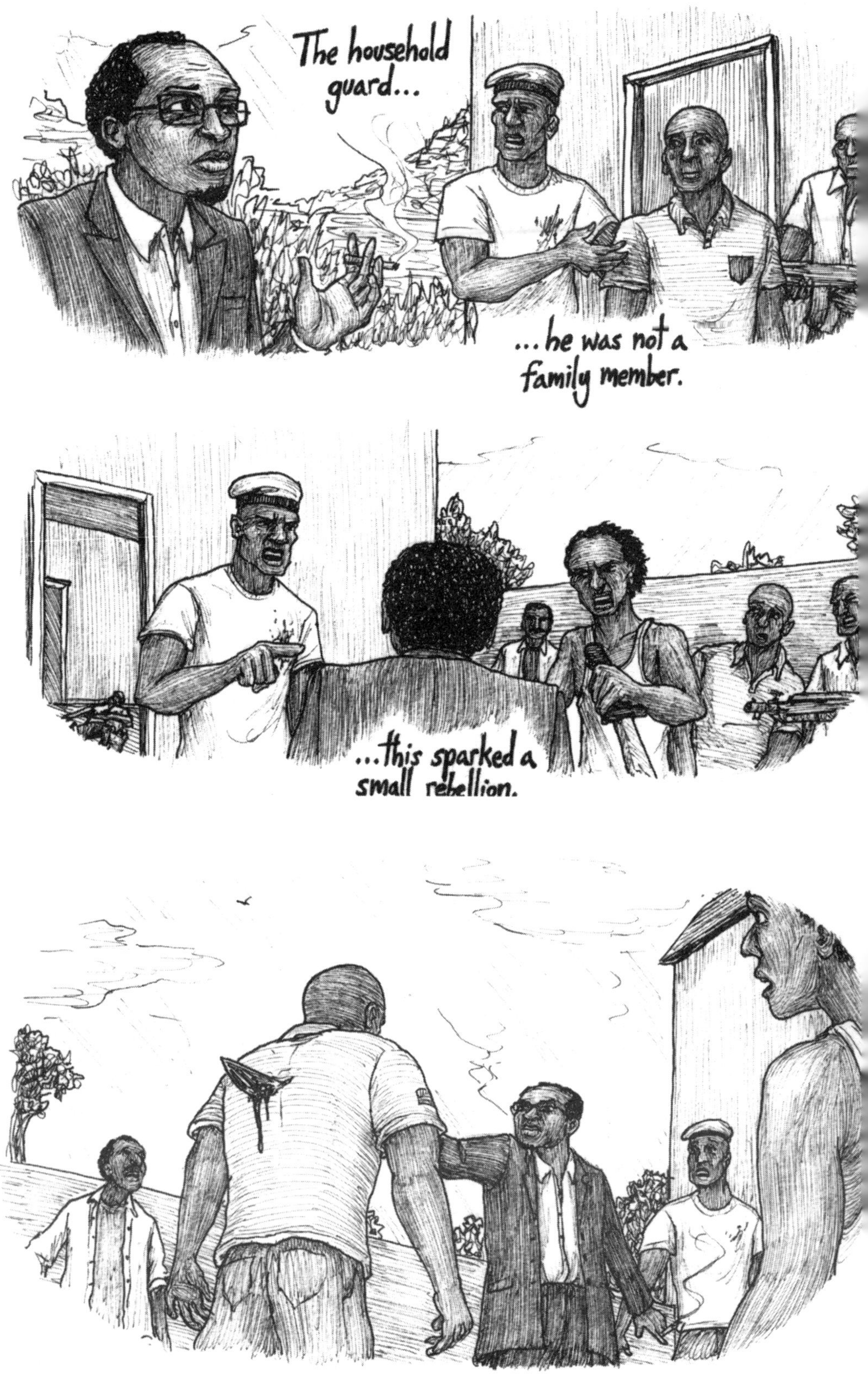
The household guard...
...he was not a family member.
...this sparked a small rebellion.

It wasn't a simple matter to induce his men to kill...

...had to keep a close eye on them to ensure that they complied.

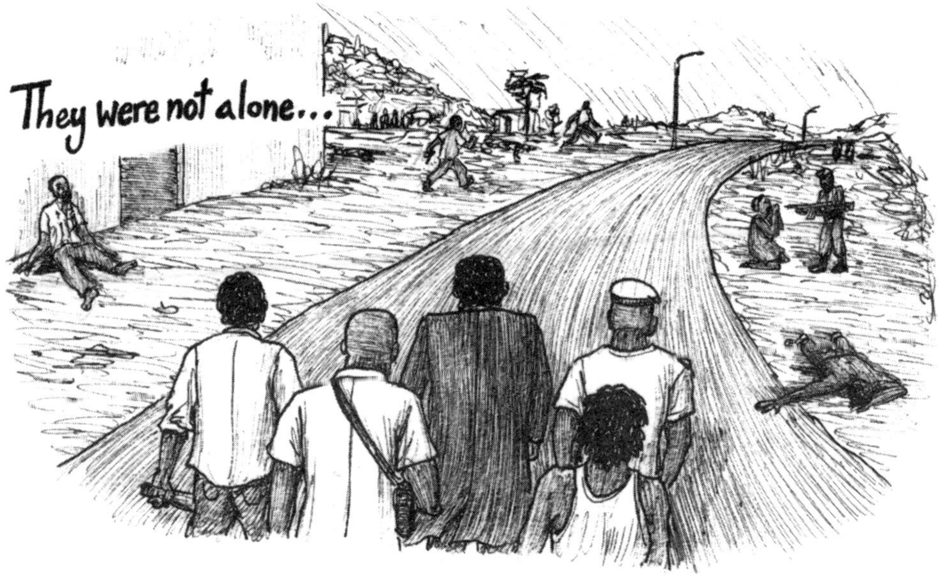
They were not alone...

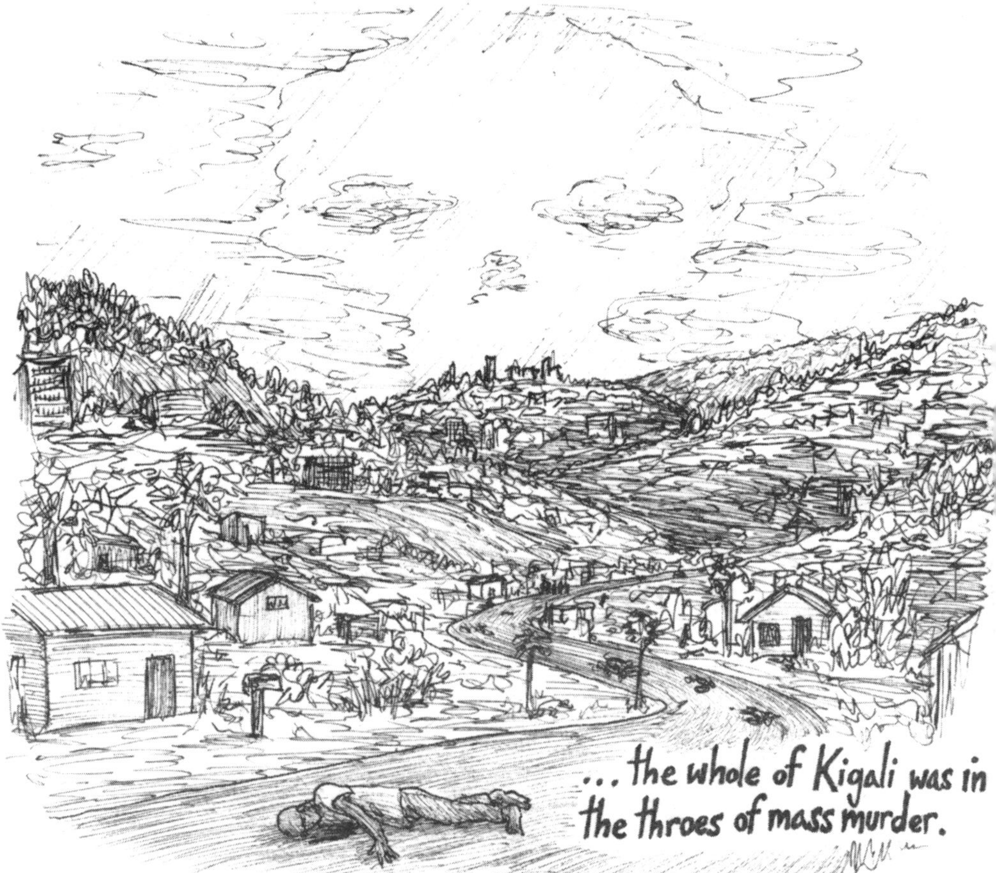
... the whole of Kigali was in the throes of mass murder.

Still, there must have been one or two reluctant killers...

...and if there was one insubordinate who still held back?

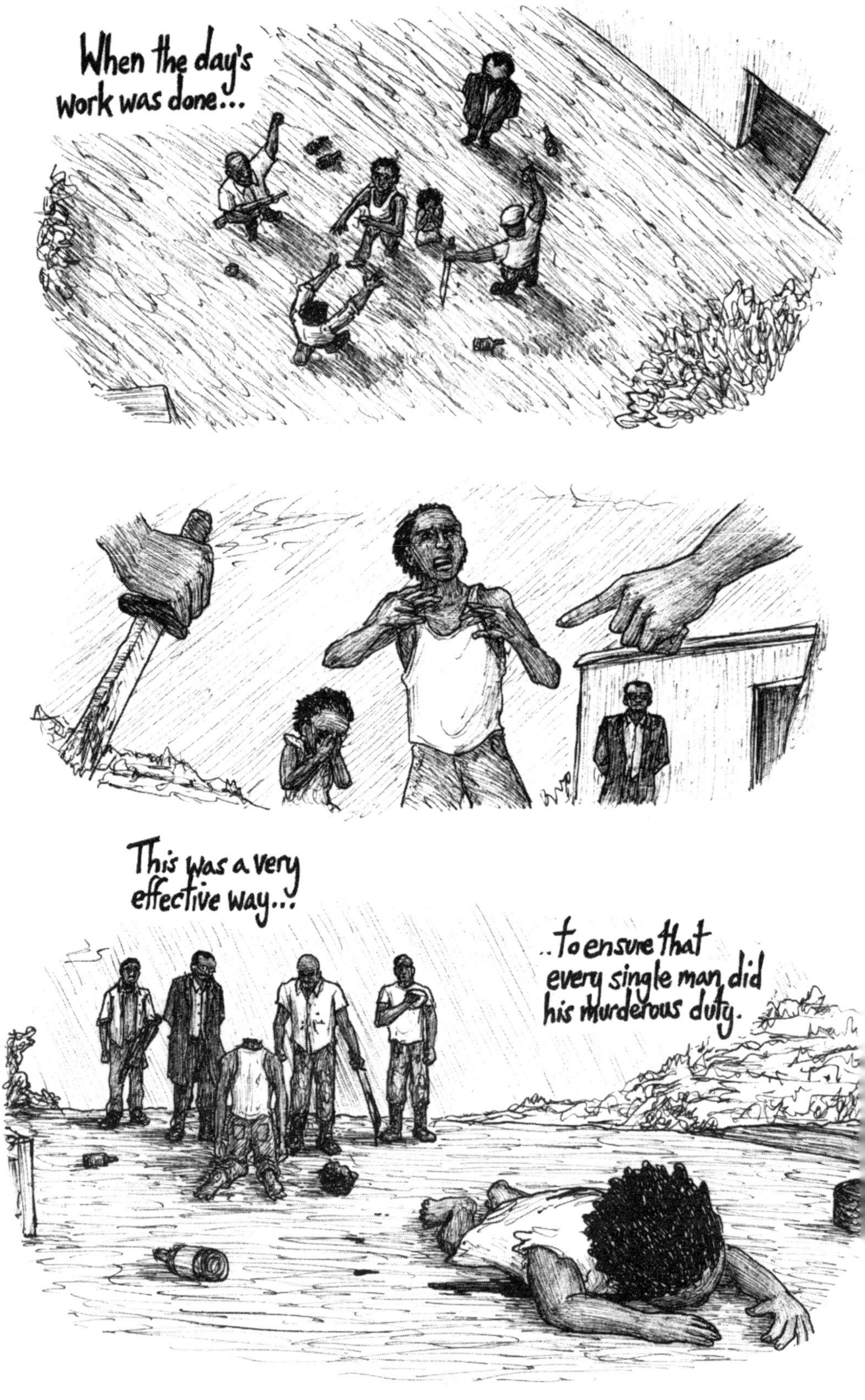

When the day's work was done...
This was a very effective way...
..to ensure that every single man did his murderous duty.

Josette Umutoniwase

Very early on the morning after the downing of the plane, Josette's father Augustin received a call from Gromo Alex, in whom he had great confidence. Gromo reported that roadblocks had been established throughout Kigali, and that government troops and Interahamwe were murdering many of the supposed enemies and their accomplices. It was probably best for all UN employees to remain indoors for the next few days. Order would soon be restored, Gromo hoped.

Suddenly there was a violent knock on the front gate. Josette's father was once again confronted with a band of armed soldiers. They said that they were looking for cockroaches and wanted to check that none were hiding in the house.

Her father replied that he worked for the United Nations and they had no right to come in. They pressed for entry, but her father stood firm. At last they agreed to go if he would give them money for beer. After all, they said, Augustin worked for the UN so he must be a rich man.

He gave them a sum of money and they trooped off, but not before threatening to be back. And if he were found to be hiding a cockroach, they warned, Augustin and his family would be killed.

That evening Josette's father called his boss and requested to be allowed to come to the office the following day. He thought that being seen as part of the UN's essential staff would give the family more protection. At least it would provide him with more information on what was going on. His request was refused. Stay at home, he was told.

Two days later, Gromo came by. Would the family be willing to take in some staff members who lived in more isolated parts of town? They didn't have much space, but Augustin accepted. The next day the five members of the Bunani family – Alphonse, his wife and their children – came to join Josette's household.

The soldiers continued knocking at the door, demanding money for beer. Josette's father was in great distress, fearing that his money might run out before the killing stopped. But he was part of the UN – surely that meant that he and his family would be safe from harm?

Gromo Alex

Only essential UN staff were allowed to come to the office the day after the shooting down of the president's plane. Gromo was among them and he made sure that the international members of his team were included in the essential group. Gromo tried on a daily basis to talk to as many of the UN Tutsi employees as he could. He tried to reassure them, and when one felt particularly threatened he would arrange for a soldier from the UN military mission to check up on them.

Senegalese Captain Mbaye Diagne, a tall gangly figure armed with nothing more than an infectious laugh, was often tasked with this job. The captain travelled alone in his white UN vehicle through the lawless streets of Kigali, seeking out the families of Tutsis and ferrying them to safer locations. Gromo came to admire his extraordinary courage.[*]

As the days went by, Gromo and his team also started to take food and water to the houses of staff. He frequently visited the homes of Florence Ngirumpatse and Josette's father. He helped other UN staff members who were located in more isolated parts of town to find temporary refuge in one of those two houses. Florence, having the bigger house, received the largest number. Gromo then took steps to ensure that both households were kept stocked with supplies adequate for the increasing number of inhabitants.

---

[*] Captain Mbaye was not alone in demonstrating such selfless courage. His boss, a Fijian, Colonel Tikoca, organized the fifty military observers under his command to conduct emergency evacuations and random visits to those they could not evacuate. But to Gromo, Mbaye's formidable laugh meant that he was exceptional.

Gromo, who participated in the crisis management meetings of the heads of the UN agencies, was shocked to see how ill-prepared the UN had been for the eventuality of violence. Many of the UN heads (including the UN representative) seemed to be tired, depressed and lacking above all in initiative. They kept waiting for instructions from New York. In those first ten days, New York sent requests for situation reports, but issued no instructions.

Lieutenant Fiacre Mboki

On 8 April, Fiacre was ordered to stand ready to join an RPF advance that would attack along the east side of the country. His platoon was to be part of a planned three-pronged offensive. Simultaneously, the RPF also planned to engage government forces in Kigali and to the northwest. By maintaining pressure on the northwestern corner of Rwanda, from which many members of the Habyarimana regime originated, General Kagame hoped to pin down the better-trained elements of the government forces.

But before launching the offensive, General Kagame proposed that the RPF, the UN and the Rwandan army form a coalition force with the sole objective of stopping the massacres. Since it was clear that the killings were for the most part being carried out by the Presidential Guard in Kigali, a joint force of 900 troops, he judged, would be sufficient to end the slaughter.[2]

The Rwandan army rejected the proposal. The UN did not respond. General Dallaire was still waiting for instructions from New York when the deadline passed.[*]

The failure of this initiative gave the RPF the justification it needed

---

[*]   Though still very much irritated, General Dallaire had started to get used to the lack of UN headquarters' response. It had almost become a pattern, and six months into his first UN command, he still found it difficult to understand why it had to be so. General Dallaire was a soldier's general, far more comfortable with his men than VIPs. Gromo used to say that the general was such a straight shooter because he had trained as an artillery officer.

to launch its offensive. In the first week, with some difficulty, the rebel force, of which Fiacre's platoon was part, defeated a sizeable Rwandan government force in the northeast. The government troops, though well entrenched, were not disciplined enough to resist the rebel assault. Simultaneously, a RPF mobile unit pushed through to the capital, arriving on the afternoon of 11 April. There they joined up with an RPF force that had broken out of its cantonment, and had, with the help of the few thousand local RPF sympathizers, established small pockets of safety in Kigali for Tutsi populations who were fleeing the killings.

Father Vjeko Curic

On 10 April, Father Vjeko found himself officiating mass in a church bursting with the faithful. Both Tutsis and Hutus had come to his service and all appeared to be anxious, frightened, desperate for comfort. The father gave them the spiritual reassurance they needed. He focused his sermon on generosity, the need to reject violence, and Jesus's teachings on the importance of loving each other. It seemed to work. The faithful were in tears. Some Hutus even crossed the ethnic divide to embrace their fellow Tutsis.

Father Vjeko felt encouraged after the service. Of course, he was worried, but he thought the message of Christ had been understood. He hoped that his parish might remain an island of tranquillity amidst this hurricane of hatred.

UN Security Council[3]

In April 1994 the UN Security Council* consisted of the five permanent members (China, France, Russia, the UK and the US), five members who

---

* The UN Security Council is the executive body of the United Nations, while the General Assembly nominally takes the decisions. Though the General Assembly is democratic in the sense that each member has a single vote, the Security Council is made up of five historical super powers of the world that can take unilateral action by vetoing decisions.

were starting their second year (Brazil, Djibouti, New Zealand, Pakistan and Spain), and five new members who had been elected the previous October (Argentina, Czech Republic, Nigeria, Oman and – of all countries – Rwanda). The Security Council had at this time several issues to deal with: Bosnia and Herzegovina, above all, but problems also in Georgia, Iraq, El Salvador, Israel, and in the relationship between Libya and Chad.

Of course, as always in the Security Council, there was debate about the extension of various UN peacekeeping mandates. On 5 April UNAMIR had been extended. The United States was wary of peacekeeping operations after the Somalia debacle. Discussions in Washington in response to Somalia had culminated in Presidential Directive No. 25, which created a 'vital national interests test' for any US involvement in a foreign intervention. US officials on the Security Council understood this as an instruction to thwart any attempt to mandate new missions, and thereby to avoid for the US the embarrassment of a refusal to participate.

In the afternoon of 6 April, the Security Council learned of the catastrophe at the airport in Kigali. Was the plane crash that killed the presidents of Rwanda and Burundi an accident or an assassination? Rwanda's permanent representative to the UN, Ambassador Jean-Damascène Bizimana, strongly asserted that this was an act of terrorism perpetrated by the RPF. France quickly backed up this claim, but the other members of the council were more hesitant.

Over the next days, the Security Council met repeatedly without coming to any conclusion. Then the Belgian government announced it was withdrawing its troops. Finally spurred into action, the council requested the UN Secretariat to prepare a report on available options. The report was promised immediately. By the end of the first ten days of the genocide, it had still not been provided.

Between day one and day ten of the genocide more than thirty thousand people –
Tutsis and moderate Hutus – had been killed.

14

The Withdrawal of the Belgian Peacekeepers[4]

On the morning of 7 April, Lieutenant Thierry Lottin was dispatched with a platoon of ten Belgian paratroopers to protect Agathe Uwilingiyimana, a moderate Hutu politician who was prime minister-designate of the new coalition government. His specific instructions were to escort her to the national radio station, Radio Rwanda, where she was to make an address calling on the population to remain calm.

But the Presidential Guard, commanded by a member of the Akazu, had been ordered to stop the prime minister from reaching the radio station. When at 05h00 the Belgian platoon approached the prime minister's house, they came under fire. Lieutenant Lottin informed his battalion headquarters and then moved his paratroopers into the prime minister's garden in search of cover.

An hour later, Lieutenant Lottin contacted battalion headquarters again, this time to report that his platoon was coming under mortar fire. Twenty minutes later, after the Presidential Guard had surrounded the compound, he informed battalion HQ that he was moving his men into the house.

During the initial clash, the prime minister-designate had been able to jump over the fence into an empty compound and hide there with her children. Her children escaped, but Agathe Uwilingiyimana was caught and murdered with extraordinary brutality.

At just after 08h00, Lieutenant Lottin again contacted his headquarters and explained that the Presidential Guard were threatening to use grenade-launchers and the guns of their armoured vehicles if he and his men did not surrender. Stand firm, he was told. Three armoured vehicles of the UN Bangladeshi contingent were on their way.

Minutes later, two of the Belgian paratroopers were captured. The Presidential Guard informed Lieutenant Lottin that the platoon would be escorted to UN headquarters if they first surrendered their weapons. The lieutenant contacted the Belgian contingent headquarters for advice. He was told that it was his call.

At about the same time, the Bangladeshi armoured vehicles that had been heading towards them were forced to turn back. When Lieutenant Lottin learned of this, he decided there was no option but to surrender in order to preserve the lives of his men. The platoon was loaded, hands-over-heads, into a minivan.

But rather than being escorted as promised to UN headquarters, they were taken to the barracks of the Presidential Guard, where they were accused of having shot down the president's plane. The unarmed Belgian paratroopers were kicked and beaten.

Lieutenant Lottin managed to secure a radio from the Togolese UN observer inside the Rwandan barracks. He contacted his battalion commander and explained what was happening. His men were being beaten, he said, and he feared they would all be lynched. It was the last contact the UN had with the ten paratroopers.

Between 09h00 and 10h00, the paratroopers were kicked, clubbed and stabbed by frenzied Rwandan soldiers. Four of the Belgians died immediately. The Togolese UN observer tried to intercede, but he was threatened with a similar fate and manhandled out of the barracks.

A Belgian company commander had been listening in on the communications and heard what was going on in the barracks. His unit was only a hundred metres away. He pleaded for permission to mount a rescue mission. Permission was denied.

Somewhere between 12h00 and 14h00 the remaining paratroopers were killed. The Togolese captain, the first outsider to see all the bodies, was unable to make out if the remains belonged to ten men or eleven.

Stunned by the deaths and afraid of Belgian public opinion, the Belgian government announced that it would withdraw its troops from the UN mission. The last of the Belgian troops left Kigali on 15 April.

When the returning paratroopers stepped down from the plane onto the military airfield in Belgium, some of them made a show of cutting their UN berets to pieces. They vowed never again to fight under the UN flag.

15

Days 11–20: Killings Extend to the Rest of the Country

In Kigali, the killers targeted not just opponents of the regime, but any who were Tutsis or moderate Hutus – men, women and children alike. Killings started to spread to the rest of the country, where women and children were for the most part spared.

Kamana Rumbashi

According to the same two key initial witness statements mentioned previously, Kamana Rumbashi was allegedly seen at the gate of a house near the Baobab Hotel, explaining to the men with him that Sam, who lived there, was a rebel sympathizer, and that he and his family must all be killed. The house girl opened the gate at their knock. The men brushed by her and went into the compound. If the witness statements are correct, Rumbashi is then reported to have instructed three of the men

116

accompanying him to go into the house and kill everyone. Instead they brought out Sam and his wife. Rumbashi is alleged to have told them to sit down. He then explained to them that they would be killed for belonging to the rebels. He then supposedly told one of the men to undertake the task. Sam was shot in the chest, while his wife in the head.

According to a single witness statement, Rumbashi and the men stopped in front of the gate of a nearby house belonging to Joseph, who worked in a nearby petrol station. The gate to the compound was open and the group walked straight in. Joseph's wife opened the door of the house, and Rumbashi is reported to have gone in with the other men. Joseph's children, aged twelve, nine and five, ran into the back of the house when they saw the armed men. Only Joseph's wife remained in the living room. When the men started to go after the children, Rumbashi is alleged, by the same witness, to have ordered them to stop and first take care of the wife. 'If you leave her when searching for the children, she may escape' were supposedly his words. The mother was shot and then the children taken care of. There was no one else in the house. The witness did not know what happened to Joseph. He assumed that he must have died at another point in time.

The next day Rumbashi, in his UNDP capacity, was supposedly called to a meeting, allegedly with the head of UN administration and the UN representative. He was told that all international UN staff were to be evacuated. There is some confusion as to whether he was entrusted with the responsibility of officer-in-charge of the UN or he just assumed the role. A witness statement confirms the former, but Rumbashi has repeatedly denied this. Whatever the case, Kamana Rumbashi found himself in control of the UN's vast resources: the logistical capabilities (vehicles, fuel, spare parts); the cash and supplies; and also, importantly, the communications.* He was able to monitor the activities of the small UN force on the other side of the city. With the satellite phone, he had direct access to the outside world.

Josette Umutoniwase

The days turned into weeks but the violence was far from dying down. The targeted political killings that dominated the first hours were supplemented by the frenzied involvement of the Hutu population in the murder of all Tutsis, whatever their politics. Day and night, there was the unrelenting sound of whistles, screams and shouts. It was now impossible for Josette and her family to venture outside of the compound. They were dependent, as were other UN Tutsi staff, on the supply and support provided by Gromo Alex, Captain Mbaye and their team.

By mid-April, with no end to the killings in sight, the Tutsis among the UN staff were increasingly alarmed. The government-sponsored RTLMC radio had escalated its rhetoric, with speakers trying to outdo each other in attempts to fuel hysteria and hate. Cockroaches were everywhere, it was said. They needed to be annihilated – all of them.

A particularly ferocious presenter on the RTLMC radio was a French-Italian called Georges Ruggiu.** He did not speak Kinyarwanda, the official language of Rwanda, but this didn't stop him from being one of the chief propagators of extremist Hutu propaganda, exhorting his audience to kill all Tutsis and 'disloyal' Hutus. It is Ruggiu who is credited with finding the most effective phrase to spur the killings on: 'Graves,' he urged, 'are waiting to be filled.'

---

*   As attested to in numerous witness statements and by Gromo Alex to me.
**   Later to be condemned to twelve years' incarceration by the ICTR.

Meanwhile the UN continued to insist through its own radio channels that all staff would be protected. Even when the French and Italians evacuated their nationals, the UN message remained clear: WE WILL NOT ABANDON YOU!

Ten days into the killings, Josette's father was able to persuade Gromo to let him join his effort. A UN-marked vehicle was allocated to him and parked in front of his house. Very early every morning, when the killers were still sleeping off their beer from the night before, Augustin would venture out to collect supplies from UN headquarters, and he then dropped them off at various UN staff houses. At UN headquarters he also gathered information.

One morning, Josette's father re-entered the compound and took Josette's mother aside. They talked for a few minutes, head against head, and then beckoned Josette towards them. As the eldest child, her father told her, she needed to be strong. The UN was abandoning them. All the internationals were to be flown out over the next few days. The nationals would now have to fend for themselves. It was important that they stay home, lock the house and open the door to no one.

That night on the UN radio, Josette and her family heard the same voice that they had heard every night insist that the UN would not abandon its staff. Yes, the internationals were relocating to Nairobi, but it was only temporarily. Arrangements were being made to take care of UN staff who remained behind. Josette's father took comfort from the message.

The next morning there was a new voice on the radio. An unknown person explained that the UN military mission had taken over the security network. Those staff with radios must listen carefully to the information that he would broadcast three times a day, must keep the channel clear and try to keep their radios hidden. The voice gave another frequency to use in case of urgent need.

That afternoon, Clothilde Murebwayrie and her child, and three other children, came to join Josette's family in the already-crowded house.

Gromo Alex

Working closely with Captain Mbaye, Gromo had moved the Tutsi UN staff who were most at risk, along with their families, to join the households of other UN staff. Josette's father and Florence took in a great many. Gromo was at pains to ensure that the houses were adequately supplied.

Gromo continued to attend UN security management meetings. Initially the meetings were focused on providing situation reports for New York, while little was received in return. And then suddenly ten days into the killings the order came for all international staff to evacuate. French, Italian and Belgian paratroopers, who had flown in to evacuate their nationals, agreed to stay behind to supervise the departure of the UN, beginning the next morning, while US marines remained stationed in Bujumbura to intervene if the necessity arose.

The instructions coming out of New York stipulated that only UN internationals were to be evacuated. No national staff, and especially no Tutsis. The rationale? If the UN evacuated the Tutsi staff, it would risk losing its 'neutrality'.

A number of UN international staff were horrified at the idea of leaving their Rwandan colleagues behind. Since they could not be evacuated by air, a small group of internationals decided to attempt a land convoy to Burundi. Gromo thought the plan, however courageous in intention, was misguided. He feared that an attempt to take Tutsis colleagues and their families through the roadblocks out of Kigali would simply expose them to the killers. He was overruled. The convoy was formed and took off. None of the Tutsis in the convoy survived past the first few checkpoints.

Gromo did not want to be part of the evacuation. But the UN representative told him that there were to be no exceptions. Gromo couldn't help feeling that he was being denied permission to remain behind because it would reflect badly on those hightailing it out. So, it was with a heavy heart and anger that Gromo clambered aboard the C-130 and left Kigali. He remained on standby in Nairobi, hoping to return as soon as Mbaye could get General Dallaire to intercede on his behalf with the UN bureaucracy.

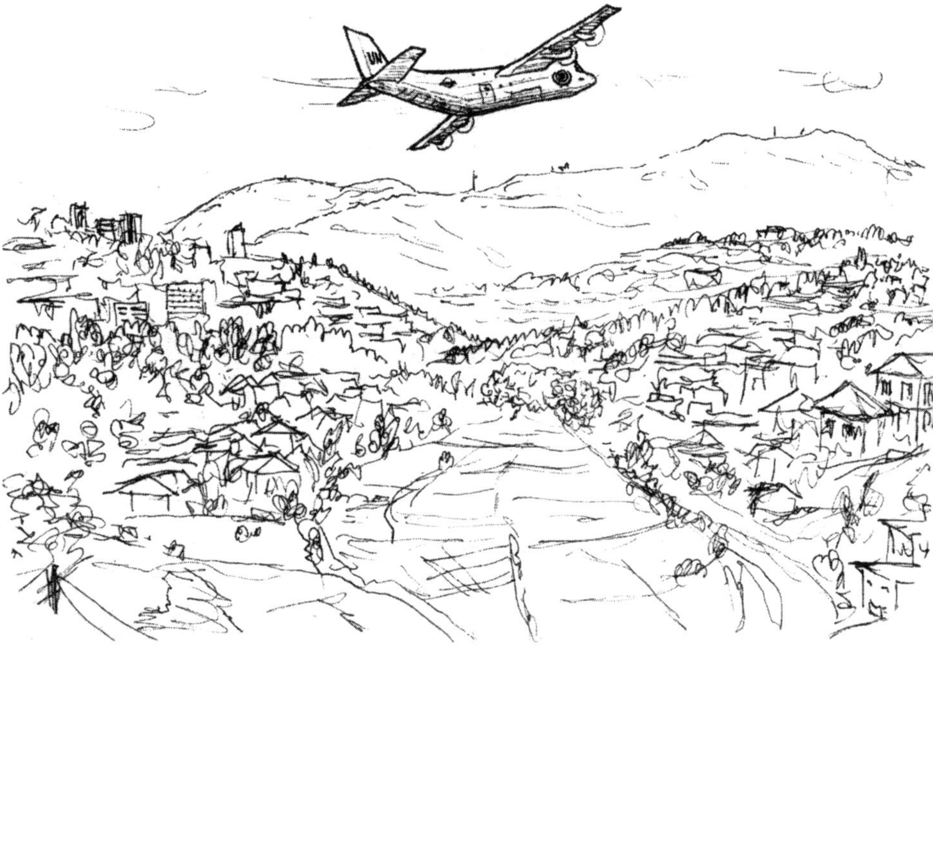
UN

Father Vjeko Curic

Sometime towards the end of the second week, Father Vjeko was woken up in the middle of the night by frantic knocks. He opened the door to find the entire Tutsi population of Nyamabuye huddled in the courtyard. Some of them had been attacked by a band of Interahamwe, who had been joined by young men from the village. They begged Father Vjeko for help. He opened the doors of the church, and urged them to rest. Tomorrow they would find a solution.

The next morning, Father Vjeko went to meet the elders of the Hutu community. He asked them why they had allowed an attack to take place, and why had they not prevented their own youth from participating? It was beyond the elders' control, he was told. Leaders of the Interahamwe from Gitarama had come and had explained how Tutsi rebels were attempting to take over the country. And how, in other places, even long-standing Tutsi neighbours were helping the aggressors. 'How can you be sure it is not the same here?' the father was asked.

Unable to sway them, and appalled by this turn of events, Father Vjeko warned the elders that he was placing the Tutsis of Nyamabuye under the protection of the church. Under no circumstances were they to be harmed.

He then identified a large field, towards the back of the church, where the frightened Tutsi population could set up shelter. They could use the water and cooking facilities of the presbytery. That afternoon, he went off to Kabgayi to see the archbishop. The archbishop listened while Father Vjeko made his case. He agreed with the initiative but urged the father to remember that he was responsible for the wellbeing of all Rwandans, not only Tutsis. Father Vjeko, knowing that the archbishop was a card-carrying member of the Hutu majority party, was not unduly surprised by this response.

That Sunday, only the Hutu population of Nyamabuye came to the service. The Tutsis were too scared to join in. Father Vjeko reminded the assembled crowd of their commitments and their tears of a week before. What had happened? he asked. His question met with a deathly silence. Again, he asked: what had happened? And again, nothing. Not even a cough.

Father Vjeko thought for a long moment. There was no place for the sacrament, he decided, in a world without charity and forgiveness. He announced that he would not officiate another mass until both communities were sitting together under the church's roof.

UN Security Council

Within the UN Security Council, the mass killings were a continuing subject of discussion. The picture was confused. The long-awaited report from the UN Secretariat had yet to appear. The only information provided by the UN Secretariat was that the killings were increasing rather than reducing in number.

Two conflicting positions emerged within the council. In tandem, the Rwandan and French permanent representatives, backed by Djibouti, framed the killings as part of a civil war. But the other council members weren't convinced.

The Czech representative drew the attention of the Security Council to a *New York Times* opinion piece written by Frank Smyth from Human Rights Watch.[5] Drawing on information from experts in the NGO community, the article argued that the slaughter was not an accidental side effect of civil war, but was deliberately instigated and organized. Rwanda was ruled, the article explained, not by the late President Habyarimana, but by a small Akazu clique led by his wife. Slaughtering their opponents, Tutsis and moderate Hutus, was the only way the Akazu could hold on to their twenty-one-year-old rule. The Akazu needed weapons, and had found an ally in France, which was concerned above all with maintaining *la francophonie* in Rwanda.

When the Czech representative raised the article in the Security Council, the French ambassador immediately dismissed the analysis as nothing but rumour. The Rwandan and Djiboutian ambassadors then did their best to disparage the article further. That may have been the wrong tactic, for it only strengthened the impact the article had on a number of Security Council members. In particular, those members representing smaller nations refused to accept the simplistic interpretation of events advanced by Rwanda and France.

The Security Council pressed yet again for the UN Secretariat to present its report on options for the UN mission.

By day twenty of the genocide more than one hundred thousand Tutsis and moderate Hutus – men, women and children alike – had been murdered.

16

Days 21–30: Killings Pick up Pace Throughout the Country

During the fourth week of the genocide, killings picked up pace still further, especially in the south. The prefect of Butare, who had initially opposed the violence, was replaced and killed. The butchery accelerated.

Kamana Rumbashi

Rumbashi's de facto role as officer in charge of the UN gave him access to resources and a base in the UNDP office, which was located almost dead centre of the Interahamwe positions on Nyamirambo. Were he to have command of a militia, as it is alleged by some witnesses, at the beginning of each day, he would have walked out from his office to check that the men were in their place at the checkpoints, with shortwave radios tuned to RTLMC. Were the statements to be correct, he would have reminded them of the importance of rigour in their examination of identity cards, so that no Tutsis slipped through. By the end of the month, it had become the practice to conduct the actual killings further away from the checkpoints, in order to keep the swarms of fatty black flies at bay.

Confident that the checkpoints were in order, Rumbashi would then have set off. One day, the group is reported to have found a dead Rwandan soldier lying on the road. According to two key witness statements, bystanders told Rumbashi that the shots that killed the soldier had come from a nearby house where a crowd of people were said to be hiding. The men were then positioned around that house and the adjoining one, and instructed to kill anyone who attempted to leave. Rumbashi reportedly set off to the Presidential Guard to get more support.

Two hours later, a tank lumbered up. According to the same two witnesses, behind it in a black vehicle without UN markings was Rumbashi. The tank came to a halt, belching a thick black cloud of diesel, at a point that allowed it to cover the front of both houses. The turret of the tank turned to the house on its left. It fired three shots, then targeted the one on the right, and did the same. The process was repeated again and again until both houses caught fire. Occupants who ran out were immediately gunned down. The few who made it into the watching crowd were clubbed to death.

After a while nothing could be heard but the crackling of flames and the explosion of air pockets. One of the men walked forward, knelt in front of a body and smeared his face with its blood so he would not be bothered by their spirits.

That over with, according to a different witness statement, the men went to the house of a businessman. He was called Pascal and worked for the Caisse Hypothécaire. The witness statement alleges Rumbashi explained that the house belonged to a Tutsi and should be killed. Pascal came out of his house with his wife. They pushed the wife to one side and then shot Pascal. According to the same witness statement, someone then said 'Let's see what a Tutsi's sex organ looks like.' They took her back inside. Some twenty minutes later she was dead.

Next, according to two other witness statements, came the killing of Guido. Initially, the men checked every corner of his compound but found no one. The neighbours explained that they had not seen the family leave. Inspecting the house again, Rumbashi is believed to have noticed that one of the plasterboard squares of the ceiling was bulging as if it supported a heavy weight. The men were ordered to shoot into the ceilings. Guido called out that he was coming down. He jumped to the floor and attacked the militiamen. Guido was very good at karate. He fought with the men, until one of them shot him. The rest of the family was nowhere to be found.

According to one of the more detailed statements made to the ICTR, Rumbashi then consulted his list and announced that he knew that Sakufi had moved houses, and was now living with relatives not far away. He asked his men to go find him. An hour later they returned with Sakufi walking in front of them. He was very frightened. They walked Sakufi to his house and asked for beer. He said he didn't have any, so they asked for money. Sakufi climbed up into his ceiling and came back with around 300,000 Rwandan francs. He thought he had saved himself.

He was taken to a playground nearby. They ordered him to sit down and then a witness alleges Rumbashi ordered one of the men to shoot him. He shot him once in the head, and they all left.

The following day, Rumbashi and his group, according to three witness statements, were seen to enter the compound of Michel Rugema. Michel worked for UNICEF and as a result had a handheld radio. A number of times he had contacted the UN for help, but each time was told that no assistance could be provided. Michel's wife testified seeing Rumbashi enter her compound at the head of a group of armed men. Rumbashi allegedly wore a military shirt and civilian trousers, and was carrying a gun.

There was a lot of shouting and whistles from the group as they entered the compound. Michel's wife escaped, while a friend of the family, who was also there and later also testified, went into hiding in the back of the house.

The men found Michel and took him into the living room, where his four-year-old daughter also was. They shot him three times in front of her. The men then tore the clothes off the little girl. But when they saw how young she was, they left saying they wouldn't kill her, as someone else probably would.

According to one witness statement, the final house attacked that day belonged to Katabarwa, who worked for an NGO. Rumbashi and a number of armed men were seen entering the house. Supposedly he found a handheld radio and was alleged to be heard saying that this was proof of complicity with the rebels and that all in the house should be killed. Katabarwa, his wife, three of the five children and the house girl were shot. When after a little while, two other children, both less than five, were seen coming towards the house. One of the men suggested they be taken to the Catholic orphanage. 'Why?' someone else is alleged to have asked. 'Why do you save these children? They must be killed.' And that is what happened.

Gromo Alex

From the moment Gromo arrived in Nairobi, he started campaigning to be allowed to return to Kigali. He pestered Captain Mbaye to find out if he had approached General Dallaire about his return. Far from being exasperated, the captain liked Gromo's impudence and determination. But the only thing Captain Mbaye could tell Gromo was that he was waiting for the favourable moment to raise the issue with the general.

While in the middle of his attempt to return, Gromo learned of my refusal to join the mission in Kigali. He called one night when I was still in Somalia. 'What are you doing, Chuck?' he asked. 'Stop dicking around and come here.' He explained that what was happening in Rwanda was beyond anything that he or I had encountered before. It was pure evil. He was determined to move back to Kigali, and needed me to join him.

But I continued to resist the pressure, and he called me three nights in a row. I explained to Gromo that I had no wish to be forced to witness the price that would be paid for the international community's failure in Somalia. But he wouldn't buy it. 'Your reasons are intellectual bullshit. They don't hold up to the reality of what is happening in Rwanda.' And so, on the third night of discussion, I relented.

Josette Umutoniwase

In the last days of April, a group of soldiers arrived in front of Josette's house. Unlike those who came by regularly to get their money for beer, this group had a commander and was bigger and better organized. The commander shouted for everyone to bring out their identity cards. If they did not comply, he yelled, the door would be broken and all of them would be dragged out.

Augustin, Josette's father, was the first to step forth. The commander ordered him to lie on the ground with his identity card visible in his right hand. One by one, the others emerged, and were given the same instruction. Only Esther, Josette's little sister, refused to lie down. The commander told her to stand to one side.

Mao, one of the children who had come to stay in the compound, asked the commander why he was going to kill all these people when they were friends of his father, whom the commander knew well. The commander asked Augustin what was his relationship with Mao's father. Augustin pretended that Mao's father was his brother-in-law. The commander then demanded that Augustin give him two million Rwandan francs. Augustin, who had no such sum, offered instead whatever he had, which was fifteen thousand francs. The commander accepted the money. He walked Augustin through his and the neighbouring compound, indicating better hiding places. Then he and his men left. Augustin and his household had escaped. For a time.

Lieutenant Fiacre Mboki

In the first part of the rebel advance, Fiacre's platoon had had a pretty hard time. They had engaged in combat with a sizable force of government soldiers south of Byumba, had serious exchanges with their retreating elements, and launched a successful attack on a well-entrenched government position at Muhuru. After that, the little resistance they met came from local militia groups – more bound together by ideology than discipline – and from Interahamwe. They had little difficulty advancing.

The RTLMC broadcasts that Fiacre listened to at night touted the successes of the government forces, but Fiacre was deeply sceptical. His disbelief was confirmed when he heard a militia leader boast that his battalion had successfully defeated an RPF unit – but it was Fiacre's unit, perfectly intact, that had supposedly been destroyed. If many of the 'successes' of the government side were like this, Fiacre saw every reason to hope that the conflict would be over soon.

Fiacre and his men laughed at the boastful and inaccurate report, but not at what happened next. His platoon had been ordered to conduct a sweep of a number of hills. The operation went well until they hit a village that Fiacre knew had been the home of some of his men. He was concerned: how would he maintain discipline if these men came upon the bodies of their families?

It was two in the morning and pitch black when Fiacre gave his orders to the section leaders crouched around him. He commanded two of his sections to encircle the village. At first light, he said, the others would conduct the actual sweep.

Slowly the veil of darkness lifted. It gave way to a thick white fog, hugging the ground, revealing only the tops of a set of low-lying hills. From his position on the ridge overlooking the village, Fiacre saw the church emerging from the fog. It stood on the highest hill, imposing and defiantly alone.

Fiacre gave the order to start the sweep. From his position he watched his men move soundlessly towards the village, their silhouettes becoming fainter as they were swallowed by fog. For a long while, an unbearably long while, there was total silence.

Suddenly Fiacre's radio sprang to life. First one and then the other section leader informed him that they had reached their destination. The village was empty. Not a living soul was to be found. Nor a dead one.

As Fiacre ordered his men to take up positions throughout the village, his attention was drawn to the gigantic figure of Christ that stood in front of the church, arms thrown wide open in a gesture of welcome. Spread out over the entire hill were hundreds of banana trees which seemed to mimic the gesture, their broad leaves sprouting heavenwards. He couldn't understand what had happened. Where were the bodies? Could it be that all had escaped? That, unlike the other villages they had seen, the Tutsis in this area had survived?

The men to whom the village had been home were as perplexed as Fiacre. Then suddenly one of the soldiers shook himself, as if struck by a bolt of lightning, and rushed to the nearest banana tree. It was a mature tree and yet the earth surrounding it had been recently turned. He saw then that the other banana trees had the same loose soil around their bases.

The soldier knelt and placed his weapon on the ground. He opened his folding pocketknife and slowly, cautiously, inserted the blade into the soil. It met resistance. He put the blade away and began to brush the earth lightly with the tip of his fingers. Working methodically, and with increasing tenderness, he uncovered a skull with shrivelled skin and tufts of hair attached. He stopped, stood up, tears welling in his eyes, and looked at Fiacre. Together they scanned the hundreds of banana trees, each with fresh earth at its base.

Father Vjeko Curic

On the Wednesday evening after Father Vjeko had made his Sunday pronouncement in the church, he once again heard frantic pounding on his front door. He opened the door and once again saw the entire Tutsi population of Nyamabuye in front of him. They dared no longer stay where they were, an elder explained. All afternoon they had seen Interahamwe in the hills close by, and the killers were now starting to regroup at the bottom of the hill. They feared for their lives.

Father Vjeko walked to the edge of the open space in front of the church, and peered down to the bottom of the hill. On seeing the lamps and torches heading towards the temporary camps that he had offered to his Tutsi parishioners, Father Vjeko knew he could now no longer protect them.

Leaving the crowd of frightened individuals waiting outside, Father Vjeko called the archbishop's office in Kabgayi. He explained to Father Sibomana, the priest who answered the phone, that he was bringing the entire Tutsi population of his parish on a three-hour walk to Kabgayi. Father Sibomana agreed to mobilize as many of his colleagues as he could to provide an escort for the column.

Father Vjeko then dashed off to speak to a Hutu village elder whom he knew and trusted. The man and four other elders agreed to join them on the walk to Kabgayi.

The column of a few hundred people started their long march. Father Vjeko and one of the Hutu elders walked at the front, while the other elders grouped at the back to protect the rear from attacks. Barely had they left Nyamabuye when the group hit a roadblock manned by a drunken bunch of Interahamwe carrying machetes and nail-studded clubs. Father Vjeko instructed the column to sit. The Interahamwe leader roared that he knew these people were cockroaches, and he had every intention of killing them. 'You'll need to kill me first,' Father Vjeko replied. He refused to move. The Interahamwe leader stepped forward, brandishing his club, but the priest stood firm. The fraught standoff lasted for minutes. Then Father Vjeko, looking over the shoulder of the fighter, saw a large minibus overflowing with staff from the archbishopric barreling down the road with Father Sibomana behind the wheel.

The minibus stopped behind the Interahamwe and some twenty people in religious robes stepped out. The Interahamwe, overwhelmed by the numbers, dispersed. Father Vjeko said a brief prayer of thanks and embraced Father Sibomana. The column set off again, now protected by a phalanx of clergy, while Father Sibomana shuttled to and fro in the minibus ferrying villagers to the archbishopric. The daring paid off. The column was saved and a camp was created for the refugees under the window of the archbishop's office.

UN Security Council

It is only towards the last days of April that the UN Security Council received from the UN Secretariat the much-anticipated report on options for the UN mission for Rwanda. Following the withdrawal of the Belgian contingent, the UN mission was down from its initial 2,500 men to 1,700.[*] The UN

---

[*] General Dallaire had refused to leave and had insisted on keeping as many troops as he could get. Canada, alone among all the nations involved, then sent in about a dozen military officers to cover slots abandoned by the Belgians.

secretary-general presented three options for the UN mission. One of them was a total withdrawal of UNAMIR; the second, to leave only 270 soldiers in the country; and the third, to beef up UNAMIR to several thousand soldiers, with a new use of force mandate under Chapter 7 of the UN Charter.

The report didn't end the disputes within the Security Council. The non-aligned nations wanted to strengthen UNAMIR. The United States pressed for a complete pullout. No mention whatsoever was made of a role for the UN in stopping the ongoing carnage.

The resolution that was finally adopted allowed for 270 UN troops to remain in the country, while the rest would withdraw to a nearby base in East Africa. They would become an over-the-horizon reserve without an explicit mandate to intervene.

The new resolution was regarded as a disaster by a number of the representatives, especially those from smaller countries. Not only would UNAMIR not be strengthened, it would be reduced to a minimum military force capable only of its own protection. Thousands of civilians who until then had had some protection from the UN had effectively been handed over to the killers. General Henri Kwami Anyidoho of Ghana, who was the deputy force commander in Kigali, posed a chilling question: did the UN feel able to abandon Rwanda because the killings only concerned the 'dark continent'?

The New Zealand representative, Colin Keating, had been shocked by reports he had received from NGOs working on the ground – reports far more detailed than those that the UN Secretariat had provided for the Security Council. He tried to use his position as President of the Security Council for the month of April* to push through a presidential statement

---

* The President of the Security Council is the head of delegation of the UN Security Council member state that holds the rotating presidency. The presidency of the UN Security Council is handed over in alphabetical order every month from one member state to another.

that would clarify events in Rwanda. But he faced strong opposition. The French permanent representative refused to attribute the killings to the interim government. It was the Tutsis and the RPF who were the aggressors, he insisted. The British representative argued that to base a presidential statement on information obtained from NGOs would turn the Security Council into a laughing stock. The US representative, keen to avoid any discussion of the deployment of a bigger UN force, attempted to downplay events in Rwanda altogether.

The text of the statement took days to negotiate. It seemed that some of the member states were trying to prolong the process beyond the end of the month of April, knowing that no new President of the Security Council would want to pick up the agenda of his predecessor.

On the evening of 28 April, the smaller countries effectively called the opposition's bluff. New Zealand proposed to submit a new resolution. While a statement needed endorsement from all members of the Security Council, a resolution – unless it was vetoed by one of the permanent five – could pass with only a majority vote. This placed France in an uncomfortable position. If it wanted to prevent the resolution going through, it would have to publicly veto an expression of concern for Rwanda.

A frantic new round of discussions started, aimed at finding common ground between France's insistence that blame be divided equally, and the insistence by New Zealand, the Czech Republic and several others that the killings be declared the work of Hutu extremists. The UK permanent representative saved the day by suggesting a phrasing that ran as follows: 'Attacks on defenceless civilians have occurred throughout the country, especially in areas under the control of the armed forces of the interim government of Rwanda.'

*By day thirty, approximately three hundred thousand Tutsis and moderate
Hutus had already been murdered.
Five hundred and fifty thousand more were yet to die.*

17

Days 31–40: Routine Sets In

Tutsis in Kigali go into hiding. The southeast of the country is emptied.

Kamana Rumbashi

Thirty to forty days into the genocide, with victims less readily available, the rate of killings slowed, at least in Kigali. Those Tutsis who had survived the initial savagery were in hiding.

It has been suggested to me, by a surviving member of Florence's family, that it is around this time that Rumbashi could have started to realize that the 'enterprise' in which he was involved would not necessarily succeed. He would thus have begun to be more cautious, avoiding to be seen near any of the killings by any of the UN international staff remaining in Kigali.

Josette Umutoniwase

This time the banging on the door was even more violent. By now Josette's family had run out of money. The family had handed over possessions when the cash ran out, but now everything was gone.

When, the day before, Josette's father had told the soldiers he did not have enough money to buy them a few beers, he had been badly beaten with rifle butts. Now he was lying on the living room couch in great pain, barely able to move.

Josette heard the pounding on the door from the back of the compound where she was hanging up the laundry. With laundry hanging from the line, a small bathhouse was hidden from view, and Josette quickly stepped into it.

From her hiding place, Josette saw armed men burst into the compound with, as she alleged,* Rumbashi in the lead. They shouted for everyone to come out of the house. Josette's mother stepped out and was stabbed in the stomach with a bayonet. Josette's younger sister, Esther, followed. One of the men swung his machete and severed her arm at the shoulder. She staggered around the compound in a state of shock.

Augustin finally made his way out. He pleaded to be allowed to look after his daughter, but instead he was held against the wall of the house and one of the men demanded that he surrender his UN radio. Augustin attempted to strike out but they all turned on him and beat him with clubs and the butts of their AK-47s, and hacked him with their machetes.

When Esther stumbled to a position near the bathhouse, Josette grabbed her and pulled her into the hiding place. She snatched a piece of cloth from the washing line, tied it to Esther's upper arm and tore away the flesh that had held the arm to her body. Delicately, Josette placed the arm on the ground. Dazed, Esther turned back towards the front of the house. 'No, stay and hide with me,' Josette pleaded, but Esther refused to remain alive with

---

*   Josette Umutoniwase's deposition is more unclear as to Kamana Rumbashi's involvement in the murder of her family than the subsequent interview she gave to journalist Ginny Stein, in her Australian Broadcasting Corporation's 21 February 2007 piece entitled *Rwanda – Questions of Murder.*

her parents dead. She begged of Josette – 'Afterwards will you bury my arm with the rest of my body?' – and then stumbled away.

Esther joined the rest of the family. Her mother looked up and screamed when she saw Esther returning. Another of the men raised his club and crushed her mother's skull. Ten members of the household aside from Josette and Esther remained alive – Alphonse, his wife and their three children, Clothilde and her daughter, and three cousins. The men cocked their weapons and opened fire. Ten more dead.

As they prepared to leave the compound, one of the men aimed his gun at Esther. But another is heard to have said, 'Don't waste a bullet, she will soon be dead.' Esther lay down among the bodies of her family.

The men then moved on to the next house. When one of them came back alone, Esther raised her head and begged him to kill her. He fired a single shot.

Through all this, Josette lay crunched up in a ball against the inner wall of the outhouse. Her tears flowed, her body trembled, but she was silent. After a long period of quiet outside, she rose to her feet and, peering through the crack of the door, saw the bodies of her family, lying near the open gate.

Josette waited some more. Straining to listen, she heard some activity further along the street, but it was faint. When there was absolute silence, she made a dash for a gate at the back of the compound that gave onto the neighbour's plot.

The gate creaked as she entered the compound, and a dog barked. The seven-year-old son of the neighbour came to the window. He spotted her and shouted, 'Cockroach! Cockroach!'

Josette ran to the gate of the compound and out into the street. Nobody seemed to have been roused by the noise. At one end of the street, a group of Interahamwe were grilling meat over a fire that had been lit in a ten-gallon drum. The other end of the street was empty. Hugging the wall with her

THE TRIUMPH OF EVIL

back, Josette crept into the next compound. There was a light in the window of the house. She went to it and peered in. A man and woman whom she knew well were sitting around the table. Josette tapped on the windowpane. They looked up at her. There was a moment of hesitation. The man then got up, walked to the window and drew the curtains shut.

Gromo Alex

By the end of the first week of May, Gromo had finally managed to get himself back to Kigali as head of the UN humanitarian assistance team.

Gromo's first act in Kigali was to organize a convoy to take him to the houses where UN Tutsi staff had regrouped. He wanted to make sure that all were okay. The first house he went to was Josette's. He was devastated to find the bodies of the thirteen members of the household lying near the gate. He tried to bury them as best he could, desperate to save their bodies from being eaten by dogs. He realized that visiting the hiding places of the UN Tutsi staff might reveal their location to the killers, so instead of going to Florence's house, he reached her by phone.

At the UNDP base, Gromo found Rumbashi comfortably seated in the UN representative's office. There were armed men in the compound, some wearing khaki uniforms, some with the red berets of one of the elite units. Rumbashi appeared to be very much in charge. Gromo ordered Rumbashi to clean up the area in front of the UNDP office that was littered with beer bottles and the debris from various parties.

Charles Petrie

I only ended up joining the UN Rwanda mission in the beginning of May, even though I had succumbed to Gromo's pressure much before. It took a few weeks for the paperwork from New York to come through. I was designated deputy UN humanitarian coordinator.

I joined the core of the UN humanitarian team that had been evacuated to Nairobi. I ended up arriving in Nairobi a week after Gromo had left for Kigali. As was the case in many UN interventions, the team in Nairobi spent most of their time writing reports of situations they did not see, or briefing ambassadors on developments they knew only second hand. My boss, the UN humanitarian coordinator, was an experienced, sophisticated and worldly diplomat. But this far into his UN career, there were limits to the discomforts he was prepared to tolerate. Those limits included almost anywhere beyond the Nairobi Hilton.

As soon as I arrived in the temporary UN coordination offices on the fringes of Nairobi, I spoke to Gromo in Kigali. He sounded in great form and was chuffed that he had succeeded in persuading me to join him. He described how that morning, while he was out taking food and water to drop-off points for the Tutsi UN staff, the convoy had been shot at by a rocket-propelled grenade. It had ricocheted off the top of one of the vehicles and exploded harmlessly at the side of the road. It was pretty cool, he said. 'Cool?' I asked, astonished. 'Cool,' he repeated. Apparently, he was compiling a list of the weapons he had been targeted with, and he was pleased to be able to add the RPG to the list. I waited a moment to absorb the information. I was horrified by what he was telling me. I asked him to get me on the next day's early morning flight to Kigali.

My first impression of the city was that it looked somehow hollow. The city wasn't empty, but the people in the streets seemed subdued and instead of the buzz of human voices, there was a constant sound of gunfire. Close to the UN compound there was a body at the side of the road. I supposed that it had been dragged there either by one of the packs of dogs I saw roaming the city, or by some good Samaritan who wanted to clear the road of an obstruction.

As I entered Gromo's office, I found the list he had mentioned behind the door. I had to admit that it was impressive. In just one week, his convoys had been fired upon multiple times. 'Hey, Gromo, my friend,' I said, 'this is crazy. Won't you and your team feel pushed to try to complete this list? And to take greater and greater risks to do so?'

Not missing a beat, Gromo laughed and wrapped me up in a bear hug. 'Good to see you too, Chuck,' he said.

Since in my newly appointed role I outranked him, Gromo suggested I deliver the humanitarian segment of General Dallaire's upcoming evening briefing, known as the 'evening prayers'. Gromo offered to provide some notes but, thinking I had a handle on the situation – after all, hadn't I prepared dozens and dozens of situation reports for New York during my UN career? – I told him there was no need. He smiled and shrugged his shoulders.

That evening, when it was my turn to speak, I offered generalities of the kind that had served as briefings for New York. I was barely into my stride when the general cut me off. 'Listen,' he said – and I did. 'If you are going to insult my men with trivia like this, you'll be out on tomorrow's plane.' He glared at me and then relented. 'Since Gromo says you know your stuff, I will give you one last chance.' Next morning, I was either to give a briefing worthy of the officers in the room or I was out.

From the corner of my eye, I could see that Gromo was working hard to hold back laughter. He didn't try to gloss over my error. 'You've really fucked up,' he said when the meeting was finished. Chastened, I asked Gromo to provide me with the notes that I'd so foolishly refused before. I stayed up late that night contacting friends who were with Médecins Sans Frontières and the International Committee of the Red Cross and gleaning what information I could. I pored through all the reports I could find.

The next morning, after I had finished my briefing, there was a moment's silence. Then, to my relief, General Dallaire said that my name could be taken off that day's passenger manifest for Nairobi.

Lieutenant Fiacre Mboki

By the end of April, the RPF had opened a corridor from Kigali to Byumba, sixty kilometres to the north. They began evacuating thousands of people to camps behind the lines, some from existing sites for the displaced, like the Amahoro stadium or the King Faisal hospital, and others collected as they moved from house to house. Displaced persons gathered by the thousands at Rutare, where the RPF established its first camp. Eventually the RPF housed thirty-five thousand people in Byumba and another hundred and fifty thousand at Rutare. In a similar way, as the rebels advanced along the eastern side of the country, they moved the Tutsis they encountered to camps further north.

As Fiacre's platoon progressed south, he was surprised by the total absence of resistance. No government soldiers, no militia, no Interahamwe. They came across an occasional Tutsi emerging from a hiding place in a swamp or forest, and sent them north to RPF camps, but even the encounters with straggling populations were significantly reduced. The area in front of them seemed empty, and this began to make Fiacre distinctly anxious. Were he and his men being led into a gigantic ambush? Were they about to come up against a well-entrenched and heavily armed enemy force?

And then came the surprising explanation. One morning, Fiacre heard on his shortwave radio that the Hutus and the local officials of this region had crossed on foot over the border into Tanzania. In one night, some two hundred and fifty thousand people had moved into Tanzania and settled near the Rwandan border in the greatest mass exodus of refugees ever.[*]

---

[*] I remember visiting the camps. How incredibly orderly they were. The Rwandan officials among them had recreated the social order of the communes from which they had left. It became quickly apparent that, rather than being a spontaneous flight, the movement of such a large number of people had been ordered by the various Rwandan mayors and community leaders.

145

Later that morning, Fiacre received new orders from his company commander. His platoon was to continue towards the Tanzanian border. Their objective was not now to fight to take control of the area, but to locate survivors.

Father Vjeko Curic

Father Vjeko had succeeded in transferring the endangered Tutsi population of his parish to the archbishopric of Kabgayi, but next morning he faced a difficult encounter with the archbishop. His Eminence was unhappy. He insisted that housing communities from one side of the conflict risked compromising the position of the Catholic Church. *What position?* thought Father Vjeko. They were not talking about two-sided conflict but about the massacre of one group by another.

For a time, it was doubtful whether or not the Tutsis that Father Vjeko had escorted to the archbishopric would be allowed to stay and shelter there. It was only when the archbishop received calls from Rome, lauding his humanitarian gesture, that he relented and agreed that the people who had arrived the night before would be allowed to remain.

Father Vjeko took this as an open invitation to bring all vulnerable Tutsis to Kabgayi – an interpretation that he knew went well beyond the archbishop's intent. The very next day, Father Vjeko drove back to his parish to see if there were others needing rescue. In the parish itself, all the Tutsis seemed to have left. He then followed the route that the band of Interahamwe who retreated from the checkpoint would have taken. Less than two kilometres on, an appalling stench led Father Vjeko to a mass of bodies in a ditch at the side of the road.

The very next day,
Father Vjeko drove back to the parish
to see if there were others
needing rescue...

The Tutsis seemed to have left...

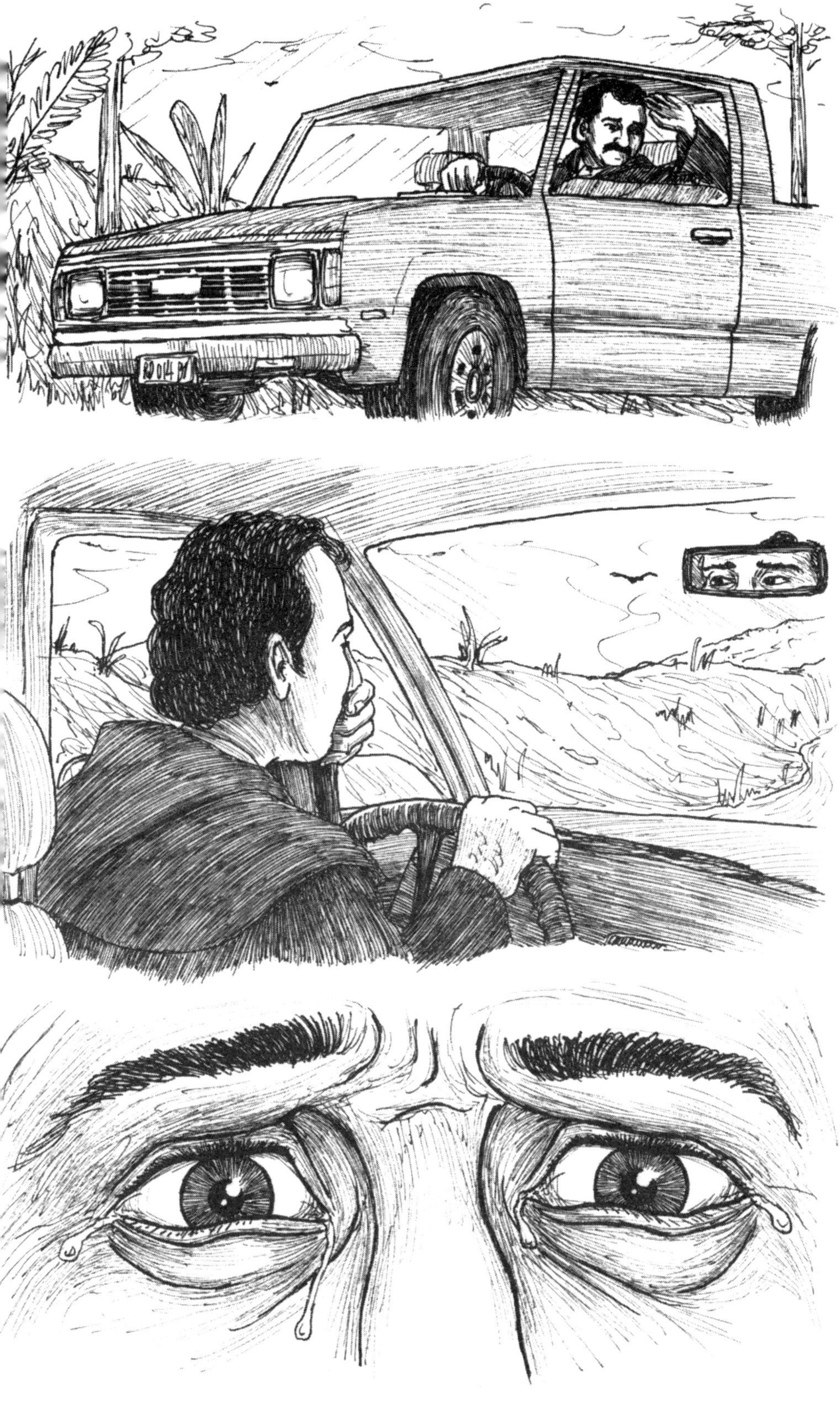

Somewhere...
deep down...
a muffled cry

Father Vjeko plunged, gagging, into the mass of bodies...

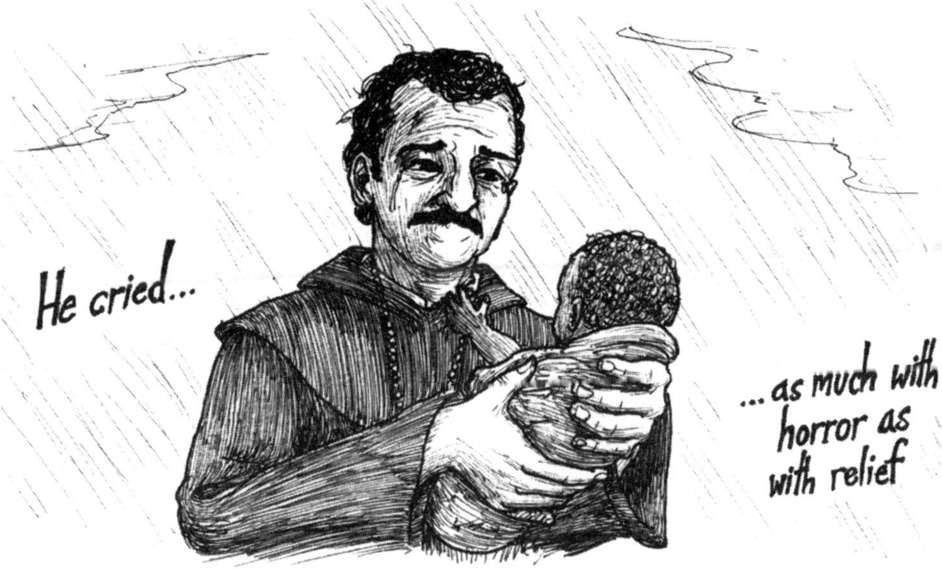
He cried...
...as much with horror as with relief

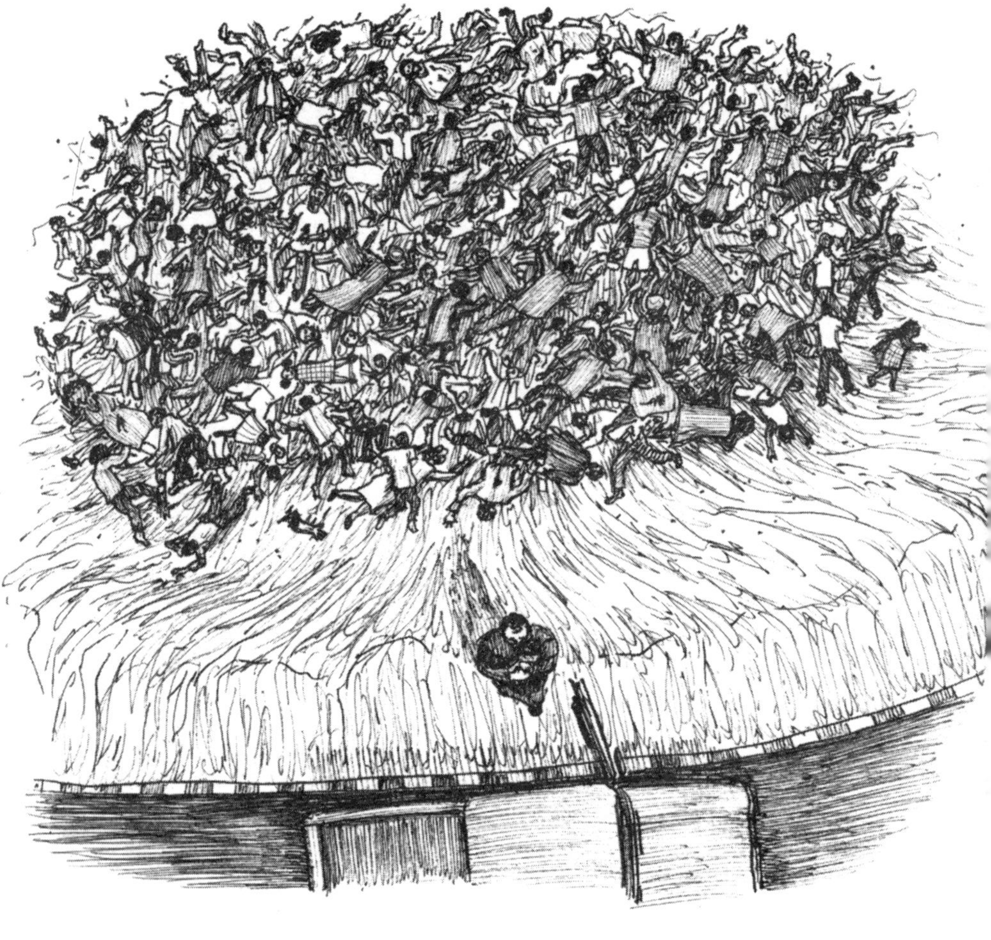

UN Security Council

The efforts in April to produce a last-minute presidential statement had highlighted the differing positions on Rwanda and the political interests behind them. After the monthly rotation of the presidency passed from New Zealand to Nigeria, the focus of Security Council debates was on the exact description of events in Rwanda. There had been tremendous hesitation and even resistance to the use of the word genocide. France was still pushing for the killings to be described as an outcome of civil war. Rwanda called it aggression. The United States wanted to avoid the word genocide as it could trigger the Genocide Convention, which brought with it an obligation for international intervention. The Clinton administration would only go as far as to talk about 'acts of genocide', which they insisted fell short of genocide itself.

Then Ambassador Jose Ayala-Lasso, the newly appointed High Commissioner for Human Rights, announced his intention to travel to Kigali between 11 and 12 May. It was agreed to defer a decision on what to call the slaughter in Rwanda until his return.

By day forty, while the world body argued over semantics, close to half a million Tutsis and moderate Hutus had been killed. More than a million people had been made homeless.

18

Days 41–50: The Rate of Killings Drops

Josette Umutoniwase

Towards the end of May, Josette had returned to hide in her house. Hours after the attack that had left her entire family and ten others dead, she had finally found refuge with her sister's primary school teacher. This interlude lasted a week. Then the Interahamwe came to the house and accused the teacher of being sympathetic to the Tutsi cause. Since she had educated Tutsi children, she must be a spy. That evening they attacked the house. It was very dark and there was much confusion, with people shouting, whistles blowing and shots fired. In the midst of it all, Josette managed once again to escape.

She returned to her family home, the site of the killings. The house had been ransacked a number of times, and was in such a state of dilapidation that it was unlikely anyone else would bother to come in.

Gromo Alex

Gromo and I agreed on a division of responsibilities. My focus would be the daily analysis of the humanitarian situation that had to be sent off to New York, and the more detailed one to be used for the evening prayers. Gromo would continue to provide support for people in the safe havens and for the UN staff members in hiding.

I had persuaded the UN administration to agree to buy a small Suzuki Vitara from one of the staff members who had evacuated Kigali. UNAMIR equipped it with a huge Codan radio antenna (Gromo said it resembled a rhinoceros) and I tied a UN flag on a pole to the back. It was with this that I started moving around Rwanda. As long as one avoided the RPF–government forces front line, it wasn't that difficult to travel around the country behind the respective lines. The killers in the government-held areas were focused on their actions, which they believed were part of a just cause.

Gromo continued to drop into the UNDP office in Kigali. Rumbashi had had the area in front of the building cleaned up, and there were fewer armed men milling around. Time and again, Rumbashi asked Gromo whether he knew the whereabouts of particular UN staff members, on the excuse that he had to give them their salaries. Gromo offered to find a way to get it to them himself, but Rumbashi insisted that he alone was accountable for the money. He pestered Gromo in particular for the whereabouts of Florence. Gromo told him nothing, but he made a mental note to get Florence moved to a safer location.

With the adoption of the new Security Council resolution defining his mandate, General Dallaire was left with an official force of 267 men, the core of whom were from a Ghanaian battalion. But through various subterfuges, the general had been able to retain an additional fifty military observers under the command of Colonel Tikoka. General

Dallaire deployed the Ghanaian troops to provide static area security. He tasked Colonel Tikoka with identifying sites not far from the UNAMIR headquarters that could serve as protected areas for the Tutsi population. Once the sites were established, hundreds of people were brought to the safe havens.

One of these havens, the Hôtel des Mille Collines (many years later of *Hotel Rwanda* fame), with a UN platoon made up of Tunisian soldiers deployed to cover it front and back, became a major regroupment centre for refugees.* It still functioned as a hotel with the owner charging exorbitant prices for the rooms.

Amahoro stadium was another important safe haven for the Rwandan displaced. Major Don McNeil, part of the UNAMIR force, organized the reception of the Tutsis, and by the end more than twelve thousand found protection there.

By mid-May, with Florence sheltering eighteen people, the conditions in her house had become intolerable. Moreover, Rumbashi's continued questions as to her whereabouts posed a threat. Gromo knew that the provision of supplies for Florence's house would not go unobserved for long. Something had to be done.

Every evening Gromo was on the phone battling it out with New York to overturn the ban on evacuation of UN national staff. His colleagues in New York refused to give way. So Gromo and Captain Mbaye put together a plan to take Florence and all those under her care to one of the areas in Kigali guarded by UN soldiers. Given the number of barriers that would have to be passed, they would need a UN armoured personnel carrier and UN soldiers. Authorization from New York was therefore essential. Finally,

---

* The Tunisians also guarded King Faisal hospital while the Ghanaians covered the airport, UNAMIR HQ and the Amahoro stadium.

a forceful intervention from General Dallaire triggered a green light from New York for Florence's move – but with the stipulation that New York would be given details of it forty-eight hours before it was to happen.

Gromo and Captain Mbaye made their preparations in total secrecy. Two evenings before the operation in the last week of May, the nightly confidential cable to UN headquarters in New York relayed details of the plan, as required. Florence was given notice to be ready.

Lieutenant Fiacre Mboki

Following the mass movement of the populations of southeastern Rwanda, Fiacre's progress was trouble-free. Some of the villages they passed through appeared to be undisturbed. The bodies of those killed had been buried. Doors were closed, agricultural tools neatly stored and streets uncluttered. The only anomalies were the absence of any people and the roaming of farm animals that had broken free. Other villages they passed seemed as if a tornado had swept through. Bodies in the fields, doors ajar, houses ransacked, half-finished bowls of food on the table – all the signs of a sudden, unplanned departure.

It was only when his platoon hit the northern edge of Lake Mugesera that they began to encounter sizeable numbers of Tutsis emerging from hiding. Each had a tragically familiar tale to tell. They spoke of apprehension immediately after the downing of the presidential plane; a brief period of calm before the alarm that accompanied the arrival of Interahamwe and government troops; the beginning of the attacks and the murder of their friends and family members. They described being tracked by dogs through the marshes and hearing the shriek of whistles when one of them had been found – screams followed by silence.

Each time Fiacre gathered together a dozen survivors, he sent them north with an escort.

Father Vjeko Curic

For the two weeks that followed the establishment of the camp for the displaced in the archbishopric of Kabgayi, Father Vjeko continued his forays into the outskirts of his parish, seeking survivors. He chartered a minibus at first, but it became increasingly difficult to negotiate the Interahamwe checkpoints with large numbers of people on board. He used his pickup truck, but that too became problematic. As the number of possible victims in the countryside dwindled, the vehicle searches of the militia at the checkpoints became more rigorous. He was forced into a desperate measure. Flying a white flag on his pickup, he hid survivors under the corpses that he was taking to Kabgayi for burial.

Father Vjeko negotiated his passage through the barriers with great craftsmanship. He acquired the names of the men at the checkpoints, and attempted the passage when individuals he knew would be present. He avoided the early evening, when the militia would be particularly inebriated. His trips saved many people. By the time ten days had gone by, Father Vjeko found fewer and fewer people to evacuate to Kabgayi, while the numbers in the camp had risen to thousands.

In order to supplement the food in Kabgayi and to obtain essential drugs, Father Vjeko began making frequent trips to Bujumbura. Between Kabgayi and the border with Burundi, there were more than thirty roadblocks, each demanding deft negotiation and undivided attention.

After a few trips, the militia came to recognize the metallic rattle that signalled the approach of his disintegrating car. This suited Father Vjeko well, since there was no advantage in approaching a roadblock unannounced. Others also heard his approach. On one stretch of road just out of sight of a roadblock, arms emerged from the dense undergrowth at the side of the road each time he drove by. To stop the vehicle might have drawn the attention of the militia. Instead Father Vjeko drove along that

159

segment as slowly as possible, tossing water and food as far as he could into the bushes on either side.

Florence Ngirumpatse

On the evening before their rescue, Florence and the members of her household were packing in preparation for their departure, when there came a loud series of knocks on the door. She signalled to people to keep still. The knocking came again, more insistently. Florence's husband was moving towards the door, when suddenly bullets from an AK-47 ripped through the door and struck him down.

With a swift kick, the door flew open, and a team of men rushed in. When the action ended, there were eighteen dead: Florence, her husband, five other adults and eleven children. In less than ten minutes, all had been shot down or hacked apart with machetes.

Later that night, Rumbashi was described in a witness statement as allegedly being in a bar near his house celebrating Florence's death.

One can't help but wonder whether it was pure coincidence that her killers converged on Florence's house the very evening before she was to be rescued.

The improbability that the timing was due to coincidence alone raises the uncomfortable possibility that someone in Kigali had been tipped off by someone in New York about the rescue plan – which in turn suggests the possible complicity of someone in the New York office in the killing of UN staff.*

---

* Gromo always suspected that Rumbashi had had something to do with Florence's death. That he learned of the impending rescue and he tipped off the militiamen who conducted the killings of Florence and her wards. While there is no proof of his direct involvement, a number of witness statements allege his intimate knowledge of her murder at the time it occurred and celebrating the event afterwards.

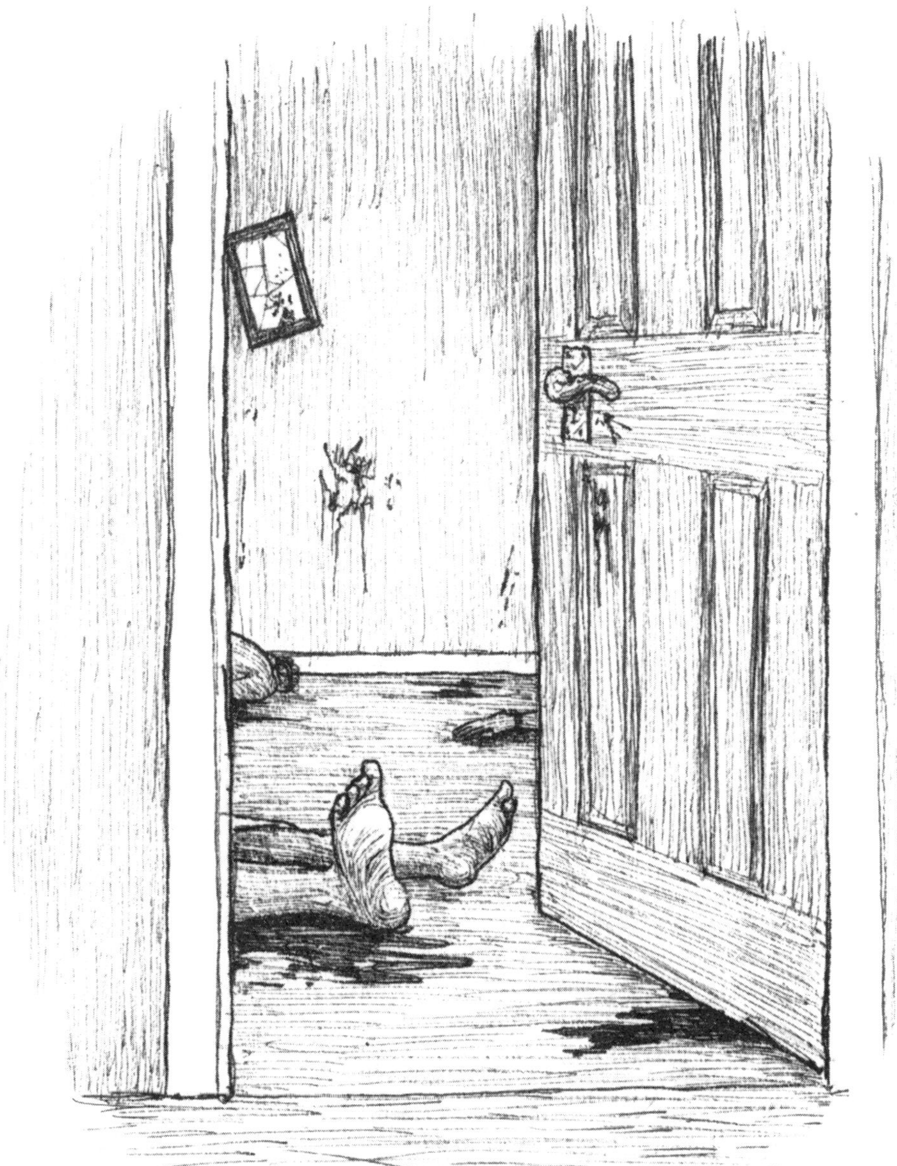

UN Security Council

On returning from his mission to Rwanda, the High Commissioner for Human Rights sent a report to the Security Council. He had travelled to Kigali and Byumba, and had spoken to representatives of both the interim government and the RPF. His report called for a strong condemnation of the mass killings of civilians. He concluded that extremely serious violations of human rights had taken place in Rwanda, and were continuing. He refused, however, to attribute responsibility.

The members of the Security Council did not consider the report particularly helpful. Most of the positions within the council remained fixed, though there seemed to be a shift in the American stance. The US representative suggested the creation of a protective zone with an international force providing security along the Rwandan border. This approach, she argued, would be less complex and require fewer troops than a new UN mission.

The subtle shift in the US position notwithstanding, the Security Council passed Resolution 918, which imposed an arms embargo on both parties, and demanded that a ceasefire be agreed and the massacres end. A UN force of 5,500 troops was authorized. Efforts were afterwards concentrated on finding the troops to make up the force.

During an open debate on Rwanda, held in mid-May, the Czech representative questioned the description of the situation as a humanitarian crisis. This is not a famine or a natural disaster, he said. In the view of his delegation, the only accurate description was genocide.

He started his statement forcefully, saying that the crocodiles in the Kagera river and the vultures over Rwanda had seldom had it so good. They were feeding on the bodies of thousands upon thousands of children, of women and of men, people who had been hacked to death during the past six weeks by what had turned out to be a most vicious regime.

This was the very first time that a member of the Security Council had publicly used the label genocide to describe events in Rwanda. But even this did not spur the Security Council into action. In lieu of decision-making, the secretary-general's representative informed the council that another mission was being sent to assess the situation.

By day fifty of the genocide, some six hundred thousand Tutsis and moderate Hutus had been killed, and many others were in hiding.

19

Days 51–60: Tutsis Start Coming Out of Hiding to Be Killed

After a first bout of frenzied activity in April and much of May, the killings took on a different form. By the time Florence had been killed, close to 80 per cent of those who would eventually die in the genocide had already been killed.

The killings that did occur towards the end of May and the early days of June came not from hunting Tutsis down, but from Tutsis giving themselves up. Having run out of supplies, they emerged from hiding, tired and defeated. They approached the checkpoints voluntarily. What killing there was now, was done on the barriers. Those who could afford it paid money for a quick finish with a bullet.

Gromo Alex

On the very last day of May, Captain Mbaye was driving back to UN headquarters when a mortar shell landed behind his jeep. Shrapnel entered through the back window and hit Mbaye in the head, killing him instantly. The mortar had been one of the many fired by RPF forces at the Rwandan army checkpoint.

Gromo made it to UN headquarters just as Captain Mbaye's body arrived. General Dallaire received the body and placed it carefully on the table that had been set up in the main lobby of the Amahoro Hotel, located next to the stadium. The shrapnel had created a small entry wound. Captain Mbaye looked as if he was only sleeping.

Gromo followed the body to the airport. The full Senegalese contingent stood at attention. Standing rigid, Colonel Tikoka, General Dallaire and General Anyidoho saluted the coffin of the captain as it entered into the bowels of the C-130.

I was in Nairobi when I heard of Captain Mbaye's death. I was only able to reach Gromo that evening. He was distressed. 'I can't continue, Chuck,' he mumbled. 'It is just too much; first Florence, and now Mbaye.' I could hear him crying over the line. 'I need to get out.'

Gromo got on the plane the next morning.

Lieutenant Fiacre Mboki

Having almost reached the border with Burundi, the battalion of which Fiacre's platoon was a part was given the order to march westward. Their new objective was to cut off the Kigali to Bujumbura road at the level of Kabgayi. The RPF were now in full control of Kigali airport, and wanted to lay siege to the part of the capital still in the hands of government forces.

Josette Umutoniwase

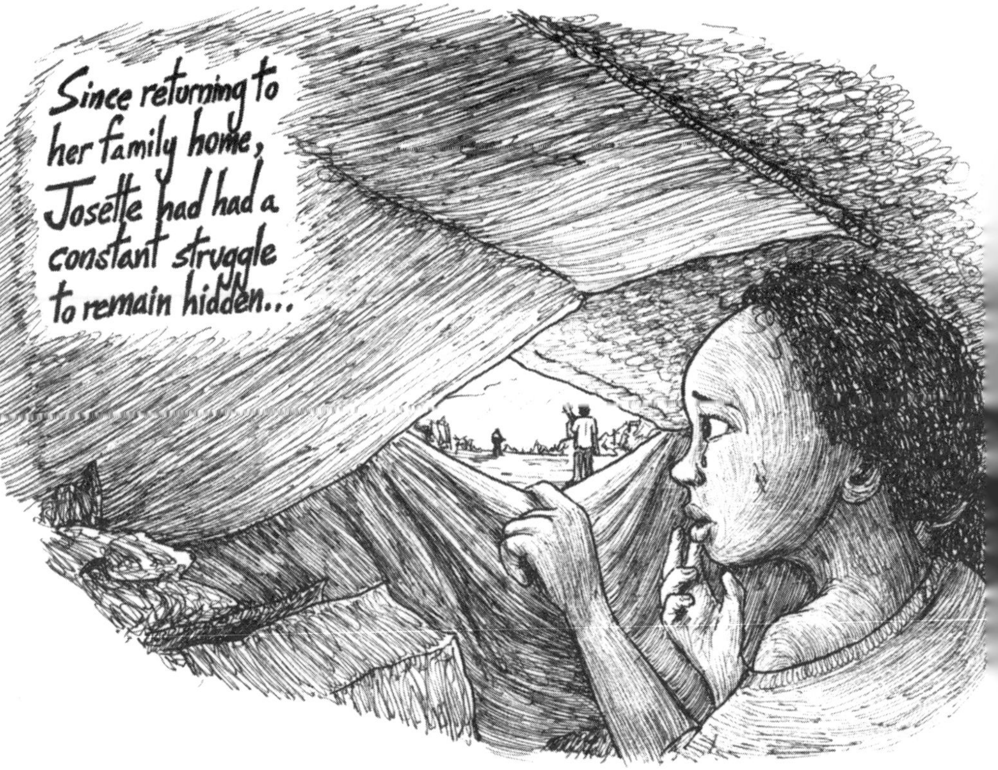
Since returning to her family home, Josette had had a constant struggle to remain hidden...

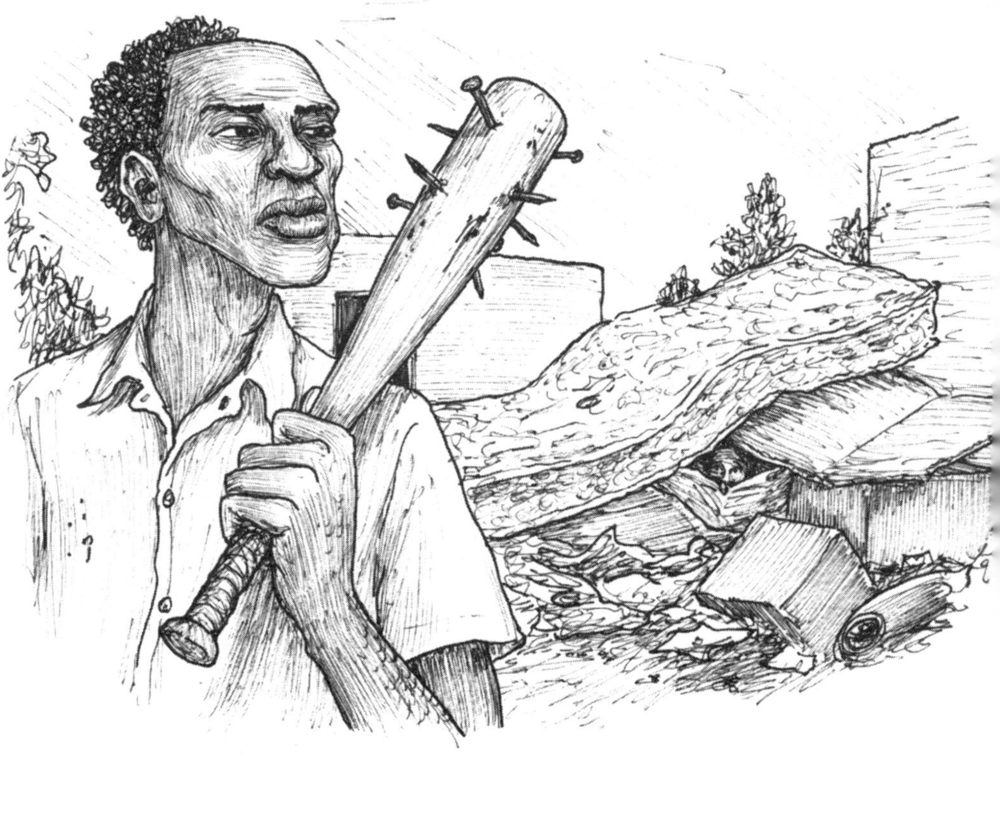

... During the night, she scavenged for food.

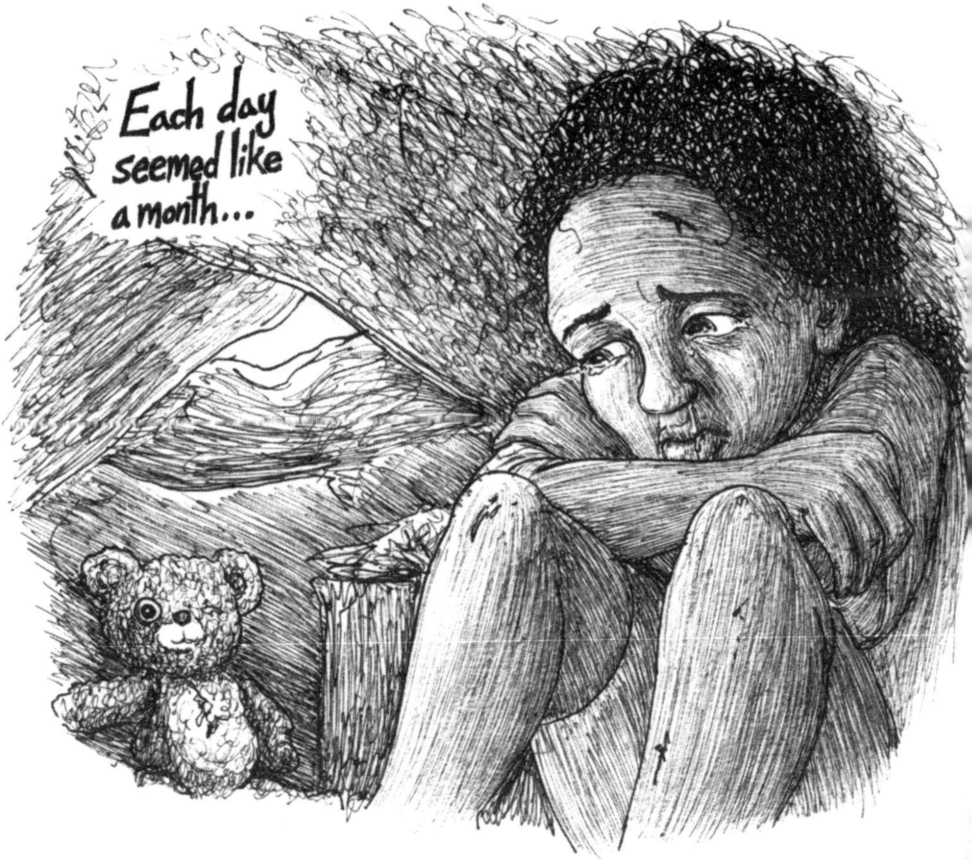
Each day seemed like a month...

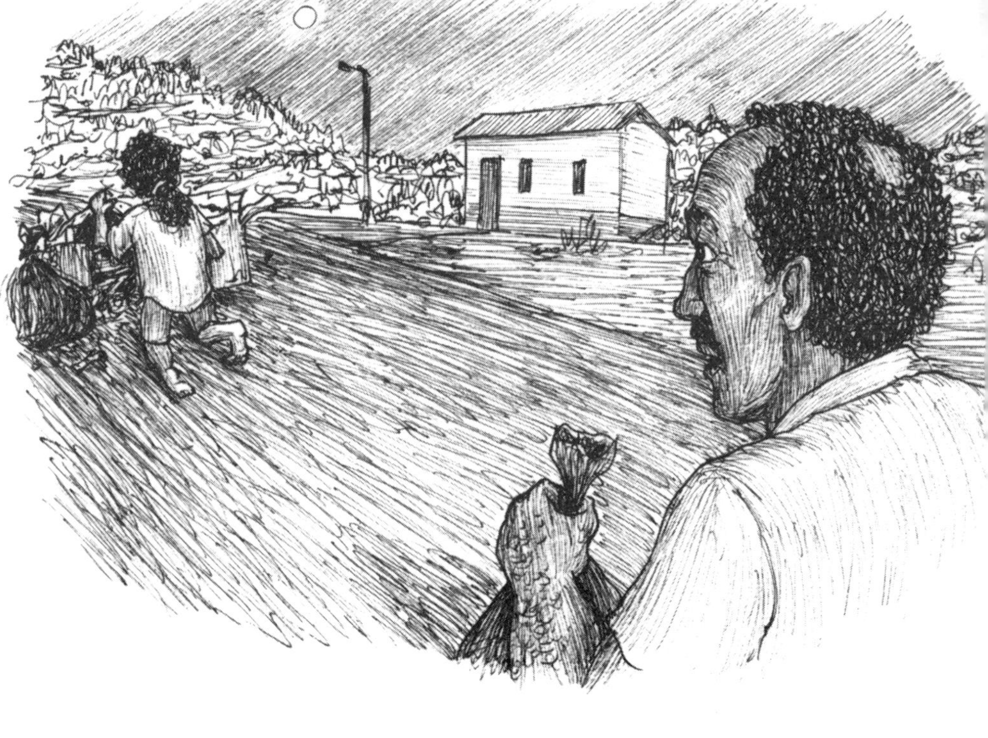

For a short period...
...she could look forward
to a warm meal.

The respite only lasted a week...

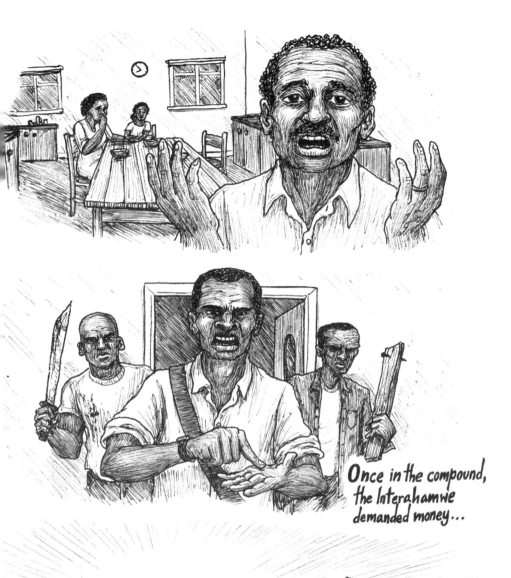

Once in the compound, the Interahamwe demanded money...

...they had none.

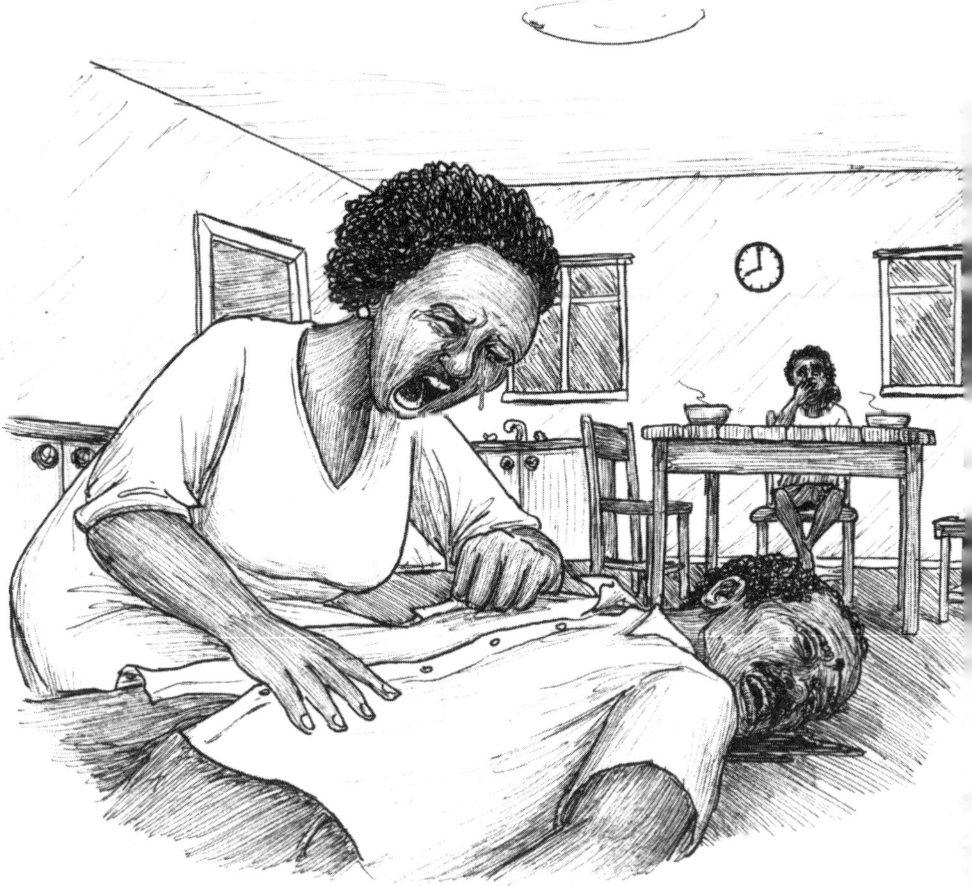

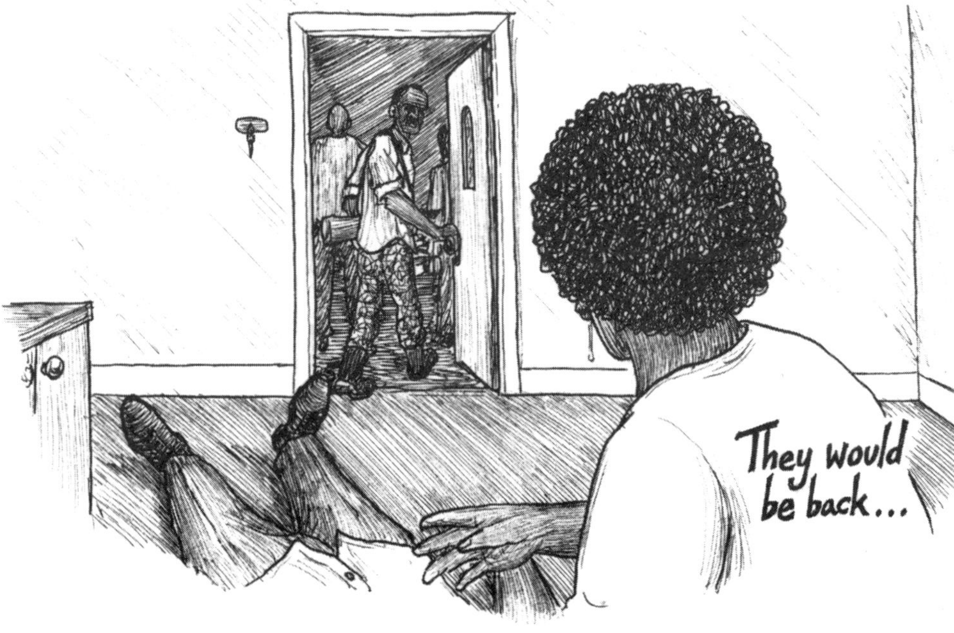
They would be back...

Without a moment's hesitation,
the driver bundled them into the car...

Hôtel
des Mille Collines

Charles Petrie

I had been sad to see Gromo go, but I fully understood his need to get out. He had been through a lot. Having arrived in January 1994, he had gotten to know many of the people killed. By the time I had joined the UN in Rwanda, all of the Tutsi staff who weren't dead were in hiding.

By early June, a dense network of roadblocks had been set up by Interahamwe militia throughout the zones controlled by the interim government. In some cases, the barriers were separated by no more than a few hundred yards, making escape virtually impossible for those targeted for elimination.

For those less at risk, and especially for foreigners, the roadblocks were agonizingly difficult to negotiate. I had to try, without benefit of the local language, to answer questions about my origin over and over again. I dreaded those moments when roadblocks were manned by someone capable of reading, and I had to hand over my British passport as well as my UN laissez-passer. The militia on the barriers were looking for Belgians, whom they blamed for the troubles of the country, and my passport had been issued in Brussels. I had to try to explain how I had lost a passport while travelling through Belgium and had to get a replacement there. During these lengthy discussions, I aimed for an unwavering stare with a slight smile to convey a feigned appearance of ease as a sign of my absolute sincerity. This tactic worked, but was each time more taxing.

One day I left UN military headquarters early in the morning, on my way to visit a camp of displaced people some distance to the west of Kigali. I had really not wanted to go. My stomach had started to act up and I was pretty tired. Not even out of Kigali, I encountered the first of the interminable roadblocks. The further I travelled, and the greater the number of times I had to make the same jokes and deal with the same issues, the less I felt up to the challenge. I started to think of turning back. But I realized that if I turned around, I'd have to negotiate the same barriers all over again. And this time I'd also have to allay suspicions as to why my plans had changed. I had no option but to continue onward. As Gromo would have put it, 'You're screwed, Chuck!'

Father Vjeko Curic

There were now more than ten thousand people sheltering in Kabgayi under the protection of the archbishopric. One morning, a novice told Father Vjeko that someone was trying to enter the camp's hospital with a list in his hands. He would not accept the insistence of the hospital staff that the space was a neutral one.

Father Vjeko confronted the individual, who turned out to be an Interahamwe leader. He found the man surprisingly sophisticated and articulate, and couldn't help asking himself how he came to head a militia band. I wondered later, when Father Vjeko told me the story, whether he could have been connected to Rumbashi. Father Vjeko tried to convince the person that the hospital was an inviolable area, but the Interahamwe leader totally refused to budge. He turned away from the priest, took his men into the hospital, and demanded to see identity cards. Three patients whose names were on his list were executed on the spot, their bodies abandoned on the floor where they fell.*

UN Security Council

In the very last days of May, the Security Council was presented with the conclusions of the special mission that the secretary-general had sent to the region between 22 and 27 May, under the leadership of his chief

---

* The bodies stayed where they had fallen for quite a while. For many weeks later, after they had been removed, the stain of their silhouettes could still be seen on the concrete floor.

of staff, Iqbal Riza. The report, the hardest-hitting to date, included a vivid description of the horrors of the weeks since the beginning of the genocide, referring to a 'frenzy of massacres'. Significantly, the report also stated that the massacres and killings had been systematic, and that there was 'little doubt' that what had happened constituted genocide. For the first time, the UN Secretariat dared use the term.

The report concluded on a bitter note: 'We must all realize that we have failed in our response to the agony of Rwanda, and thus have acquiesced in the continued loss of human lives.'

The Security Council then spent the first week of June discussing the report. The discussions occurred in the midst of preparations for the fiftieth anniversary of the Normandy landings. Nobody seemed to find it incongruous that discussions on Rwanda should be held at the same time that the victors of the Second World War – the five Permanent Members of the Security Council – commemorated Operation Overlord, launched to ensure that *never again* would the horrors of genocide be inflicted on the peoples of the world.

But to be fair, the secretary-general's report did have a sobering effect. The Rwandan representative was now much less vocal. The French representative changed from insisting that rebel aggression had to be stopped to declaring that a humanitarian tragedy had to be urgently addressed. Most significant was the full re-engagement of the US.

But much time continued to be spent rehearsing arguments about the applicability of the word genocide to Rwanda. Words have great importance in the United Nations. Sometimes words are mistaken for action.

By day sixty of the genocide, more than seven hundred thousand Tutsis and moderate Hutus had been killed.

20

Days 61–70: Close to 90 Per Cent of Those to Die Are Dead

In the second half of June, it would seem that instructions were received to clean up the area around the barriers. Bodies suddenly disappeared, even though the killings continued. Those in command must have wanted to ensure that no sign remained afterwards of the massacres.

Father Vjeko Curic

Father Vjeko was in Bujumbura collecting supplies when he heard that the RPF had cut off the Bujumbura to Kigali road just north of Kabgayi. The portion of the road south of Kabgayi was still, however, under the control of the interim government. Realizing that this would probably be his last trip, he left Bujumbura with as much food and water as he could crowd onto the front passenger seat of the car.

The trip, and especially the passage of the roadblocks, was surprisingly routine, almost as if the militia hadn't yet realized that the road further up was cut off. But when he reached the barrier immediately before the stretch that demanded his attention, he was taken aback by the particularly demented look of those manning it. They grinned stupidly at him. A little further on, he understood why. Hundreds of bodies cascaded out of the bushes onto the road, their lifeless hands no longer able to catch the supplies that had been intended for them.

Father Vjeko drove the rest of the road to Kabgayi in a state of shock, expecting at any moment to be stopped or shot at. In Kabgayi, he received his second shock. A priest rushed up to him and announced that ten priests, three bishops and the Archbishop of Kigali had been murdered. RPF soldiers had burst into their rooms in a frenzied state and shot them dead. It was supposed that the murders had been carried out in revenge for the slaughter of their own families.

Charles Petrie

A little over a week after Gromo's departure, I was in Burundi, investigating rumours of a new movement of people in the government-controlled areas as a result of the RPF advance. I received a frantic call from Kigali. A building that Gromo and I had arranged to have renovated so that all the humanitarian agencies could be housed together – a building near to, but not directly within, UN military headquarters – had just been found to be mined.

I placed an urgent call to New York and explained the situation. Since the area around the building was now under RPF control, I was told to deliver a letter from UN headquarters that would be faxed to me to deliver to the rebel General Kagame. Up to that time, the humanitarian arm of the UN had had no direct link with the rebel general. General Kagame had refused invitations to travel to Kampala to meet the UN humanitarian

181

coordinator, and the UN humanitarian coordinator had shown no inclination to venture into RPF-controlled areas.

When I received the fax, I was surprised by its accusatory tone. New York, it seemed, had jumped to the unwarranted conclusion that the rebels should answer for the security of the building. This definitely didn't suit my purposes. I was keen to persuade General Kagame to agree to a temporary truce to allow a cross-line mission into government-controlled areas so that we could locate a large number of displaced civilians. This presumptuous fax, I feared, would make that task much more difficult.

I contacted the RPF liaison officer in Bujumbura and asked him to arrange for me to deliver the letter from the under-secretary general for humanitarian affairs to General Kagame in person, in Rwanda. After discussion with his colleagues, the liaison officer agreed to pick me up the next day at 06h00 and take me to the general.

The next morning at the agreed time, no one showed up. I sat down at a table on the terrace of the Novotel swimming pool, ordered a coffee and a croissant, while watching the hummingbirds beat their wings in a nearby bush. The morning passed. It was only as I was biting into a sandwich at midday that the RPF liaison officer finally marched in.

'We go right now,' he said, and turned around and walked out. I pocketed the sandwich, and followed. We were to spend the night near the border with Rwanda and go over very early the next day. During the drive, I had debated with myself how best to give the offensive letter to the general without jeopardizing my chances of securing an agreement for the cross-line operation. I decided that it was best for the general to be forewarned of the letter's content so that he could digest it before we talked. Although this was a risky strategy – he could decide not to meet me – I thought it better for me to be seen to be transparent. That evening over a frugal dinner I showed the contents of the fax to the RPF liaison officer. He read it and shrugged his shoulders.

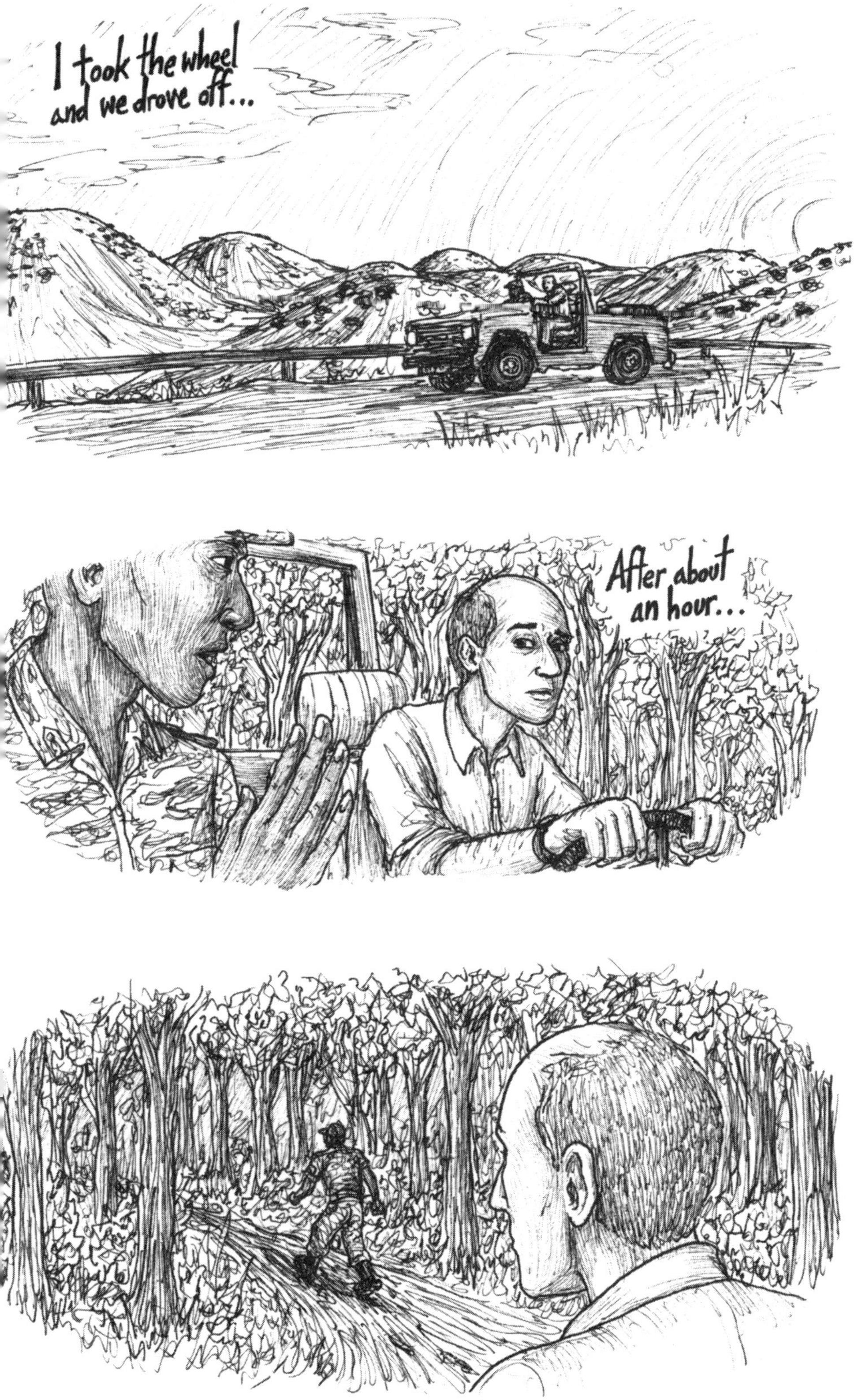
I took the wheel and we drove off...
After about an hour...

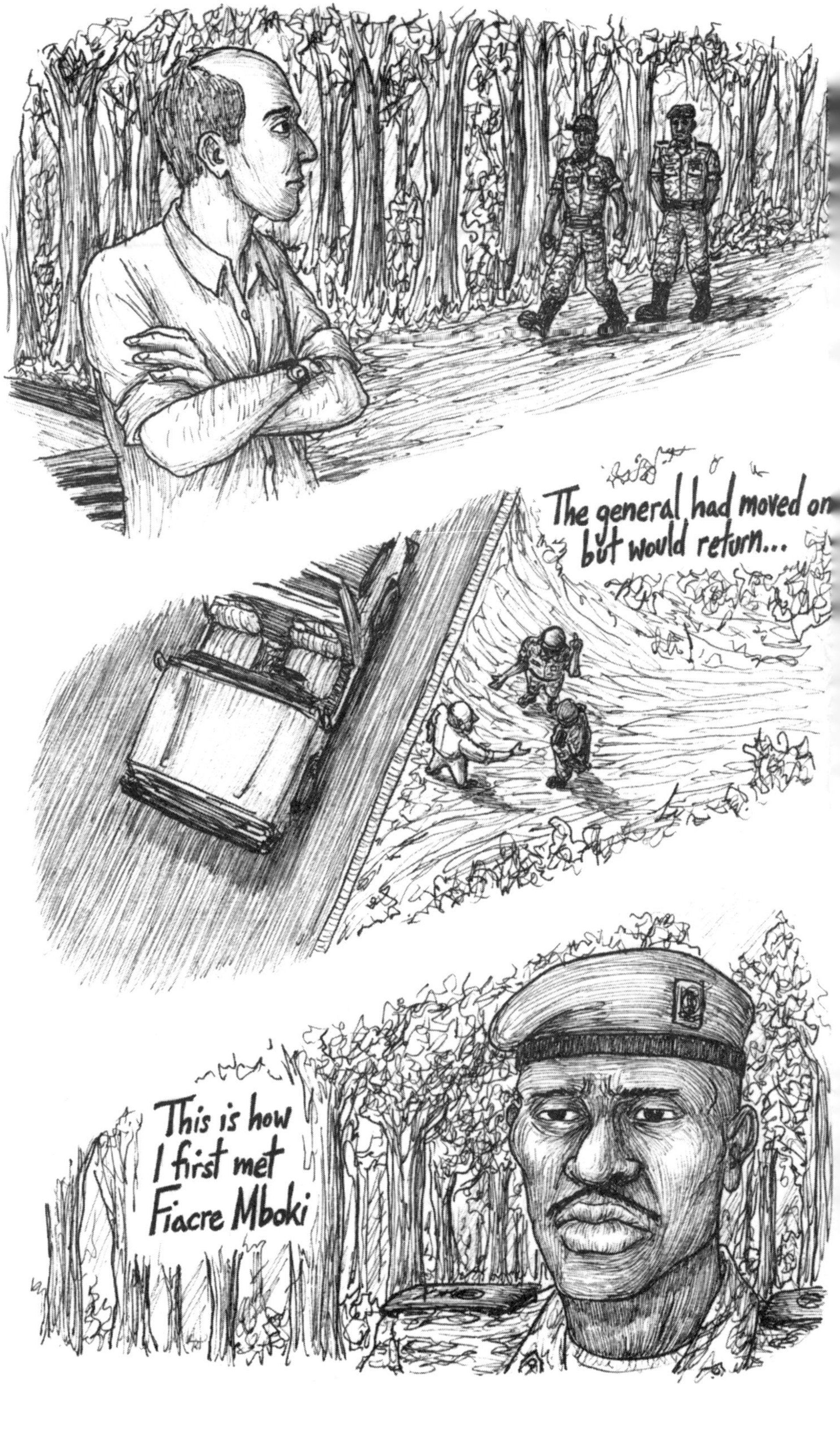
The general had moved on
but would return...
This is how
I first met
Fiacre Mboki

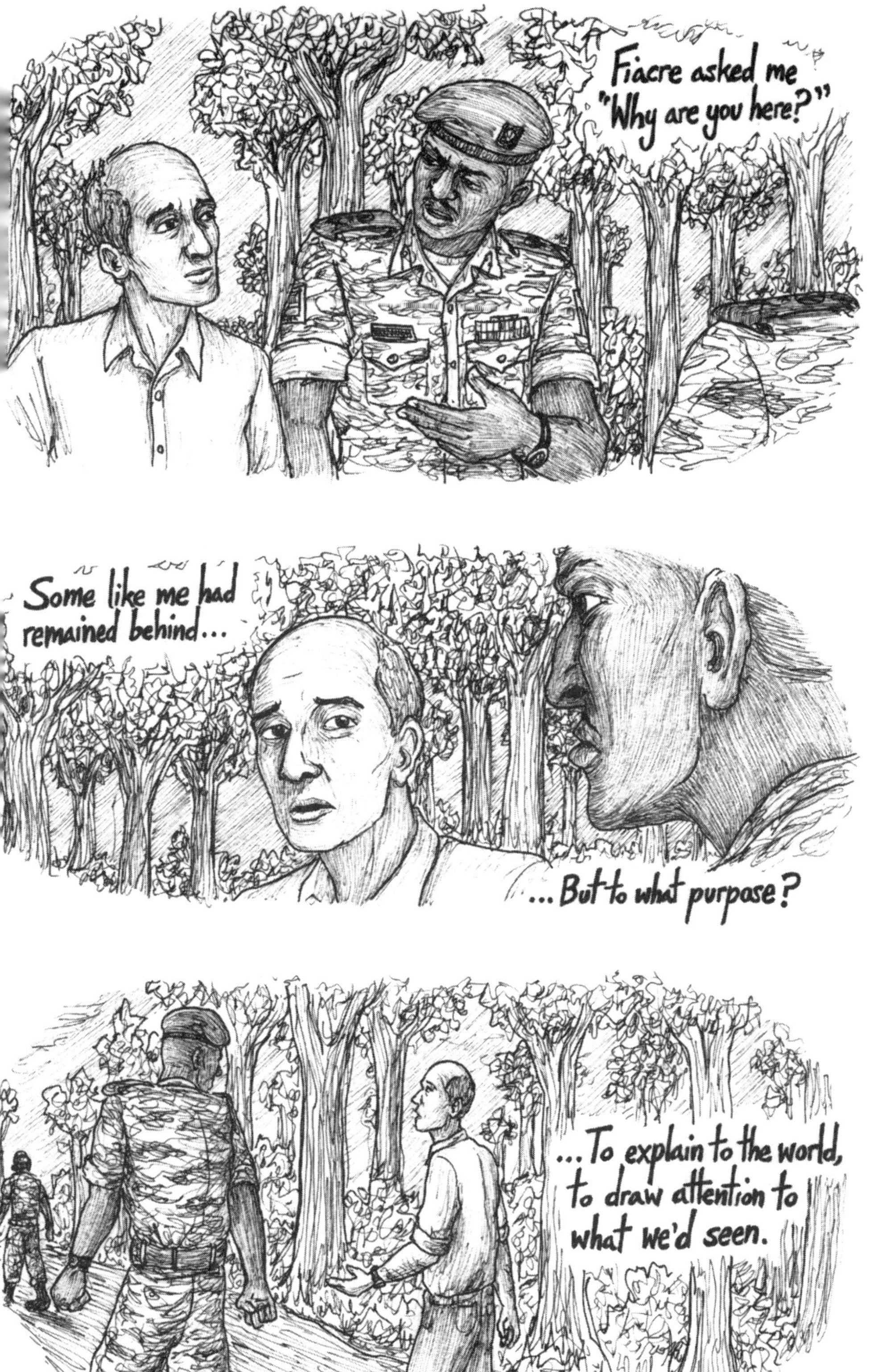
Fiacre asked me "Why are you here?"
Some like me had remained behind...
... But to what purpose?
... To explain to the world, to draw attention to what we'd seen.

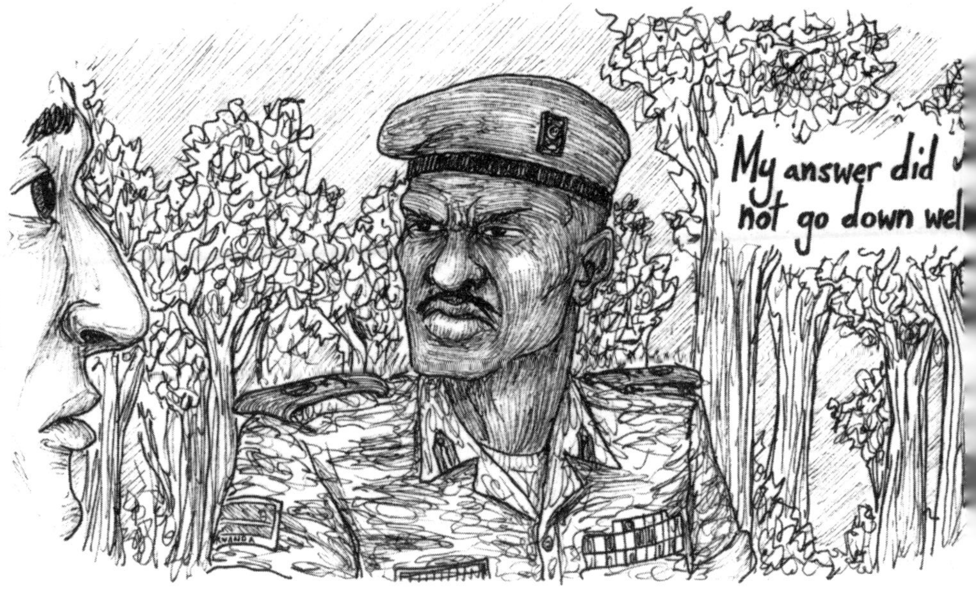
My answer did
not go down wel

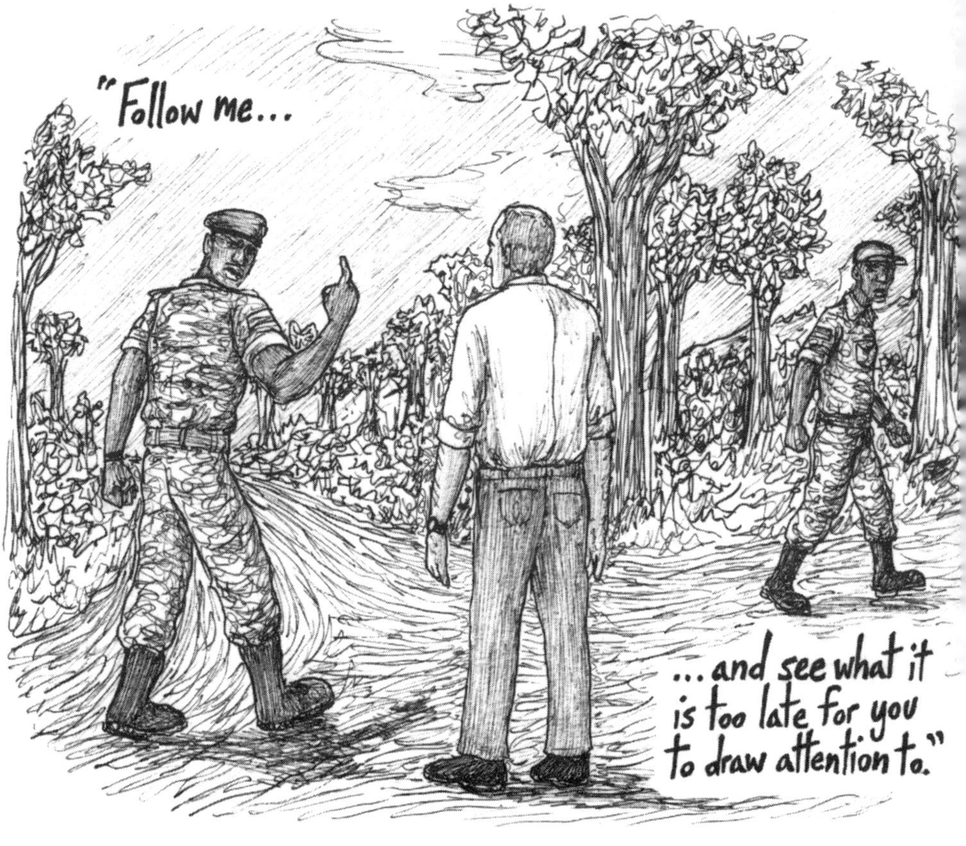
"Follow me...
...and see what it is too late for you to draw attention to."

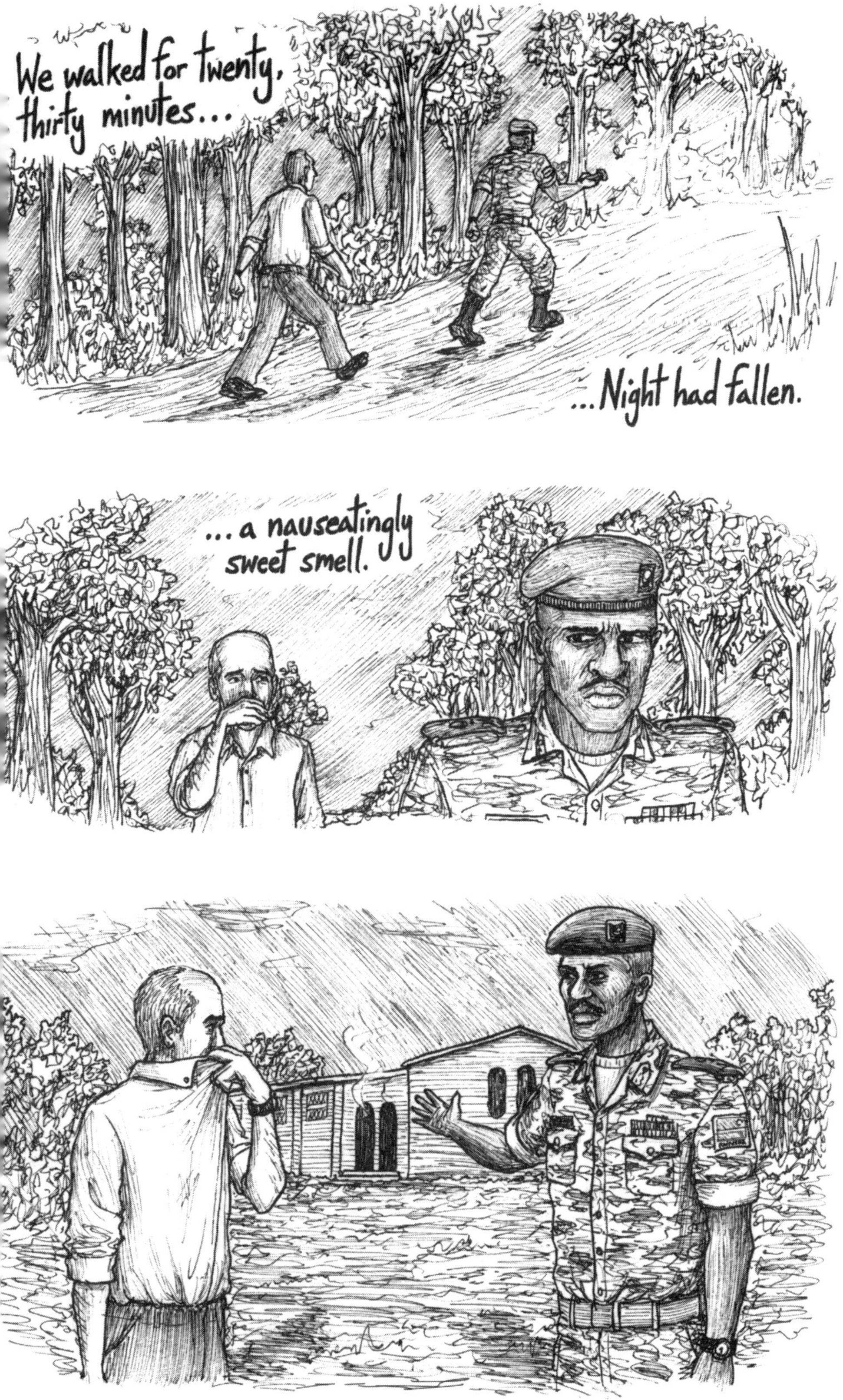
We walked for twenty, thirty minutes...
...Night had fallen.
...a nauseatingly sweet smell.

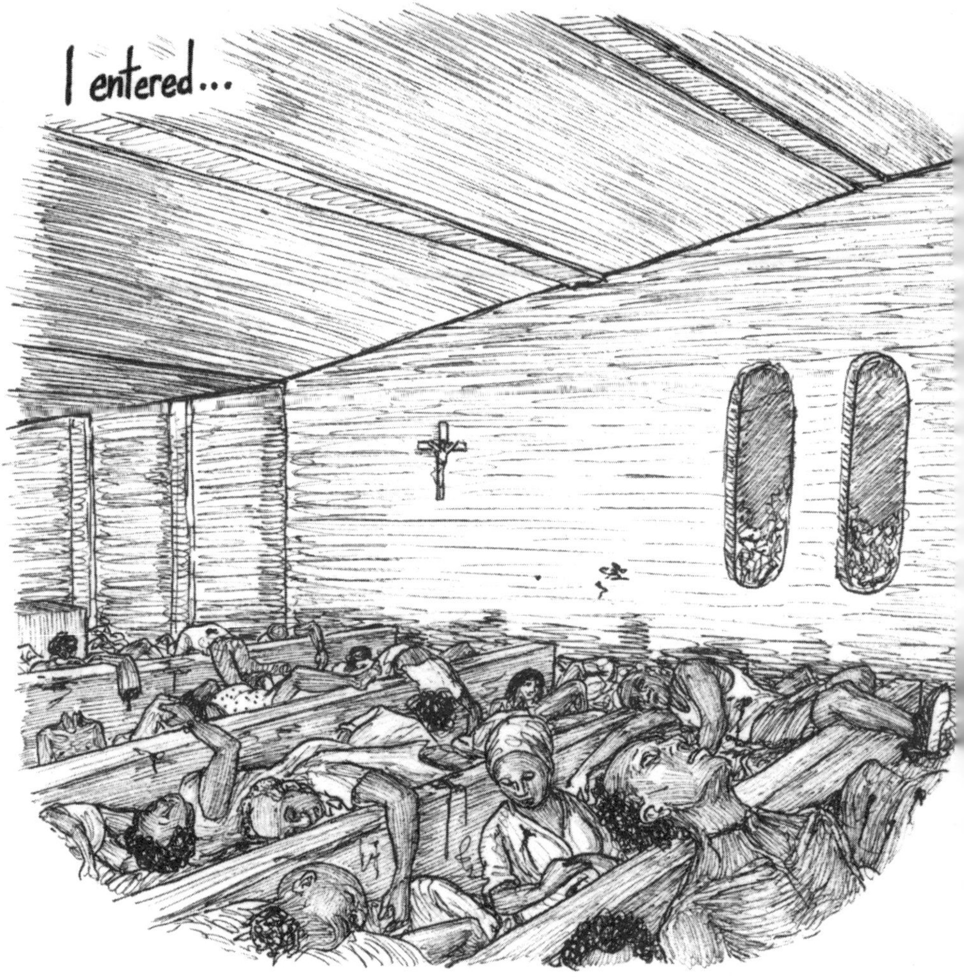
I entered...

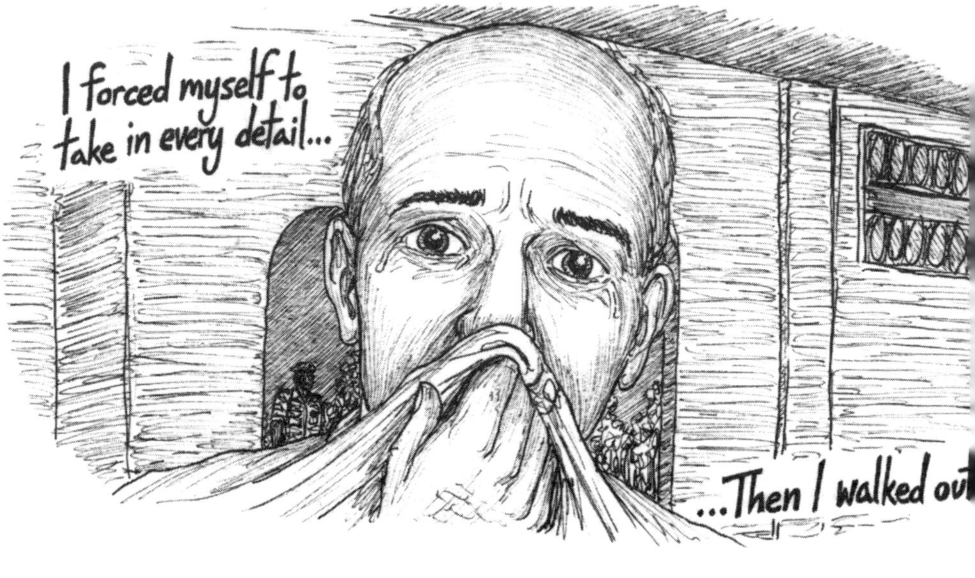
I forced myself to take in every detail...
...Then I walked out

On our way back to the encampment there was little conversation. When we arrived, the captain said brusquely that the general was waiting. We had to go. We set off again into the darkness, following a path barely visible in the dimmed lights of the Suzuki Vitara. At times we drove rapidly over open ground, and at other times moved inch by inch through undergrowth that scratched the sides of the car. We came upon a cache of upended suitcases, with heaps of clothes and personal items that must have been abandoned in a panic. Where had the people fled to? The answer soon came, as our vehicle plunged into a path lined with piles of putrefying bodies. It seemed I had been taken on a tour of hell.

In the middle of the night, we reached our destination, to be told once again that the general had just left. We were to wait for his return. I reclined the seat of the car, nibbled a bit of my sandwich, and tried to sleep.

The next two days were like the first: long and fruitless waits for the general, hurried dashes to other rendezvous, and more long waits. On the morning of the fourth day, I asked the liaison officer to return me to Kigali. Before he dropped me off, I handed him the letter intended for General Kagame. I told him that I also had had a verbal message for the general, which I now needed to tell New York I had not been able to deliver.

I had just settled behind a computer at UN headquarters when I got an urgent message that General Kagame would see me immediately. We drove to an abandoned school compound an hour out of Kigali, which had become General Kagame's headquarters. When I entered the room, the general was standing at the window, looking into a clearing that must once have been a playground. What, he asked, had I wanted to say to him in person? I presented my request for a cross-line operation to move displaced persons to safety. He asked a few questions. Then he agreed to the mission and told me to arrange the details with his humanitarian team.

The general went on to address the issues raised in the fax from New York. The RPF, he assured me, had not laid any mines near the UN humanitarian office. Though security of UN premises was hardly his highest priority, he had now placed a guard near the site. With that the meeting was over.

'By the way,' he added, as I was leaving, 'I always thought that its own security was, and always will be, the UN's primary concern. Isn't that why the UN troops are in Kigali? To protect yourselves?'

In over thirty years of being involved in conflicts, I have met many leaders. General Kagame has to rank among the most focused and charismatic. There was no time lost with him on small talk. Everything was just matter of fact. I left and wrote my report to New York.

UN Security Council

In mid-June 1994, the Security Council adopted Resolution 925, which endorsed the deployment of a UN military force under a mandate expanded and extended until December 1994. Member states were urged to respond promptly to a request for resources. The council noted that the expanded military force would continue to operate only as long as it was needed to protect displaced civilians, refugees and humanitarian aid workers.

The Security Council noted that the hostilities were still continuing, that there was no ceasefire and that the violence affecting the population had not come to an end. In particular, there were reports of genocide. The resolution acknowledged that the systematic murder of civilians was occurring and that the perpetrators were acting with impunity.

The resolution stressed the importance of the Arusha Accords as a basis for a peaceful solution to the conflict in Rwanda, while reaffirming the territorial integrity and unity of the country.

By day seventy of the genocide, seven hundred and fifty thousand Tutsis and moderate Hutus had been killed.

21

Days 71–80: The UN Security Council Mobilizes

Father Vjeko Curic

Father Vjeko pondered at length over the slaughter of the church officials. It wasn't even as if the priests had been personally involved in killings. Was their murder truly the spontaneous act of unbalanced rebel soldiers? He had difficulty imagining that a force like the RPF, which had demonstrated such a level of discipline, could tolerate a rogue element. Or were the killings – horrifying thought – part of a systematic RPF strategy of revenge?

Now no longer able to travel to Bujumbura, Father Vjeko needed more aid for the camp in Kabgayi. He contacted me and we arranged to meet in Kigali. My first impression was of an exhausted and fragile man. But as soon as he started describing the desperate needs of the camp, I was struck instead by his passion, his urgency and his actual strength. I promised to marshal the UN agencies to provide the necessary relief.

He seemed in no hurry to leave, so we continued our conversation. I confessed that I found the situation in Rwanda difficult to understand. Father Vjeko didn't agree. Actually, he said, it was pretty simple. Hutus were killed for specific reasons, however specious: because they were seen as RPF sympathizers, because they had land that someone with authority coveted, or because of old jealousies or injustices. One Hutu, one reason for murder. But on the other hand – and here lay the horror of the situation – no reason was needed for the murder of individual Tutsis. Tutsis were killed simply because they had been born. Because they must, as a category, be wiped off the face of the earth.

As we were parting, I said to the father that I hoped he would be able to take a break soon. He smiled and shook his head. 'No,' he said, 'I will never again take a holiday. With everything I've seen of human nature, I'm sure that in idleness I would go mad.'

Charles Petrie

I arrived at the Sisters of Charity orphanage early one afternoon. The sister who greeted me was in a state of great agitation, her fingers trembling as she passed the beads of her rosary over them. The nun was perhaps no more than twenty-five. Sleepless nights showed under her eyes, and she struggled to control her nerves. They had come that morning, she said, her voice faltering. They had stood her against a wall and pointed their guns. She had been sure she would be murdered.

When I asked who 'they' were, I was told the Interahamwe. And why did they do that? Because they believed that the sisters were hiding the family of a Tutsi politician. If she did not hand over the family, the sister was told, all of the orphans would be killed.

I glanced around the compound, where clusters of children sat quietly engrossed in their own private games. 'And?' I asked. The sister dropped her voice to a whisper and admitted that the family sought by the Interahamwe did in fact live under the roof of the church.

What a mess, I thought. Throughout Kigali, civilians were trying to protect themselves from the Hutu extremist militia, and at the same time to avoid the fighting that raged between the government forces and the RPF. Everywhere there were scenes of utter despair: people huddled together in stadiums, churches and schools; victims forced into hopelessness by methodical and systematic violence; furtive glances everywhere, expressions filled with an emptiness anchored in fear. My visit to the orphanage was an attempt to follow up reports that the Interahamwe had become much more agitated, targeting areas previously left alone. The sister's plight now confirmed this.

The family of the Tutsi politician had to be moved. But how? The presence of an Interahamwe checkpoint less than one hundred metres from the orphanage's front gate would make things very difficult.

'How many children are there in the orphanage?' I asked the sister. One hundred and fifty was the answer. Most had come in themselves after the killings started, or had been found wandering in the town by the sisters.

I excused myself and walked further off into the walled courtyard where groups of children played silently in the mud, their knees and hands streaked with red clay. I thought through the options. Negotiating with the thugs at the barriers was a non-starter. Asking the UN to send a covered vehicle for the family might just save the family – but as the sister had pointed out, it would be a death sentence for the orphans and their guardians. I struggled to come up with other alternatives, but couldn't. Nothing could be done.

I rejoined the sister. I started to speak, wanting to explain how very sorry I was, that I really didn't know how to help, but the sister held up her hand. 'What you must do,' the sister said, 'is to pray that the Interahamwe do not find the family.' Again, I was about to speak, but the sister stopped me with the same gesture of the hand. 'Also pray,' she started again, 'that if they do, the children are not macheted. Pray that they are shot.' Dying under the blows of the machete was a slow and painful death, the sister explained, as if explanation was needed. She was willing to die, it was her calling, but she could not bear the thought of seeing her children macheted to death. She asked me to promise her that I would say a prayer.

For a long moment, neither of us spoke. I struggled to hold back tears. What right did I have to show weakness in the face of so much courage? I clasped the sister's hand, and promised I would pray.

*

Back at UNAMIR headquarters, I found General Dallaire officiating at the promotion of a Ghanaian officer who had just been raised to the rank of lieutenant colonel. When the ceremony was over I went up to the general. He listened with a solemn look on his face as I explained the terrible danger the orphanage faced. He was visibly upset. 'I'm really sorry,' he said. 'But there is not much that I can do.' The kind of operation needed to rescue the orphans wouldn't be allowed by headquarters in New York.

Suddenly he banged his fist down hard on the counter. There were three hundred men from the Ghanaian battalion currently twiddling their thumbs in Kampala, he said. If only he could get them out to Kigali, he could protect not only the sister and her children but all of the orphanages in the city. But the defeat in Somalia had made everyone nervous, and he knew full well that he wouldn't be allowed to have those men.

'Merde!' he exclaimed. I had never seen him so furious before.

'Somalia really fucked it up for everyone,' I said.

'Yes, it did,' the general agreed. 'But I'm not sure that I would put it in exactly those terms.'

*

A few days later, the Sisters of Charity orphanage was attacked. A number of the children were killed and many more badly wounded.* The attackers had relied on automatic weapons to do their dirty work. Most of the children were shot, execution style, or caught up in the crossfire, and died from bullet wounds.

I guess on this point, at least, there had been some form of an answer.

Captain Fiacre Mboki

Towards the second half of June, Fiacre was summoned to see his battalion commander. He congratulated Fiacre for his work. His platoon had been consistent in its performance, reaching positions on time, being conscientious in their searches and never requiring additional support. As a result, the upper command had decided that Fiacre was to be designated as the new liaison officer to the UN mission. Fiacre smiled. All the flowery praise, he was sure, had been designed to ensure that he couldn't refuse his new assignment. How many others had turned it down before him?

Fiacre was not thrilled, but he accepted it. His first encounter with the UN came as a surprise. He had expected the UN mission to occupy a well-equipped and comfortable headquarters, but instead found that the operational centre was nothing more than a hotel lobby partitioned with plywood. The UN officers were hardly the desk-bound pen pushers he had expected. They displayed a sense of purpose, exited the building with their

---

* I was never able to find out if the sister was among those killed.

197

flak jackets on and took their responsibilities seriously. And they were far more open and welcoming than he had anticipated. Even the liaison officer for the Rwandan government was friendly.

When we met, Fiacre seemed genuinely happy to see me again.

UN Security Council

The United Nations expected to complete the first phase of the UN military operation, the strengthening of the UN command in Kigali, in week one of July 1994. But the Security Council was informed by the secretary-general that a date couldn't be set for the deployment of the second phase because they were awaiting details of the resources required. In the circumstances, would the council consider an offer to undertake a multinational operation under French command?

There was heated discussion with representatives of the smaller countries who were now totally wary of France's intentions. But eventually, having no other option, they gave way.

The French proposal to send troops into Rwanda puzzled a number of Security Council members. Why, they wondered, had France suddenly become so solicitous? A number of the members started to suspect that France's real motivation was to halt the advance of the RPF and protect French protégés among the Hutu leadership. These suspicions could not be raised openly, but they found expression during the vote on the French draft resolution, from which Brazil, China, New Zealand, Nigeria and Pakistan abstained.

On 23 June 1994, Operation Turquoise was launched. The first element of special forces moved to the Zairian town of Goma, on the border with Rwanda. The 2,500 French troops were gathered from elite units within the Foreign Legion, marine infantry and parachute regiments. The Rwandan Patriotic Front expressed its strong opposition to the French move but announced that it would not seek confrontation with French forces.

By now, day eighty, more than eight hundred thousand Tutsis and moderate Hutus had been killed. Another fifty thousand were still to die before the genocide was finally brought to a halt.

22

Days 81–90: The International Community Responds

Kamana Rumbashi

By late June, it must have been clear to Rumbashi that the tide had definitely turned against the regime he was supporting. The possibility of succeeding to resolve the 'Tutsi problem'* was definitely over.

On the evening of 3 July, Rumbashi was told that the RPF would open the next morning an exit route out of Kigali for government forces. Those inside Kigali would only have three hours to leave the city.

Charles Petrie

A friend working at the US embassy in Nairobi informed me that President

---

* For want of a better term to describe an ideology that remains so difficult to understand.

THE TRIUMPH OF EVIL

Clinton's envoy for Africa, after travelling to South Africa, was scheduled to make a short stop in Nairobi. She offered to arrange for General Dallaire to brief the envoy. The general agreed to attend, making this the first time since the beginning of the conflict that he would have left his theatre of operation.

Having arrived in Nairobi the day before, I watched the Canadian C-130 turn off the main runway and coast towards the terminal. When it reached Gate 14, General Dallaire stepped off the plane and walked briskly towards me. He announced that he had exactly two hours before he needed to leave again. What had I prepared for him? I explained that the president's envoy was in the VIP lounge with a delegation of fifteen people. The delegation was interested in briefings on the situation in Kigali and in the rest of Rwanda.

The general instructed his aide-de-camp, a smart-looking Senegalese captain, to get the headquarters battle map of Rwanda from the plane, and to meet us in the VIP lounge. I trotted behind the general as he marched towards the meeting.

On entering the rundown lounge where the envoy waited, General Dallaire immediately set the tone. He thanked the US envoy for finding the time to see him and then announced that the pilot had given him only two hours on the ground if he wanted to make it back to Kigali that night.

The envoy skipped the courtesies and plunged straight into conversation. Did the general share the assessment that the situation in Rwanda was far worse than those in the US administration had imagined? In a briefing he had had earlier, the word genocide had been used. Was this accurate, in the general's view?

General Dallaire chuckled. 'I am only a soldier, not a politician,' he said. 'People can use any term they choose for what is happening in Rwanda.

But what I can say with certainty is that we are witnessing the systematic murder of innocent people every single day.'

The aide-de-camp spread out the map of Rwanda on the low table in the middle of the room, and the envoy and his delegation gathered round. General Dallaire explained that the fighting had reached a stalemate. The front line had cut the country in half. The RPF controlled the east of the country, the government held onto the western half, and Kigali was smack in the middle. His view was that General Kagame was planning to mount an attack on the southwestern part of Rwanda.

Why the south and not the north? asked the envoy. The general explained that most members of the government – including the assassinated president and his wife – came from the northwest. Their best troops were stationed there. If Kagame could secure the southwestern part of the country, he could then concentrate all his forces on the remaining portion. Furthermore, the south, which was heavily forested, provided the sort of hostile environment in which the RPF – who were expert guerrilla fighters – had an advantage. The government forces would be no match.

The offensive would start later in the month, Dallaire predicted. Not before. In the meantime, General Kagame aimed to capture Kigali. The government held the western part of the capital. Their only exit point was the road which led to Gitarama, where the government had relocated in early May. The rebels had been trying to close this exit.* When they succeeded, General Dallaire feared, there would be even more violence. In fact, there would be panic.

Knowing the Interahamwe as he now did, the general was convinced that they would try to kill every single Tutsi in the city – including the

---

* At the time of the briefing, the RPF had not yet completed the encirclement of Kigali nor offered a time window for government forces to escape.

fifty thousand displaced people under UN protection in the regroupment centres. He would not have enough troops to defend the centres if the Interahamwe attacked.

The envoy was horrified. 'When do you see this attack happening, General?' Possibly even this very night, the general responded, which was why he couldn't accept their kind invitation to remain overnight.

What did General Dallaire need to protect these centres? The general's answer was crystal clear: authorization from the Security Council for airlift capacity to transport to Kigali the Ghanaian battalion that was currently in Kampala, and ten more armoured personnel carriers. 'Is that all?' the envoy asked.

'Yes,' replied the general. He had only asked for what he knew could be provided by the US within forty-eight hours.

I whispered in General Dallaire's ear that Kigali airport had been shelled and the pilot suggested an immediate take-off. General Dallaire looked the envoy straight in the eye. 'Ambassador,' he said, 'you provide what I have asked for, nothing more, and tens of thousands of innocent lives will be saved.'

UN Security Council

On 1 July 1994, the council adopted Resolution 935, requesting the secretary-general to establish an impartial Commission of Experts. Their brief was to reach conclusions 'on the evidence of grave violations of international humanitarian law committed in the territory of Rwanda, including the evidence of possible acts of genocide'.

On 4 July 1994, the RPF captured Kigali. The genocide was for all intents and purposes over.

Only remaining to be murdered were a few thousand Tutsis who had been hiding in the areas that fell under French control. Believing they would be protected by the French forces, they unwisely left their hiding places and revealed themselves to their killers.

The genocide officially ended on 18 July 1994.
By that date, more than eight hundred thousand Tutsi and fifty thousand
moderate Hutu lives had been sacrificed to the genocide.

PART FIVE

THE SEARCH FOR JUSTICE

23

Evil Made Banal

I was not to know that the end of the genocide would be the beginning of a prolonged and bitter ordeal for me. I say this knowing full well that my petty troubles were nowhere on the scale of what took place in Rwanda.

Rwanda, in the first weeks after the genocide, was a country devastated. Vast parts of it were totally empty. The reason was simple. After the fall of Kigali, faced with increasing military pressure from the rebels, the genocidal government had retreated to the northwest. They then decided to deny the victorious rebels a population to govern. Months before, a quarter of a million people had been instructed to flee from the southeast of Rwanda into Tanzania. Now the leadership issued further instructions and another million and a half Rwandans crossed into Zaire almost overnight.

They left behind emptiness – and the stench of decaying bodies. In Kigali, the smell could strike at any time and in any place. It could be found in the garden of a house about to be rented. It could leap out at the unsuspecting as they passed a garbage heap, an abandoned well, or latrines.

The devastation permeated everyday conversations. Sometime in August, in habitual small talk, I mentioned to the tea and coffee 'assistant' that I had to go down to Butare the following day. Bernard, a boy barely into his teens, answered that he came from there. Great, I responded. Perhaps I could deliver a letter or a parcel to his family?

He gave me a bewildered look. 'They are dead,' he said. 'All except me.' Bernard took from his wallet a worn picture of a family gathering, possibly a wedding, and identified each murdered relative in turn.

I felt so callous, so stupid. In my subconsciousness the genocide was over. But for Bernard, it would remain forever present.

24

Not Aggression, but Self-defence?

If my clumsy comments to Bernard about his family showed how much I had still to learn, my encounters with French forces in the first weeks after the genocide were a foretaste of how much I did not realize I had to understand.

On 30 June, General Dallaire asked me to accompany him to Goma, in the then Zaire, to meet the newly established command of Operation Turquoise. When we got off the UN helicopter, there was a massive Antonov An-124 quadjet plane at the other end of the landing strip. The Antonov was so huge that the inside of its opened nose was like the entrance of a dark tunnel burrowing through an Alpine mountain. Out of it marched elements of the Foreign Legion's 13th Demi-Brigade, including the tall commanding officer whom I had encountered walking from the airport to the K4 roundabout in Mogadishu.

While the general went off to brief his French equivalent, I was taken to another tent, where I was told – and it was news to me – that a lieutenant colonel from the French marines was looking forward to my briefing. Lt.

Col. Chollet's welcome was perfunctory to say the least. He merely pointed me to a seat at the table in front of which had been unfolded a map of Rwanda, and instructed me to provide an assessment of the humanitarian situation. I attributed his brusqueness to the inability of a reserve officer to adapt to the sleepless nights that initial deployments demanded. I was wrong. What I did not know was that Lt. Col. Chollet had previously served in Rwanda as the head of French support to the Rwandan military. He had been a key advisor to former President Habyarimana and was even at one point the de facto head of the Rwandan armed forces.

I launched into my off-the-cuff briefing, without the sense of caution that this background information would have instilled in me. Very quickly, I met resistance. In fact, as soon as I uttered the word genocide, the lieutenant colonel cut me off, rejecting the term outright. His pushback was so strong that I thought it was best to ignore the outburst, forsake the use of the word, and just continue with my briefing.

I went on to explain, now with much greater care, the movements of populations within Rwanda, the positions of the front lines and the anticipated actions of the RPF. Lt. Col. Chollet's questions surprised me. He wanted to know in great detail about the situation in Kigali. Surely, I thought, the French weren't planning to go that far into the country? Chollet drew a line on the map that went north to south, cutting off a third of the country from the rest, and explained that it would initially be the new front line. *Initially?* How far into the country did the French intend to go? Were they actually seeking military confrontation with the RPF?

At lunch, I found myself seated next to Lt. Col. Chollet. Finding him in a far better mood, I broached again the subject of the genocide. Why, I asked, had he reacted so strongly to the use of the term?

He took a long look at me. He seemed to hesitate before launching into his explanation, an explanation underpinned by a great sense of certainty.

There had been not one but two genocides in Rwanda, he declared – the quick one and the slow one. The former Tutsi elite had conducted a slow genocide against the majority Hutu population that continued for decades, and resulted in hundreds of thousands of deaths. The quick genocide that I'd witnessed was the spontaneous reaction of an oppressed majority against the aggression mounted by their former masters. It was nothing other than legitimate self-defence.

I was astounded by the analysis, and even more so by the strength of the conviction that seemed to lie behind it. Did Chollet really think it possible that the Tutsis, who constituted less than 15 per cent of the population, would attempt to exterminate the other 85 per cent? Astounded or not, I decided it was best to remain silent.

General Dallaire, too, had his doubts about the true agenda of the French operation. On the helicopter ride back to Kigali, he charged me with a mission into the security zone that the French were planning to establish in Rwanda. The French would never accept one undertaken by UN military officers, but he felt confident that there would be little resistance to a humanitarian assessment.

*

When I returned to Goma less than a week later, with other humanitarian colleagues, Lt. Col. Chollet was much more welcoming. He explained that the French military had just established the Zone Turquoise, a 'safe humanitarian zone' put in place by Operation Turquoise covering the prefectures of Kibuye, Cyangugu and Gikongoro in southwest Rwanda. The mission I was leading would help underscore the humanitarian nature of France's intervention.

Chollet suggested that the mission enter Rwanda from the South Kivu town of Bukavu. Though it meant a one-day drive on the Zairian side of the edges of Lake Kivu, he said, it was safer than driving along the Rwandan edges of the lake that were not secured by the French. He was right.

We took the roundabout route, the road snaking up and down through dense forest and jungle, along dirt tracks that hugged the sides of hills and dipped into and out of ravines. Our view of the lake as the road peaked over the summits of the two mountain ranges was breathtaking. We reached the Orchid Hotel in Bukavu late that evening.

Early the next morning, we made an easy crossing of the border back into Rwanda. This had traditionally been a challenge, if not an extraordinary pain. It was now a casual formality. But almost as soon as we had crossed the border, we found ourselves swamped by rejoicing Hutu Rwandans. Everywhere signs were up welcoming the French. Signs with 'Vive la France' and 'Vive President Mitterrand' covered the walls and lampposts of Cyangugu. The Hutu population clearly felt that the French presence confirmed their blamelessness in the tragic events of the past hundred days. Ecstatic crowds came out of nowhere and ran towards us waving handmade French flags. Suspecting that this hysterical reception was probably only meant for French nationals, I suggested by radio to the other vehicles in our convoy that communication with the crowds be left to those who spoke French.

Our next destination, the Nyarushishi camp, was home to more than eighty thousand Tutsi refugees. The International Committee of the Red Cross (ICRC) coordinator of the camp told us that, with the arrival of the French, the security situation had improved. Attacks on the camp had ceased and it was easier to get relief supplies in.

Some hundred metres from the ICRC tent was the bivouac of a small group of French soldiers. From the insignia on their green berets, I recognized them as part of the same elite Foreign Legion 13th Demi-

Brigade that the Antonov An-124 had disgorged a couple of weeks before. Over a cup of coffee, I mentioned to the sergeant, in charge of the group, that I had seen his unit in the streets of Mogadishu. He smiled and said, yes, he had been part of that deployment.

The first thing that struck me in talking to the soldiers was how disoriented they were. They had been told, before their deployment, that they were being sent to stop a massacre of Hutus by Tutsi rebels. The problem was that they had yet to find any armed rebels. On the other hand, they had had to prevent roving bands of Hutu militia from attacking Tutsis. They had encountered so many bands of militia that they had been forced to set up positions all around the edges of the camp. As recently as the night before they had intercepted militia attempting to infiltrate the camp.

One of the soldiers asked me why things were the reverse of what they'd been told to expect. Could it be, he wondered, that the presence of French military was giving Hutus confidence, for the first time, to take revenge on Tutsis for the massacres of the last hundred days?

The soldiers were clearly astonished when I explained that most of the violence over the last three months had come from the Hutu side. The people in the camp were mainly Tutsis who had fled the killings that started after the downing of the presidential plane. They were alive thanks to the constant negotiating skills of the ICRC and the support of the very few within the Rwandan administration who had retained some level of humanity. The French soldiers around me fell silent. One of them muttered that they were too late. I shook my head. The important thing, I said, was that they were here now. They had helped bring this horror to an end.

Perhaps I would have answered differently if I had known then about the killings in Bisesero. This locality in the high mountains that plunged into Lake Kivu had become a centre of Tutsi resistance to the killings in the early days of the genocide. Though subjected to repeated attacks coordinated by Dr Clément Kayishema, a Hutu and the prefect of the region, the fifty thousand Tutsis who had found refuge there resisted. By the time the French established Zone Turquoise, in which jurisdiction Bisesero fell, only two thousand survivors remained. All of the women and children had been killed.

However, the victims' ordeal was not over. When, on 27 June, the survivors saw the first elements of the French contingent driving along the base of the mountains, they came out of hiding and asked for protection. The French officer in charge promised to return with more troops. But by emerging, the Tutsis had revealed their presence to the Interahamwe. When the French finally returned, three days later, only eight hundred of the two thousand remained. The rest had been hunted down and killed.

If the confusion of the French soldiers as to the true nature of the genocide had surprised me, I was even more startled when, seated on under-sized plastic chairs, I spoke to the French commander of the Gikongoro sector of Zone Turquoise. In his sector of responsibility, the colonel insisted, terrified populations were fleeing from the RPF-controlled parts of the country. They were seeking protection from the rebels, whom he called the 'Khmer noir'. The colonel could barely hide his contempt and hatred for the RPF.

At dinner that night, as we sat with the colonel and his entourage on one side of the tent, I saw a table at the other end filled with Rwandans. Some of the faces were familiar. I recognized them as Hutu officials of the Habyarimana regime whom I had seen in magazines and on the television during the genocide. When I asked who they were, the colonel said they were Rwandans whom the 'Khmer Noir' had targeted for assassination. These were the people that the French military force had come to protect.

On my return to Kigali, General Dallaire asked me what I thought the French were up to. I replied that in my view the French had come to rescue the government from total defeat. I told him how much it distressed me that the French government would continue to assist the killers, when so much was now known of what they had done.

General Dallaire smiled sadly, and muttered: 'Politics.'

25

Acts of Delusion

When on 14 July the genocidal leadership had instructed a million and a half people to move with it into Zaire, the rebels had been left in control of the whole of Rwanda. Well, almost all: the French still had control of Zone Turquoise in the southwest of the country. But the genocide was definitively over.

Aid agencies in Zaire found themselves struggling to cope with the biggest refugee influx since the Second World War. Not only was the international community challenged with the need to feed and shelter the numbers, but almost as soon as the refugees crossed into Zaire, cholera struck. In an extraordinary twist of fate, the lake beside which the town of Goma was located was one of the only water sources in the world capable of sustaining the choleric bacilli. The methane gas that Lake Kivu contained provided a natural habitat for the bacteria, and it was from this lake that the refugees drew their water. Within a very short while, the daily death toll among the refugee community reached well into the thousands. Ultimately, more than forty thousand people, this time mainly Hutus, died within a period of four weeks. I watched the tragedy unfold, fighting off the uncharitable thought that this might be seen as divine justice.

After receiving the report of the mission into the French protection zone, New York asked me to go to Goma for a fortnight to assist UN colleagues there in understanding the situation in which they now found themselves. When my helicopter landed in Goma, I was shocked by the extent to which the landscape had been transformed. The airport itself was overflowing with relief planes coming from all parts of the world. Goma had become a massive sprawl of makeshift tents set up by the aid community to shelter the millions who had crossed over. The French command centre was now nothing more than a cordoned-off speck.

Inside the arrival hall, a senior UN official was holding a press conference. I went up to him when it was over and introduced myself. He welcomed me having heard that I was being sent from Kigali. He invited me to travel with him to a humanitarian coordination meeting that was being held on the other side of the lake.

As we drove through the heavily congested town, we passed lines of bodies, victims of the epidemic, waiting to be collected. They had been wrapped in white shrouds and neatly placed at the sides of the road.

At one point, the official turned to me and asked me whether I had ever seen anything as bad as this. 'During the last three months inside Rwanda – was it as bad as this?' he asked. I was astounded by the question. Was it possible that this man had a wicked sense of humour?

'Have you ever seen anything like this?' he repeated.

'In Rwanda it was different,' I said slowly, pretending to search in my inner memories. 'The bodies weren't shrouded. They weren't conveniently placed on the side of the road. Bodies were everywhere. They lay two or three deep between church pews. The bodies of babies lay below the traces of the point of impact their heads had made against a wall.'

My fellow traveller was clearly unsettled, but he smiled at me and shook his head. Regretfully, he said, it was difficult to take care of everything.

The head of the UN refugee agency was chairing the meeting, which had already started when we arrived. I stood at the back and listened to a long discussion on logistics and supplies. At the end, the chair motioned to me to join him. He explained to the others that I had been inside Rwanda during the 'events' and invited me to make a few points. As concisely as I could, I explained how the situation had unfolded. The refugees had not spontaneously fled into Zaire, I explained. They had been instructed to flee by those who had commanded the killings – and who were now hiding among them, receiving humanitarian aid.

My intervention was met with total silence. There were no questions and the meeting was adjourned. When I tried to mingle, most of the crowd of aid workers avoided me. It was only when a stranger approached me and, agitated and angry, harangued me for being a Tutsi apologist that friends from before came and rescued me. They offered excuses for my behaviour. 'You are tired, Charles,' they said. 'You must have lost perspective. You should rest.'

I was dumbfounded by their reactions. I couldn't understand their refusal to face the truth. And then it dawned on me that they couldn't accept that they were aiding the perpetrators of a violence that the international community had allowed to rage unchecked. They wanted – perhaps needed – to remain convinced that their efforts were saving innocent victims. Clearly, they thought they were involved in something historic, as the unbridled excitement of the senior UN official at the airport had made so clear. And in many ways the cholera, a natural calamity that they could do something about, was even redemptive for them. The cholera swept away the guilt of the inaction that had defined the recent months.

I called the UN in Kigali that evening, and asked when I could get on the next helicopter ride back.*

---

*   For years I remained perplexed. How could the UN have been so complicit in protecting the killers in the camps? Slowly I came to realize that the UN had been set up. UNHCR was at the height of its glory. It had demonstrated its ability to mobilize and provide assistance in the former Yugoslavia. It was natural that it would be seen to do likewise in the camps of Goma. The only problem was that in the Balkans it was responsible for only one of the three components of the international intervention. NATO provided the political and military pieces of a complex response. In Zaire, UNHCR was alone, without any international political support, and it found itself unable to cope with it (though it never admitted as much).

26

Reconciliation, Not Justice?

In the final days of the genocide, when the Rwandan regime had moved to Zaire, it took with it all of the money contained in the Central Bank. In government and UN agency premises alike, everything had been removed or destroyed, though whether or not this had been done on government instructions wasn't clear. Rumour had it that, immediately after the fall of Kigali, General Kagame had given his men forty-eight hours to take what they wanted, before discipline was restored.

Whoever was responsible for the gutting of Kigali, ministers of the new government found themselves without desks, chairs or stationery. While hundreds of millions of dollars of humanitarian aid was being pumped into the camps in Zaire, almost nothing was allocated to rebuilding the capacity of the new administration in Kigali. The sight of many UN officials driving around in brand new Toyota Land Cruisers while government officials had to move about on foot was, to say the least, rather awkward.

My return coincided with the visit to Kigali of the UNDP regional director for Africa. From the moment she landed, she only had one word on her mind: reconciliation. She announced the convening of an international reconciliation conference in Nairobi at the end of the year. Perhaps the massive media attention other UN agencies were getting for their work in Zaire made UNDP eager to get into the act. To me it seemed absurd to push for reconciliation when there had been as of yet no proper acknowledgement of the genocide. And no attempt whatsoever to bring justice. It was then that the real significance of the Nuremberg trials hit me. The trials had brought a symbolic end to the Second World War. Through the process, the suffering of the victims had been recognized and the culpability of the perpetrators acknowledged. The trials had allowed Europe to 'move on'. But in Rwanda, both the victims and the perpetrators of the genocide had been denied this level of clarity.

Doggedly, the preparations for the reconciliation conference in Nairobi steamed ahead. A team of eager young bureaucrats and less energetic UNDP officials was dispatched from New York. I was sent to Nairobi to meet the UN representative who would lead the team that was to prepare the conference. He wore pink-tinted glasses. He literally looked at the world through rose-coloured spectacles. We didn't hit it off. When I questioned how one could expect a traumatized people to reconcile in the absence of justice, I was sent back to Kigali.

*

And where was Kamana Rumbashi in all of this? He had apparently disappeared. I raised the need for an investigation into the use of UNDP resources during the genocide with the regional director, but the suggestion was brushed aside. Rumbashi's name came up in discussions about individuals who were now seen to have been close to the former regime, but for the most part these were discussions conducted between international staff. The UN local staff who had survived the genocide remained silent.

27

Not Killers, but Victims?

In late October, I was invited to a conference held in Washington DC on the crisis in Rwanda. I had been ready to intervene, but I ended up saying nothing. Not a word. Almost from the very beginning of the conference, I was struck dumb by the strength of anti-Tutsi sentiment. I was particularly shocked by the aggressiveness of one human rights activist who had barely escaped being killed by the Interahamwe in the first days of the genocide. She, like others, acknowledged the horrors of those hundred days. But she made the same point as Lt. Col. Chollet of the French marines: that at least as many Hutus had been killed over the decades in Rwanda and Burundi as Tutsis had during the recent hundred days. Once again, I heard the theory of the double genocide, the quick one and the slow one.

What was being said took me so much by surprise that for a long while I thought I was mishearing. I was totally confused. How could a straightforward genocide be so misrepresented? Though some would like to argue that the Hutu majority had been severely oppressed over many years, to compare this with the horrific massacre of some eight hundred thousand Tutsis over a hundred days was like equating a slow intensity burn with a thermonuclear conflagration. In fact, was there any actual evidence to support the claims about numbers of Hutu deaths? And were the intentions the same? Was there any evidence that the objective of the minority Tutsis during their rule was actually the total elimination of the Hutus?

The discussion during the conference opening was not the worst of it. I found myself seated over lunch next to a senior US government official responsible for refugees. When I mentioned the presence of killers in the camps I was cut off in mid-sentence. You are absolutely wrong, I was told. There are no killers in the camps. There could not be. Being a refugee was a legal definition. As soon as an individual crossed a border, he or she became a refugee, and by the very definition of the term had an absolute right to assistance. The people I described as 'killers' in the camps were just victims in need of assistance, regardless of what they may have done before. Startled by this outburst, and by her anger, I remained silent.

The refusal to accept that what had happened in Rwanda was a particular form of violence extended beyond the boundaries of the conference. When I visited the newly opened Holocaust Museum in Washington, I found the images horrifyingly familiar. I even imagined I caught a whiff of the sickly sweet smell of death that I recognized from Kigali. I found a chance to speak to the museum's head of external relations. I told him how moved I had been by what I had seen, and how much it reminded me of what I had witnessed in Rwanda. Wouldn't it be possible, I asked, to set up a small exhibit recounting what the victims of the Rwandan genocide had just gone through? 'Impossible!' was the museum official's abrupt response. One could not equate the two events. The genocide that was the Holocaust was totally unique.

28

Reinventing the Past

Towards the end of the year, I decided to travel through all the camps along the Rwanda–Zaire border to see how the 'refugees' would celebrate their first Christmas in exile.

On the morning of my arrival in Goma, I searched for a priest whose name Father Vjeko had given me. When I found him, he was in a rush, as a high-level delegation headed by a cardinal from Rome was in town. The cardinal was about to officiate a mass and the priest invited me to join in. It was extremely well attended, with thousands of refugees present. The cardinal in his sermon talked about faith and fortitude, but there was little about forgiveness and reconciliation.

The next day I drove down to Bukavu, but this time taking the shorter route, along the Rwandan shores of Lake Kivu, through Kibuye. The astonishing beauty of the landscape, with the imposing mountains on the Zairian side, provided a dramatic counterpoint to the human tragedy that had now shifted into Zaire.

On the morning of Christmas Eve, I visited a camp managed by the Order of Malta where a distant cousin of mine was working. On arriving at the camp, I saw an old man whom I had talked to a number of times in Kigali during the genocide. As he had been the Rwandan ambassador to a number of countries, I had taken the habit of calling him 'Ambassador', and it clearly pleased him to have his past status acknowledged. I asked him about the genocide.

'What genocide?' he countered.

I had just driven through Kibuye, I explained, and had seen bodies that had yet to be buried. I had been told that of the one hundred and seven thousand Tutsis living in the prefecture before the genocide, only seven thousand had survived.

'All lies,' the ambassador declared. 'Everything you have been told is a lie.' He insisted on taking us to meet the prefect of Kibuye, Dr Clément Kayishema, who was in the camp, and who could tell me what had really happened there. Initially I hestitated, knowing too well the reputation of the prefect, but then curiosity got the better of me and I agreed.

My cousin, whom I had invited to accompany me, and I were then ushered into a dark storeroom behind the clinic and seated on a bench with our backs to the window. The prefect and his aides came in and sat down opposite us. The ambassador explained that I wanted to understand recent events in Kibuye.

I was granted permission to take notes. The prefect launched into a painfully long and detailed explanation of his every movement from the moment the president's plane had been shot down until his arrival in this camp. At the outset, he was nervous. He kept looking around, hesitating over his words, until he gained confidence in his tale. His explanation took more than three hours.

The prefect reported that soon after the president's plane was shot down, he and all the other prefects travelled to Kigali to meet with the

new interim government. They were told to try to ensure that their respective prefectures remained calm. However, he said, popular anger had already been unleashed and the journey back to Kibuye was, as he put it, a nightmare. The prefect was convinced that had it not been for the photocopies he carried of an official 'ordre de mission', he would not have made it back alive. Such, he said, was the spontaneous fury of the people.

The people were angry, the prefect explained, because they knew that the country was confronting a coup d'etat by the RPF and the Tutsis, who were determined to re-establish their former feudal domination. The Tutsis had prepared a genocide against the Hutus, which had backfired. It was common knowledge, he insisted, that in the Kibuye prefecture alone forty thousand armed Tutsis had attacked their Hutu neighbours. This was an astounding assertion, but more was to follow. Every Tutsi house, he insisted, had a deep hole dug in the centre of the living room, covered by planks and rugs, meant to hide the bodies of the Hutus they would kill. Everybody knew this.

I had difficulty keeping a look of disbelief off my face. 'If the Tutsis were conducting the massacres,' I asked, 'how then do you explain the very many bodies of Tutsi children?' With a perfectly straight face, the prefect replied: 'Murdered by the Tutsis themselves.' 'But why?' I asked. In order to gain the sympathy of the international community. And look, he said, sweeping his arm in our direction. It worked.

The prefect reported that on his long journey back from Kigali to Kibuye he passed by several collines where, yes, the killings of Tutsis had commenced. But we must be aware, he said, of the atrocities committed by Tutsis themselves. He had heard that the priest of Mugunda had been killed by his Tutsi parishioners. His deputy told him that the Tutsis had been found to have papers listing the names of people to be killed. Not surprising then, he said, that the popular anger among Hutus in his prefecture was so intense. It would have been impossible to stop the killings. He himself tried to save the Tutsis by directing them to the stadium and the Hom Saint Jean church. It wasn't his fault that security there was short-lived – the Hutu population had risen spontaneously and killed them all.*

As the conversation continued, I felt increasingly sick. I took copious notes, all the while wondering how I could avoid shaking the prefect's hand at the end. I couldn't bear the thought of wishing him a Merry Christmas. When the meeting finally finished, I stood up, thanked the prefect for his explanations and moved quickly. Holding pen in one hand and pad in the other, I bowed and walked out.

Outside, I thanked my cousin for his welcome and support. But I warned him that he was involved in something far darker than just providing relief to victims of a civil conflict. The numbers of killings in Rwanda was extraordinarily high, my cousin agreed, but why did I believe that this was so different from the ethnic violence that had for centuries characterized many parts of Africa?

I was so astounded by his response that I found myself unable to answer. Was he right? Was what had happened in Rwanda just like the random deaths in any other civil war? It would take a year for me even to start shaping an answer.

---

* An interesting outcome of this discussion is that I became the first person to make a deposition to two investigators of the ICTR on 8 and 12 September 1995. The court was convinced that the prefect would never be caught. So, in lieu of interviewing him, they wanted me to explain his logic as he had presented it to me.

29

Politics and Arrogance

As the beginning of 1995 started to unfold, I found it increasingly hard to relate to many of the new UN staff who appeared in the weeks after the end of the genocide. I was surrounded by keen colleagues who hadn't experienced Rwanda during the preceding months and who, to my mind, were too intent on 'moving the country forward'. It really bothered me that their genuine sense of responsibility for the present and the future seemed to obliterate a concern with the recent past. Even the new Rwandan authorities appeared determined to ensure that the past not impede their plans for the future. In those early days, the people who were quickly forgotten in all of this were the survivors, who could not simply 'move on'. No one seemed to understand that they could not be asked to leave the pain of the genocide behind.

The one new colleague with whom I felt an affinity was the new UN representative. He was Japanese. Having grown up near Hiroshima and the ashes of the atomic bomb, he understood trauma. We had a detailed discussion shortly after the UNDP reconciliation conference. He found it particularly unacceptable that, although everyone accepted that the new government was in desperate need of technical and financial assistance, the French government and the World Bank insisted on a reconciliation process as a precondition for the delivery of aid. We were in agreement: surely it was no solution to ask people immediately to 'reconcile' to pretend a coming together, a burying of past differences – without so much as an acknowledgement of the great suffering that had occurred.

In late January, I was offered a position in Gaza with the UN body responsible for supporting Palestinian refugees. I accepted it. Before leaving, I organized a dinner with those of the UN local staff who had survived the genocide. As I was one of the very few UN international officials left in Rwanda who had had any direct association with those hundred days, I wanted a chance to tell them how much I felt for what they had been through. (Self-centered, I suppose, to have organized a dinner to express the sadness *I* felt for *their* suffering, and yet I was totally sincere.) It was a profoundly sad dinner, haunted by the ghosts of Augustin and Florence and many, many others of their friends and colleagues.

A few days later, my UN colleagues organized a farewell dinner for me. At the end of it I was given a gift, and they insisted, against my wishes, that I should make a speech. I did. And I didn't hold back.

I announced that the greatest gift they could have given me was for 90 per cent of those present to resign. There was shocked silence in the room. Most of those present, I said, didn't understand how difficult it was to work in an organization where most conversations revolved around entitlements, promotions and salaries. How nauseating this was for the rest of us. But the 90 per cent should go also because their presence actually caused harm. As they drove around the country in brand new Land Cruisers, the struggling population came to believe that help was really on the way. And in anticipation of this help, people postponed difficult decisions. By the time those who had a right to expect assistance realized that it was not coming, they had forfeited a whole series of interim coping measures, and so they found themselves with far worse and much more painful choices to make.

My impromptu outburst was clapped. Perhaps everyone in the room imagined themselves to be part of the less blameworthy 10 per cent.[*]

---

[*] With hindsight, what arrogance on my part!

30

*Trauma as a Justification for Violence and Oppression**

In July, I joined the UN mission in Gaza. I found a small apartment not far from Norwegian Square, in Gaza City. Its most appealing aspect was a closed veranda with a partial sliding French window at waist height. I spent many late evenings looking out onto the street below, drinking a glass of wine, and just thinking.

At 5 a.m. on my first morning there, when the muezzin called the faithful to prayer, his voice was so loud that I was convinced he was next

---

*   This chapter has not been a particularly easy one to write. The question of the plight of the Palestinians is fraught with passions and wilful misunderstandings. Ultimately, it is included because of what it brings to the discussion on the nature of evil. In order to protect him, I have modified the name and function of the main protagonist. Though the content of our discussions is faithful to how they devolped, the circumstances in which they occurred have been slightly changed to tighten the pace. I am also indebted to Nasra Hassan for all of the insights she provided on the question of suicide bombers.

to me. The apartment was located next to one of the most radical mosques. Over time, I learned to resist his pre-dawn call, and to sleep peacefully through to a more respectable hour.

Strangely, it was in Gaza that I came fully to understand how, inescapably, the trauma of a people would be shouldered by future generations. I was officially assigned to work on the Palestinian issue, but when I first arrived I spent a significant amount of time in Israel trying to understand the politics of that country. I read all the books I could find on the plight of the Jewish people in Europe during the inter-war years, the build-up to the Holocaust, and the Holocaust itself. So keen was my interest that rumours started circulating among the Palestinian staff that I was an Israeli plant.

I'd known in an intellectual sense how a traumatic past could define the future of a people, but I was fascinated by the opportunity to actually observe this process in action. The Holocaust was everywhere. Almost daily, at least one article appeared in a major paper on an aspect of that horrific tragedy. The ghosts of the Holocaust impregnated the present-day politics of the country. It had become commonplace for the concern to protect sufferers and their descendants to be used to justify policies of oppression towards another people. Perversely, every subsequent generation seemed to be even more militant towards the Palestinians than its predecessor.

At least, that is how I understood the situation. At one point, when I was flying back to Europe from Tel Aviv, I was seated next to a survivor of the camps, a kind and considerate individual. We talked a bit about Rwanda. He told me not to let go of the truths that I had seen, but also not to let them destroy me. We went on to talk about life in Israel. In a very quiet voice, my neighbour explained that he didn't fully understand why the relations between the Jewish and Arab peoples had become so antagonistic. When he had first arrived from Auschwitz, he had been well received by his Arab neighbours. They had become friends. But now, such a thing was unthinkable.

Of course, I had come to the Middle East with Rwanda still very much on my mind. At some point, I even managed to get a meeting with the director of the Simon Wiesenthal Centre. I wanted to talk about possible assistance to Rwanda. I was very surprised to discover that the understanding of what had happened in Rwanda had evolved. The Centre was now involved in an effort to help Rwanda document its past, which included the building of a genocide memorial in Kigali.

But when the director asked me what I was doing in Jerusalem, I explained that I worked for the part of the UN that provided services for the Palestinian people in Gaza, the West Bank, Jordan, Syria and Lebanon. There was an awkward silence. It turned out that he was one of the settlers living on occupied Palestinian land. He didn't see it that way, and had very little good to say about the Palestinians. In his mind there seemed to be no connection between the two parts of the discussion we had just had. It was so strange.

A similar level of moral compartmentalization emerged in a discussion I had with a senior Israeli Ministry of Foreign Affairs official. When I mentioned I had been in Rwanda, the foreign affairs official immediately launched into an account of how fantastic his government's intervention had been in providing an emergency medical field hospital in the camps of Goma. When I tried, as tactfully as possible, to say that the medical intervention had ended up providing support to the killers rather than the victims our meeting was cut short.

*

Early on during my stay in Gaza, I discovered a hole-in-the-wall pizzeria, in a garage on the side of a secondary road. The garage, with an enlarged chimney breaking through its ceiling, housed the pizza oven, and a few standing tables on the sidewalk constituted the eating area. But it made the best pizza that I had ever tasted. I became a regular and became friendly with the owners – a Palestinian who had returned from the US and his American wife. They were full of optimism and gave off a great deal of positive energy. And it is there, one evening enjoying one of the pizzas, that I first met Osman Ahmed.

A recent graduate with an accountancy degree, Osman had started working with a local religious organization providing assistance to the most destitute Palestinians. The more he opened up about his work, the more I came to see how much more effective than the UN such local structures were in supporting the most vulnerable in Gaza. Getting to know Osman confirmed my suspicion that the UN was missing the mark.

The Gaza Strip is a very confined area: less than forty kilometres long and only fourteen kilometres at its widest point. When I was there, 30 per cent of the land mass was occupied by seven thousand Israeli settlers, who were protected by fifteen thousand soldiers. Close to two million Palestinians were crowded into the remaining two-thirds of the territory. Even when the situation was at its most stable, only about forty thousand Palestinian workers were allowed to cross into Israel on a daily basis to find work. Except through the UN Relief and Works Agency (UNRWA) – which had twenty thousand employees providing education, health and basic support to Palestinian refugees – there was virtually no regular employment in Gaza itself. Gaza was a prison, a pressure cooker of desperation waiting to explode. The international community was involved in trying to contain it.

The Oslo Accords, which had kicked off the peace process between Israel and the PLO, started to unravel while I was in Gaza, and its end brought the resumption of suicide bombings. More and more young people started finding a purpose to their existence by taking the lives of others in actions that ended their own. From 1994, when the first suicide bombing took place in the West Bank, to 1998, the year I left Gaza, thirty-seven human bombs exploded in shopping malls, on buses, at street corners, in cafés – wherever people congregated. I would be walking around Tel Aviv, hear an explosion not far off, and then wait for the wail of ambulance sirens. Another young person, possibly two, had gained martyrdom. Another ten or twenty Israelis were dead. Of course, the Israeli retaliation that followed resulted in many more additional deaths.

Through my conversations with Osman, I came to appreciate the depth of the desperation that existed in Gaza. But I couldn't accept this as justification for suicide bombings.

One day Osman set it out for me, the usual openness of his expression wiped away.

'You see the news, Charles. You know what's happening,' he said. 'Palestinians armed only with slingshots and stones are being mown down by rifles and missiles in confrontations with Israeli soldiers. Palestinians need greater pushback.'

It was Osman's hope that if human bombs could inflict real damage on Israel, then maybe the cost of the occupation to the Israelis would become unbearable.

'But the bomber dies too,' I argued. 'What does that accomplish? And what kind of fanatic would blow himself up in pursuit of some distant goal?'

Osman said that I needed to understand how much support the tactic had among the general population. He told me that the youths who were blowing themselves up were not, as imagined in the West, the rejects or delinquents of society. None were uneducated, desperately poor, simple-minded or depressed. Many were middle class and mainstream and, unless they were fugitives, held paying jobs. Two were even the sons of millionaires. More than half of them were refugees from what was, as he put it, now called Israel. All were deeply religious.

Over the subsequent months, suicide bombers became a regular topic of discussion whenever we met. I raised again and again the suffering of innocent victims that was caused by indiscriminate violence. Difficult to justify, Osman agreed. But I needed to understand the level of desperation that led to an unceasing stream of volunteers. The biggest problem was dealing with the overwhelming numbers who were clamouring to be sent. I thought it was another one of his jokes, but he insisted it was not. It struck me that Osman may have been more politically engaged than he had let on.

Osman was very convincing. But colleagues in the UN, who had been in the region for much longer, were sceptical. I was told that the candidates were brainwashed into believing that suicide bombing was an act sanctioned by the teachings of Islam. Nasra, a UN colleague, explained that the suicide-bombing candidates she had met all used the same phrases: 'the West is afraid of Islam', 'Allah has promised us ultimate success', 'it is in the Koran', 'Islamic Palestine will be liberated'. It sounded very much like a mantra. And every candidate she had talked to exhibited an unequivocal rage towards Israel. Over and over again, she would hear: the Israelis humiliate us, they occupy our land, they deny our history.

Friday 31 October was the last time I saw Osman. I had just come back from a short mission to the Democratic Republic of the Congo. Osman as always bombarded me with questions – about my mission, about the situation in the Congo, and how it felt to return to the Great Lakes region. And then we turned to our perennial topic.

Osman explained that the act of suicide bombing did not end with the explosion. After the bomber's death, his act became the subject of sermons in mosques. It was the inspiration for leaflets, posters, videos, demonstrations and coverage in the media. Aspiring martyrs performed mock re-enactments of the operation, using models of exploding cars and buses. Graffiti on walls praised the martyr's heroism. The families of the martyrs were given pride of place in the community.

Just as we were about to part, Osman said one last thing. Did I know, he asked, that the martyr was guaranteed a place in heaven? That he would find himself in the presence of Allah? And that on meeting the Prophet Muhammed, he could intercede for his loved ones so that they, too, could be saved from the agonies of hell? I never saw Osman again.[6]

*

The series of suicide bombings fuelled my deepening conviction that the place was completely messed up – a place where promising young men and women could see an acceptable future for themselves only through killing and violent self-destruction. So, when asked if I would be interested in taking up a position in the eastern part of the Democratic Republic of the Congo, I jumped at the opportunity. My interlocutor in New York said he understood that I wanted to get out of Gaza. The suicide bombings were just pure evil.

But were these acts purely evil? I was not so sure. The more I thought about it, the more it struck me that the term was not applicable. The violence in and around Gaza was linked to politics, economics and control. But there was no issue – as there had been in Rwanda – of one group wanting the total elimination of the other. Displacement and departure, yes; total elimination, no. Perhaps the act itself could be qualified as 'evil', but the intent was not necessarily so.

My experiences in Gaza made me think more deeply about the nature of evil. The suicide bombers each committed a brutal act in the bombing of innocent civilians, but I knew from my discussions with Osman that they might be complex individuals (like most individuals, perhaps). They were not evil men. Could it be that there was no such thing as evil? It was all just a question of context and interpretation? For example, the Palestinians did not see the act of suicide bombings as being dishonourable or vile; they simply represented a just form of retribution.

I remained obsessed with the issue of 'evil': was it something that actually existed? Intuitively I believed there had to be such a thing. After all, I had seen something like it unleashed in Rwanda. And then the beginning of an answer came to me as I read a speech made by Heinrich Himmler, the head of the SS, to ninety of his senior SS leaders at Posen, Poland, in October 1943. He started off by saying that he wanted to be completely open in this company about a very difficult subject. 'It should be discussed amongst us, and yet, nevertheless, we will never speak about it in public. I am talking about the "Jewish evacuation": the extermination of the Jewish people ... The tough decision to make this people disappear from the face of the earth.' Himmler was acknowledging – though only to a select few – that he knew perfectly well that the extermination of the Jews was beyond the pale.[7] And therein lies a proof that evil exists – the fact that one of the main perpetrators of the Holocaust could acknowledge that there were acts that went 'beyond the pale'.

Of course, it has never been as clear-cut in Rwanda. My many discussions there during and after the genocide demonstrated that its perpetrators were perfectly capable of portraying those vile acts not as beyond the pale, but as retribution for past wrongs, or as less dishonourable than preceding events. So even though there was, even is still today, no acknowledgement that evil was unleashed, the genocide remains the epitome of evil, in part because the motivation, the trigger, was so absolute. Father Vjeko expressed it succinctly: Tutsis were killed, not for money, not for gain, not in retaliation, but for the simple reason that they had been born.

31

The Roaming of the Beast

In August 1998, en route to eastern Congo, I made a brief stop in
Rwanda. Gromo had returned to Kigali a year before to run the UN's
humanitarian coordination body, and I was hugely pleased when he
turned up at the airport to greet me. On our way to his house, he told
me that he had organized that very evening an informal get-together of
friends.

In the course of a pleasant evening, I was updated on how much had
changed in Rwanda. Gromo explained that the vast majority of Hutu
refugees were now back, many forced to return in 1996 by a series of
attacks by the former RPF – now Rwandan military – on the refugee
camps. The action had been strongly condemned by an international
community that until then had been unable to stop the armed incursions
into the northwestern part of the country. Attempts to reintegrate
the returning refugees were working. In an effort to deal with ethnic
tensions, the new government refused any reference to ethnicity, aiming

instead to forge a new national identity. Local reconciliation mechanisms were being encouraged. But, Gromo explained, there was still a very long way to go, and the international community was becoming more and more impatient with the new government.

None of us knew what had happened to Rumbashi. Gromo recalled how, during the genocide, Rumbashi had allowed UN assets to be used by the killers. He referred to Rumbashi's possible involvement in the killings. But he had an even more troubling suspicion. It couldn't have been a mere coincidence, Gromo felt, that Florence and her family were murdered just hours before they were to be saved – and after New York headquarters had been informed of their imminent rescue. Gromo was emphatic that Rumbashi must have known – must have been informed – of the secret plan to rescue Florence.

At some point during the evening, the name of Father Vjeko came up. Gromo had last met him in the course of a boring diplomatic reception. The father was no longer that slim, energetic young man whose face had radiated kindness and good humour. He had put on weight and his features were almost frozen into a perpetual scowl. Had it not been for his collar, Gromo might never have recognized the priest.

Gromo recalled seeing Father Vjeko standing alone, a half-finished glass of beer in his hand. He seemed not to recognize Gromo, who reminded the priest that they had met a few times before and during the events of 1994. The priest shuddered at the mention of the genocide and asked Gromo when he had left. June, Gromo told him.

'June,' mused Father Vjeko. 'Well then, you saw much of what happened. None of them,' he declared, making a gesture that took in the crowd of foreigners, 'were there. Everyone wants to move on, forget the past and only think about the present and the future. Nobody cares. Even the government doesn't care. Worse still, they want us to bury what they did in the past.*

There was silence for a moment. All of us – Gromo, the other guests and I – thought of the tragic final state of that extraordinary man. Father Vjeko was killed in early January, Gromo reported. Nobody knows who was responsible. Maybe – let's hope not – the very people he had tried so desperately to help.

It was at this point that one of Gromo's guests spoke up. She was a survivor of the genocide and her voice was solemn. Father Vjeko's experience is like that of so many other white people, she pointed out. He came to Africa and gave of himself unselfishly. But he finished disappointed. She looked at us around the table and smiled. 'He had thought he could change things, but it wasn't so.'[8]

*

The next day, I left with a UN security officer for the border with the Democratic Republic of the Congo. I had been assigned to make initial contact with the new Congolese rebel movement. The UN believed that my former links with the Rwandan rebels, who now formed the government in Rwanda, would facilitate this contact since the RCD (the Rassemblement Congolais pour la Démocratie) was itself supported by the Rwandan government.

En route, I received by radio an urgent instruction: UN headquarters insisted that I was not to cross into the Congo. I was to meet the rebels on

---

* The Rwandan government is accused of having committed massive atrocities in 1996 in Zaire (DRC today), and especially in an area south of Kisangani where tens of thousands of refugees fleeing from the camps along the Rwandan–Zairian border were massacred. Some estimates have the overall number of killings as high as two hundred thousand.

Rwandan soil. But, not unexpectedly, when I made contact with the rebels, they categorically refused to come to me.

This impasse would have continued, had I not bumped into Fiacre on the poolside patio of the Serena Hotel. He was now in the uniform of a captain in the new Rwandan army. We greeted each other warmly. I explained my predicament. In a matter of hours, Fiacre arranged a covert crossing into the Congo for that evening. He assured me that no one would know. However, my UN security officer, who understandably didn't want to jeopardize his career, was adamantly against the idea. After a while, I made an excuse to retire early, agreeing with the security officer that we had no choice but to return to Kigali the next day.

Much later that night, without my security officer, I crossed over to meet the Congolese rebel commander, a lawyer called Maitre Mudumbe. We had a long discussion. He explained that when the genocidal leadership entered into what was then Zaire in July 1994, they brought with them the defeated Rwandan army and their Interahamwe associates. They settled in the Kivus, the region of eastern Congo that extended along the border with Rwanda and Burundi. This region was already in political turmoil. It had for three decades been under the dictatorship of President Mobutu Sese Seko. Anxious to counter the democratic wind that swept Africa in the early 1990s, Mobutu and his cronies triggered a number of ethnic conflicts throughout the country in the hope of demonstrating that he alone could establish control. The six months of fighting that ensued in North Kivu in mid-1993 resulted in an estimated ten thousand deaths and the forced displacement of up to a quarter of a million people. It was only after much effort and risk to themselves that local community elders were able to calm the populations down.

When the genocidal regime crossed from Rwanda into Zaire, they introduced the notion of extermination to an already receptive audience.

What's more, they brought with them the means to implement it. The Hutu extremist leadership from Rwanda found it easy to fan the flames of local hatred. The Interahamwe allied themselves with local Congolese Hutu and Mai Mai militias. They went further inland and systematically cleared the hills of all Tutsi inhabitants. They massacred tens of thousands, raped, and forced more than two hundred and fifty thousand to flee into Rwanda and Burundi. It was because of these mass killings, which had the support of the government in the DRC capital, Kinshasa, that the Congolese rebels had launched their offensive.

I listened sympathetically. Maitre Mudumbi was an articulate and kindly man, who didn't really fit the profile of a rebel commander. But I couldn't quite figure out the role of Kagame's Rwandan government in the Congolese rebel offensive. They were providing nothing more than logistical support, he assured me. It seemed hard to believe. I was unable to chase away the impression that the rebel movement could actually be little more than a front for Rwandan interests. Nevertheless, the suffering he described was real, and I couldn't help but feel that evil, having seen the light of day in Rwanda, had settled now in the eastern part of the Congo.

The next morning, I met the UN security officer for breakfast. I told him, that during the night, I had met the commander of the rebel movement. 'No!' he exclaimed. 'How could you have crossed the border against explicit instructions?' I replied that there was absolutely no reason for him or anyone else to believe that I had. Let's just stick to the facts, I suggested, and until there was some indication to the contrary, agree that the instructions from New York had been respected. The UN security officer didn't seem comfortable, but he finally agreed.

On arriving in Kigali, I wrote my report. I launched directly into the objectives of the rebel movement and my impressions of them. I kept the issue of where we had met vague. The report was well received in New York. There was great excitement at the prospect that, this time, the UN might engage with both sides of a civil conflict early on.

32

Tracking the Acceptance of Evil

I became responsible for initiating and maintaining contact with all of the rebel movements in the Democratic Republic of the Congo. My duties also took me to Kinshasa to engage with the UN presence there.

From the outset, my interactions with the heads of the UN agencies could only be described as rather hostile. In my first meeting with them, they seemed only concerned with whether I had crossed into the Congo to meet the rebels. Or had I met them on Rwandan soil? Initially I ignored the question, as it was a trap. If I'd met them in Rwanda, it would only confirm their belief that the rebels were merely proxies of the Rwandans; if, on the other hand, I had crossed into the Congo, I would have contravened their instructions. But they insisted and I continued to refuse to answer directly. Why were they asking the question rather than allowing us to focus on what could be done? I asked. And anyway, did they have any cause to believe I had contravened any instructions? They didn't! And, I added rather undiplomatically, I really didn't care what they believed. The meeting became heated. The UN representative intervened. He said that until there was proof that I'd crossed the border, he and the others would have to accept that I hadn't. Of course, he said, looking straight at me, were he to find out later that instructions had been violated, it would be a completely different matter. My relationship with the UN country team had started out on a very bad footing, and it never got better.

Thus began three years of engagement with the various Congolese rebel movements. As the war dragged on and opportunities for individual economic gains emerged, the number of rebel movements proliferated. For example, the RCD, the initial Congolese rebel movement, fractured into two. Only slightly later, another new movement emerged in the gold-rich area of Ituri to the north. And then the son of one of the wealthiest Congolese of the Mobutu regime, Jean-Pierre Bemba, decided to launch his own movement with its base in the dictator's former home village, Gbadolite.

I continued to be preoccupied with how the region was going to come to terms with the horrors of the genocide – with how this form of absolute violence was to be tamed. In late 1999, keen to gauge the extent to which the Church in the DRC was now encouraging reconciliation between the Tutsis and the Hutus, I met the Archbishop of South Kivu.

The discussion went well until I approached the subject of reconciliation. 'Impossible,' the archbishop said. He did not believe the Tutsis were of good faith. The Rwandans were in the Congo to annex the Kivus, he said, and the populations of the Kivus must force them to leave before 'all of us' were enslaved or killed. But there were Tutsis who had lived in the Congo for generations, I pointed out. 'What about them?' I asked.

The Tutsis are an exceptionally arrogant people, the archbishop insisted. Those who had lived in the Congo for generations didn't mix and refused to intermarry. They spoke their own language. They wanted their own churches. They all had to leave, the archbishop went on, whether they wished to or not. They had forfeited their right to live in the Congo, and could no longer remain in the Kivus.

When I turned the discussion to the events of April to July 1994 in Rwanda, I realized that the archbishop's views were not dissimilar to those of the prefect of Kibuye. I decided to play a game and to put to him the very words of the prefect. In order to allow the archbishop time to reflect and respond, I punctuated every one of the statements with a moment of silence.

According to the archbishop, I said, there had never been a genocide in Rwanda. This is correct, the archbishop affirmed. I could call it whatever I wanted, but the event was triggered and managed by the Tutsis themselves. It was widely known how well prepared they were – that, for example, prior to the 1994 war, every Tutsi family in Rwanda had dug a deep pit in their house in which the bodies of their neighbours were to be placed. As the conversation went on, the items of direct correlation with the prefect's thinking mounted horrifyingly.

Was there any room for hope? I asked the archbishop. There would only be real hope if the international community, especially the US and the UK, accepted that they had been duped by the Tutsis, and withdrew their support. It was because of the international community that the Tutsis were able to continue fighting this war. If it were not for the US and UK, the archbishop insisted, the story would have been finished well before now.

It was dark when I left the bishopric and began the long walk to the Orchid Hotel. Tears were flowing down my cheeks. I didn't know who I felt most sorry for: myself being thrust into the midst of so much hate, the archbishop, or the victims of this hate.

*

Over the course of my attempt to understand the dynamics in eastern Congo, it became clear that a group at particular risk were the Congolese Tutsis living in the highlands of South Kivu. The Banyamulenge, as they were called, had lived in eastern Congo since the mid-1800s, having fled there to escape extortionate taxation imposed by the then King of Ruanda. I had heard rumours that they were being besieged. When I mentioned the reports of the danger they were in to Congolese community leaders, they were rejected as pure fabrications. I needed to go and see for myself.

It was exactly then, while I was awaiting authorization for the Haut Plateau mission, that Rumbashi came back into the picture. I received an urgent message from Gromo in Angola, where he was to take up his appointment as head of the UN humanitarian coordination office. He had gone there for an initial visit to find housing and to get a better sense of what he would need to expect of the work. It was imperative, he said, that we meet up right away.

The news when he gave it to me was a shock. Gromo had found Rumbashi. His name was on the UN staff list in Luanda. Gromo made discreet enquiries and established that this was without doubt the same person. Rumbashi was on leave, he learned.

'So, what do we do?' he asked me. It was clear that we had to find a way to get Rumbashi out of Angola to a country where he could be arrested. But to accomplish this we needed to somehow get him onto the Interpol 'persons of interest' list. Gromo knew one of the investigators of the newly established International Criminal Tribunal for Rwanda (ICTR), Tony Greig, and thought that he could help. I offered to go see the UN representative in Kigali.

33

Indifference in Luanda

Having launched the two processes of collecting testimonies and finding a pretext to get Rumbashi out of Angola, I saw Gromo off at the airport a few days later. He appeared exhausted. Before heading to the departure gate, Gromo turned to me and asked: 'Are we really going to get this bastard?' The question and the emotions that underlay it floored me. I enveloped him in a bear hug. 'Yes,' I replied. 'Yes, we are.' I thought – I believed – I hoped – that what I said was true.

But it went badly almost from the beginning. When Gromo raised the allegations against Rumbashi with the UN representative in Angola, the latter refused to believe him. He countered that Rumbashi was a popular and professional member of staff. He asked Gromo for his proof. And when Gromo explained that this was in the process of being collected, the UN representative responded that he would take no action. When Gromo informed me of the conversation, we agreed that the only option was for him to send a confidential note to New York. I agreed to work with him on the brief. It would have to be carefully worded so as not to compromise 'due process', and I offered to clear it with the ICTR investigator.

I went to see the UN representative for Rwanda, to tell him of the cool reception that Gromo had received. He was disappointed, but not surprised. He had hoped that the gravity of the case would have pushed his counterpart in Luanda to overcome his customary caution. The UN representative didn't say much more about his colleague, but he didn't have to. I easily imagined his counterpart in Angola being like many senior UN officials I had met: a bureaucrat, without a political bone in his or her body, averse to confrontation, preferring to procrastinate over difficult decisions, hoping perhaps that time and unfolding events would take them for him or her. But this was not said.

The confidential note that Gromo sent New York was very strong. Tony had done a remarkable job redrafting Gromo's note, balancing what was known with what was alleged. I fretted over whether Gromo's straightforward, to-the-point style would get through to the New York bureaucrats, but decided in the end that the facts were so compelling that the tone would actually not matter. Gromo sent the 'strictly confidential' document to the under-secretary-general responsible for internal oversight. After that, there was nothing to do but wait.

The message went off on the Monday, and by Friday nothing had been heard. The UN representative for Rwanda offered to make enquiries. Later he reported that the message had created quite a stir in New York, but in the absence of an arrest warrant, the UN hesitated to be the first to take action. I was puzzled. Why would the UN need outside support to investigate events that were directly within its jurisdiction?

'Welcome to the UN,' he replied.

A few days later, Gromo called me. Ever since sending to New York the letter with allegations concerning Rumbashi, he had been doing his best to avoid him. But that morning, Rumbashi had sought Gromo out. He said he knew what Gromo had written to New York. He had received a copy of the report, and Gromo would regret ever having sent it.

I immediately conveyed to the under-secretary-general for humanitarian affairs in New York the concern I had for Gromo's safety, and in the process tried to produce the strongest endorsement possible of Gromo's démarche. I also asked how it was possible that a highly confidential report had been leaked to the one against whom the allegations had been made.

The reaction of the UN in New York was to transfer Gromo to East Timor. Nothing was done to investigate Rumbashi. Nor were any answers provided to the point of how a highly confidential report could find itself in the hands of the person in question. This raised again the uncomfortable question: what or who was the source of Rumbashi's support in New York?

34

The Mission to the Haut Plateau

As we entered the new millennium, the Rumbashi story seemed for all intents and purposes to be over. Rumbashi had disappeared, and the principal players were scattered: Gromo was in East Timor, Tony continued to work with the ICTR in Rwanda, and I was in the Congo.

I had obtained the green light to undertake a mission into the Haut Plateau. The news coming out of the area was so confused that the leadership in New York, not wanting to be caught off guard by a horrific situation, instructed the UN in Kinshasa to grant authorization.

None of us had dropped our interest in Rumbashi. By phone from East Timor, Gromo put me in touch with a journalist from the *Sunday Times* who was interested in doing an investigative piece on Kamana Rumbashi. Jon Swain was scheduled to travel to eastern DRC. Fortunately, we were able to meet the day before I took off for the Haut Plateau.

So, early the next morning, a Twin Otter deposited three of us (I was accompanied by two colleagues) on a level strip of grass between two impressive hills. The pilot said that he would return to pick us up in five days' time. In the meantime, he'd be on standby to take us out if we found ourselves in difficulty.

As the plane taxied away, I saw the leaders of the Banyamulenge community making their way down from one of the hills. They had been deputized to accompany the three of us during our stay. After a brief discussion, it was agreed that they would escort us to the largest market in the Haut Plateau, and to a camp for the internally displaced. Since there were no cars on the plateau, all would have to be done on foot.

We left early the following morning. It took four hours of walking to get to the market. The stalls were almost barren. Our guide explained that the Mai Mai and Interahamwe had encircled the Haut Plateau and that, of the thirty-five points of access, all except one had now been closed. The only way traders made it in was with heavily armed Banyamulenge fighters – and even then, the caravans were frequently ambushed.

A few days later, the three of us arrived at a settlement for the internally displaced. As was to be expected, their conditions were rudimentary. There were no aid agencies operating in the region, and whatever support there was came from other members of the community. Most of the displaced had been forced to flee from villages and settlements located on the edges of the plateau during the last six months. This recent increase in activity seemed to confirm that the hardcore extremist militias were preparing to mount an offensive.

The more we saw, the more we realized that the credibility of our reports required that we examine an area that had been recently attacked. This could provide decisive proof that the Banyamulenge were being massacred. But given the time it took to travel on foot, such a visit would necessitate extending our stay.

I called the pilot to ask that he delay our pickup by two days. That might not be a good idea, he said. He had been told that news of our visit to the Haut Plateau was out in Bukavu, and people there were upset. I turned to the two others and asked if we should still proceed. They both agreed. Two more days, I confirmed to the pilot.

It took us well over eight hours of hard walking to make it to the village, where all that remained were the charred traces of dwellings and a few carbonized poles. We rested briefly, gazing at the dramatic view of low-lying, jungle-covered hills from the edge of the plateau, before setting off to find the survivors of the attack. They had been moved to a shelter which was two hours' walk away. Those two hours were unfortunately in the opposite direction from the one we needed to take on our return.

The sun was starting to set when we reached the small group of survivors, consisting entirely of the elderly, women and children. An old man speaking for the community described how they had been attacked in the middle of the night. The community had placed spotters, so they had had sufficient warning to escape. The men of the settlement had brought the women, children and elderly here, and had then gone off to find a place to relocate.

Our guide came to say that a group of other elders from neighbouring areas would join us for a late night discussion. He was excited, explaining that some of them were legends to their communities and represented the history of their people. It would be a true honour to meet them.

A few hours later they arrived and the discussion that followed was fascinating in unexpected ways. Close to one in the morning, when the meeting was drawing to a close, I asked if any among them remembered an Argentinian-Cuban fighter who had tried to organize them in the 1960s. An old man remembered. Whatever had happened to him? he asked. Fate had not been very kind to Che Guevara, I replied. He had met his end in Bolivia.

After a few respectful nods, we called it a night. The three of us were given space in the mud-walled school hut that housed the survivors of the attack. In the very early hours of the morning, I was jolted out of a deep sleep by a series of sharp detonations I recognized as AK-47 rounds. At first, I couldn't remember where I was. The dank odour of the mud walls brought me to my senses, and then panic set in. I heard the rounds of another automatic weapon answer the initial bursts, but it was impossible to make out if these were part of a coordinated attack or the sound of others fighting back. The warning I had received from the pilot took on fresh importance. If the militia caught us, we would almost certainly be killed.

Outside, I heard dogs barking. The two-room hut was placed on top of a small barren hill, with a good two hundred metres of open ground separating it from low-lying brush. I looked around in the dark. There was only one door to the outside, and my cot was in the room that was furthest from that door. I could barely breathe for fear. As I fumbled for my flashlight, I felt the cold metal of the CQC-6 folding knife given to me by a US marine officer in Somalia seven years before. Its touch brought a sudden sense of peace. If all else failed, this would be my escape. Another series of shots were then followed by silence. The next morning, I was unable to find out what had happened.

*

The next day, while waiting for the plane to arrive, I finalized a report that was deliberately hard-hitting. I argued that attempts were being made to exterminate the Banyamulenge. Though plenty of public and private diplomatic pressure was being applied to the parties involved on 'front lines' of the war in the Congo, very little attention was paid to the war in the Kivus. It was essential that strong international pressure be applied to check the armed bands currently operating in South Kivu – and equally, on elements of civil society to cease to broadcast messages of ethnic violence and hatred.

I concluded the report with as scathing an indictment of the international community's indifference towards the suffering populations of the DRC as any UN bureaucrat could permit himself. In fact, I smiled as I wrote the last section pointing out the international community's 'absence of will to support those local forces attempting to counter the growth of cultures of hate and incitements to violence. It has to be hoped that this report will not one day be part of reference material provided to a future commission tasked with looking into why nothing had been done to prevent a new genocide.' I knew that the last statement would hit a mark.

I distributed a copy of my report far and wide within the UN system. I understand that it was even shared with some of the members of the UN Security Council. Later I learned that my report was used by the UN to pressure the Security Council into agreeing to deploy a UN peacekeeping force into the Democratic Republic of the Congo.

35

A First Indication of UN Indifference

Approximately, at the same time as I had been in the Haut Plateau, my already difficult relations with the UN country team in Kinshasa turned very sour. Following our intial encounter, there seemed to have been one member in particular of the UN country team who had it out for me. He could only seem to understand events in eastern DRC through the lens of an Israeli–Palestinian type conflict. On the occasions when we met in Kinshasa, I tried repeatedly to get him to understand the particularities of the conflict in the east. How the genocide in Rwanda had spilled over into the Kivus. Surely, he couldn't believe that the absolutist dynamics of the Holocaust were at play in the Middle East? But I was never able to get the individual to understand the dangers of amalgamating situations.

When I found out that he and other UN heads of agencies were openly dining with representatives of the former genocidal regime who were residing in Kinshasa, I asked the Office of the Human Rights Commissioner in Geneva to remind officials of their professional obligations and the correct conduct vis-à-vis suspects of crimes such as genocide. Whatever civilities had existed between us evaporated.

And then, one day in the course of a chance encounter on the Brussels airport transfer concourse with someone I knew from Kinshasa, I was told to be very careful. Claudine, who was running a Bonobo chimpanzee sanctuary near the capital, was on her way to a much-deserved holiday in the sun. The night before she had had dinner with one of the UN representatives in Kinshasa. Present at the dinner were government officials. In the course of the dinner, the UN official launched into a lengthy and impassioned tirade on how dangerous I was for the UN. According to the person, I was blatantly pro-Tutsi and trying to bias UN action in their favour. Claudine warned me that I needed to be very very careful when next travelling to Kinshasa. There were now people in Kinshasa who would want to do me no good.

The final straw was when, a few weeks after the Haut Plateau trip, I was told by one of the few good friends I had among the representatives of Bukavu civil society that a confidential report I had written for the UN in Kinshasa following my trip to the Haut Plateau had been given to a delegation of Bukavu civil society visiting Kinshasa. The report had included a fairly honest assessment of South Kivu civil society, and their misrepresentation of conditions in the Haut Plateau. I was told that my nemesis in Kinshasa had handed it over to them. It was clearly payback for the approach I had made to Geneva.

From that moment on, accusations started to circulate in eastern DRC that I was an agent of the British government pushing the Tutsi agenda. It wasn't a particularly enviable position to be in, given the nature and levels of violence in the Kivus. It became clear that the end to my time in the region was nearing.

Though at the time I was taken aback by how casually my UN colleagues seemed to view the genocide in Rwanda, I had yet to appreciate the extent to which the system would be able to relativize the significance of its inaction and lack of guilt.

36

The First Breakdown

Six months later, on 4 February 2001 to be precise, Jon Swain's article on Kamana Rumbashi appeared in the *Sunday Times*. It was a very faithful rendering of the many discussions he had had, and the evidence he had reviewed, with Gromo and me. As a result of the publicity, Rumbashi was found working for the UN in Kosovo – and this time, it was difficult for the UN to ignore the allegations against him. His contract was terminated. He was detained while the UN administrative authority of Kosovo reviewed an extradition request made by the Rwandan government.

After leaving the DRC, I was sent to Boston, to a centre that was part of the Fletcher School of Law and Diplomacy, to write a paper on criminal economies. It should have been a pleasant respite from the tensions and privations of the Congo. Instead, I came close to collapse. At night, I was gripped by feelings of extreme anguish – heart pounding with extraordinary force, chest constricting, shortness of breath. Every morning I woke up drained, debilitated. I desperately wanted the pain to stop.

Wine became my only comfort. A good bottle of Bordeaux bathed me in a comfortable torpor that lasted for a while, and I resorted more and more frequently to this means of escape. One particular night, I found myself in front of a 1982 Chateau Margaux – a grand cru classé that was fabulous but still young enough to be affordable. I poured myself a glass and inhaled the musty aroma. I picked up what I now called my 'suicide knife', the CQC-6, and played with it. I pressed the sharp blade onto my inner forearm, lifted it, and studied the indentation it left on my skin. I pressed down again and slid it back, just enough to see the open white flesh fill with a trickle of blood. I placed it on my wrist.

I've never figured out what stopped me from ending my misery with one definitive sweep of the blade. Instead, briefly, I saw a psychiatrist. The man who was recommended to me turned out to be a voyeur rather than a doctor. He was so taken by my stories that he didn't understand the need to draw some truths from me. He was also very expensive and, after five sessions, I found the courage to drop him.

*

While I was in Boston, I was selected by the UN to partake in a gruelling three-day assessment that was the route to becoming a UN representative. To my surprise, I did well and soon found myself going through briefings at UN headquarters to prepare me for the position of UN representative in Myanmar.

While in New York, in June 2003, I was contacted by a journalist, Greg Barker, who was working on what was to become an award-winning full-length documentary to mark the tenth anniversary of the Rwandan genocide. The interview took an entire day. Most of the time was spent in a dark, stuffy hotel room with a hot spotlight beaming on me. At one point, as the cameraman was fiddling with his equipment, Greg asked what I thought of Rumbashi's legal victory.

I was astounded. I had no idea what Greg was talking about. The last thing I had heard was that Rumbashi was still in a UN-run prison in Kosovo, and that the extradition process to Rwanda was going to take years of legal haggling. I was astonished to learn that Rumbashi was not only free, but that he had successfully sued the UN for unlawful dismissal. Greg told me that the UN administration for Kosovo had dropped the case against Rumbashi, on the basis that the Rwandan government had provided insufficient proof of his culpability to justify extraditing him to a country that still had the death penalty.

As soon as he had been released, Rumbashi had gone to Paris and secured his status as a political refugee.

Immediately after the interview, I contacted Gromo. He too knew nothing about the legal action or about Rumbashi's release. Gromo contacted Tony Greig, now back in New Zealand, who was particularly surprised, since when he had left Rwanda an indictment was in the final stages of preparation. It had looked very much like a straightforward case.

By chance, Fiacre arrived in New York that same week. He opened up about his own experiences before and during the genocide. Of course, we talked about our first encounter and the trek up to the church in the middle of nowhere – his attempt, he admitted, to rub my nose in the consequences of the UN's betrayal. But we also talked about Rumbashi. Fiacre knew about Rumbashi's alleged involvement in the genocide, but he hadn't realized that Gromo and I were so committed to bringing Rumbashi to account for his actions as a UN staff member during the genocide. He volunteered to help.

I tried to get more information on Rumbashi's case while I was in New York, but getting information out of the system was like pulling teeth.

There was something very strange about the case. It had been pursued in almost total secrecy. He had had access to high-powered lawyers; they were, it turned out, the same lawyers who were defending the then UN secretary-general, Kofi Annan, in the ongoing Iraq oil-for-food scandal. Someone within UNDP had arranged it for him. Tony then confirmed that, though, in his view, a very solid indictment against Rumbashi had been prepared, one year later it was not signed by the prosecutor. The whole story was totally bizarre.

Even though the spokesperson for the ICTR prosecutor Del Ponte stated that evidence 'for or against' Rumbashi had led prosecutors to question whether the case would hold up in court, Tony maintained that a number of his former colleagues on the prosecution team did not understand why the ICTR prosecutor had dismissed the indictment. Testimonies had been collected that implicated Rumbashi directly in the killings of UN staff members and others. It was obvious that there were other factors that had complicated the case. There had to be. For example, it was known that the Security Council was putting pressure on the ICTR to start winding down and concentrate on civilian, military and paramilitary leaders, to ignore minor actors.

Naturally, Rumbashi and his lawyers saw Del Ponte's order of dismissal as representing a vindication. In a statement sent to American RadioWorks via email, Rumbashi stated he had 'lost 10 years of my life and have been separated from my family solely on the grounds of unsubstantiated allegations'. He expressed 'deep pain related to the massacres which claimed lives of many thousands of innocent people in Rwanda since 1990 and which, unfortunately, has continued beyond the end of the 1994 genocide'. Rumbashi added that the truth about the killings should be uncovered and 'justice served'.

Fortunately, such an opportunity was now presented as the UN had appealed the Tribunal's ruling. But knowing the workings of international institutions as I did, I suspected that the allegations against Rumbashi would not be thoroughly investigated. So, even after taking up my position in Yangon, I corresponded every month for an entire year with the UNDP hierarchy in New York, insisting that Rumbashi must not be exonerated through an administrative procedure. The UN was appealing the judgment of unfair dismissal that had gone in Rumbashi's favour, and it had to do everything in its power to win its case – to demonstrate that Rumbashi's dismissal from the UN was more than justified.

I introduced my monthly emails and letters to New York with new bits of information that I had been able to gather with the help of Gromo and Tony. I directed the correspondence to the highest levels of UNDP, including the administrator. To my despair, there was total silence in return. Would the United Nations ever take action to bring Rumbashi to book?

*

In early 2004, I had been in Yangon for almost a year when Jane Perlez, a journalist from the *New York Times*, came to see me. She asked for my help with a story on Myanmar, and I agreed to guide her and even to provide on-the-record quotes – if in return she would consider the possibility of investigating and writing about the case of Rumbashi. Not only did she agree, but she also went to great lengths to track down all of the key players concerned with the case, including Rumbashi himself.

When I was told that the UNDP administrator denied having left my correspondences on the subject of Rumbashi unanswered, I was so enraged that I offered to go on the record. I accused the UN of justifying bureaucratic inertia with an attitude of 'don't tell me, I don't want to know'. This phrase became the concluding statement of the article that appeared on the third page of the weekend edition on Saturday, 7 August 2004. It was impossible to miss.

Jane Perlez's article amounted to a devastating indictment of the UN. I received numerous calls from New York, most of them at ungodly hours because of the time difference, and none of them congratulatory. The article triggered an internal investigation.

The investigators interviewed Gromo in Kigali, and one of them let slip that during the genocide Rumbashi was in regular contact with someone in New York. Gromo had surmised that this was how Rumbashi had had advance notice of the plan to rescue Florence. He was confirmed in his belief that Florence had been betrayed. I myself didn't know what to make of the allegation, but I was astonished when, a few months later – even though the UNDP administrator had committed from the outset to publish the executive summary of the findings – the work was finished and nothing was published. Once again, silence.

Friends in New York told me that, as a result of the article, I had made powerful enemies. I should be careful.

Some difficult projects seem to consist of two steps forward, one step back. The attempt to bring Rumbashi to justice was better described as one step forward, three steps back. In September 2004,* Rumbashi won his appeal. The administrative tribunal ruled that he had been unfairly dismissed from the UN, and doubled his award.

---

* The internal investigation was still ongoing.

37

The Loss of All Hope

Discovering that Rumbashi had not only succeeded in his legal action against the UN but won more than double the original compensation was devastating. For weeks after learning the news, I felt as if I was at the bottom of a deep dark well – and lacked any desire whatsoever to climb back out. I tried to keep myself busy – after all, I was still the UN representative for Myanmar, so I had a job to do – but I had lost conviction. My commitment to trying to make a difference in the world was seeping away.

As a first posting as UN representative, Myanmar was a real challenge. Myanmar (or Burma, as a number of Western advocacy groups and their governments continued to call the country) was in the midst of a humanitarian crisis. The country was occupied by a military force that exploited its national resources to sustain and enrich itself, and was totally uninterested in the wellbeing of the population. The minister of planning published double-digit GDP growth statistics every year, and yet almost three-quarters of the income of the average household was spent on food alone. The human rights violations were massive. They led in turn to the application by the international community of crippling sanctions that made aid efforts more difficult and ultimately only hurt the poor. The challenge for the UN in Myanmar was to engage effectively in the best interests of an oppressed and neglected people, with an authority considered a pariah by much of the international community, which in turn applied debilitating restrictions on what could be done.

My paralysis peaked during a critical moment in Myanmar. The Global Fund was an international financial instrument set up to combat three diseases: HIV/AIDS, tuberculosis and malaria. When the all-powerful US advocacy groups that had such a hold on UNDP funding learned that some of these funds were going to Myanmar, they were furious.* They threatened to pressure Congress to pull all its funding from UNDP unless the programme was terminated, even if closure meant that tens of thousands of desperately poor and sick people would be left in need of crucial medical assistance.

I was convinced that UNDP could win a confrontation with the advocacy groups. I had argued that UNDP had a position that was anchored in the principles of the UN Charter, and that if we stood firm,

---

* These groups were pushing for sanctions on Myanmar that would mean total economic isolation for the country. This tactic seemed to me a non-starter. How could a country that met 30 per cent of the energy needs of one neighbour, Thailand, and had geostrategic importance for another, China, be isolated? It would be impossible to enforce. Undeterred by the cost or logistics, the groups pushed through Congress a series of measures that prohibited the UN from any other than strictly necessary contacts with the regime. No money was to go to or flow through the government, and contacts had to be kept to a minimum. Failure to adhere to these conditions would lead to the cancellation of all US assistance to UNDP – not just the portion of the assistance that was being used by UNDP in Myanmar, but all of the funds given to the organization. Hundreds of millions of dollars were at stake. In my initial briefings in New York, I had been warned that as head of the UN in Myanmar I had to be very careful not to rock the boat.

the US administration would be embarrassed into calling off the threat. We were effectively in a game of chicken, and it all came down to who would blink first.

I was scheduled to have a crucial telephone conversation with the Asia bureau deputy director at UNDP in New York. It was going to be another one of those 'pivotal conversations' that would define the UN's stance. The deputy director was to meet a senior US Congressman the next day. The objective of the telephone conversation was to convince him to stand firm in his scheduled meeting with the senior Congressman – a meeting that could release the pressure on the Global Fund. He only had to show that the UN had a backbone.

The call came through at around 23h00 Yangon time. It quickly became clear that the deputy director wasn't buying the need to stand firm, and it would be an uphill struggle to advance my position. Just as I was about to start doing so, the thought hit me … *Why?* Why should I push for the UN to take a principled position on something like this, when it wouldn't on Rumbashi's case? I felt that my efforts were condemned in advance to fail. So instead of pushing, I capitulated, and agreed that the deputy director's concerns were legitimate. I proposed that he listen to what the Congressman had to say and find ways to accommodate his concerns. The deputy director seemed surprised by my response, and then relieved.

That night, as I was trying to fall asleep, I was suddenly aware of a stark emptiness inside me. Through the horrors of Sudan, Somalia, Rwanda and the Congo I had been shored up by a deep-rooted conviction of the possibility of justice, and an equally strong belief that in even the most desperate circumstances, an individual with resolve and courage could make a difference. But now the beliefs that had kept me going had crumbled. Suddenly it seemed to be all a sham.

I could picture my future in the UN system: I would just do what it took to survive in the organization; I wouldn't rock the boat. I wouldn't attempt to swim against the current.

This was a future the prospect of which I abhorred. Far better that I should resign from the UN.

Gromo seemed to have absorbed the blow of the verdict concerning Rumbashi better than I had. He persuaded me out of my intention to resign. Instead, he said, I should take special leave without pay. Use the time to think through my options. I realized that Gromo's proposal made sense. Why not take time to reflect – and also, it came to me, to write. To try to lay out the full implications of the UN's inaction.

*

I was granted six months' special leave without pay. A temporary replacement was found for me in Myanmar, and I went off to France to attempt to put my thoughts down on paper. I was barely a week into my special leave when one morning a newspaper article caught my attention. It was about a competition among young French lawyers as to who could make the best closing argument.

I was so taken by the winning summation, reproduced in the paper, that I contacted the lawyer. Augustin, who had just started a job in a prestigious law firm, was intrigued by the suggestion that he might investigate what more could be done in Rumbashi's case. The partners of his firm allowed him to work on the case pro bono. Within a short time, the young lawyer found that – given that genocide was considered a universal crime, and France had given itself domestic jurisdiction irrespective of where the crime took place – there was nothing hypothetically to stop anyone from taking Rumbashi to court in France.

So together, Augustin, Gromo and I, with the help of Tony, started to collect the necessary documents and obtained copies of the testimonies that could eventually serve to prepare a case. Through Fiacre, I managed to get the Rwandan general prosecutor to agree to share the information that his government held with Augustin when he travelled to Kigali.

The more we dug into the case, the more it became evident that Rumbashi must have received some form of support from within the organization. I received a version of the report of the internal investigation – entitled 'Review of the Handling of Mr. Kamana Rumbashi's Alleged Complicity in the Genocide in Rwanda in 1994' – that had followed the *New York Times* article. It had been severely redacted, making it blatantly obvious that there was something to hide. The edited version was in itself highly damning. The review concluded that UNDP had failed, at every step, to pursue the case of '*Kamana R*' with adequate rigour. The charges against him were never properly investigated, and he was never held accountable for his management of UN property and assets during the period he was in charge of the UNDP office in Kigali. On top of that, the review pointed out, UNDP had failed to provide its national staff with even minimum protection during the genocide, and the UN had never properly enquired into the murder of a large number of UN staff.

The report stated that ICTR investigators had interviewed a number of individuals who claimed that *Kamana R* had been training a militia while simultaneously serving with UNDP for two years prior to the genocide. One witness accused *Kamana R* of belonging to a group of four Hutu extremists located within the UN system. Rumours about these activities were known to the UN headquarters by 1996 – and yet in late 1996, *Kamana R* was recruited by the UN in Angola. No references were sought prior to this appointment.

The investigating team believed that *Kamana R* had the benefit of a support network that had continued to facilitate his travelling; worked towards his renewed recruitment by the UN system whether in Angola or Kosovo; and supported him financially to retain high-powered attorneys in Angola, France and the USA. There was strong circumstantial evidence tying *Kamana R* to acts of genocide. The ICTR told the investigators that they should have been called upon to testify on the UN's behalf in the case before the joint advisory board and the UN administrative tribunal, both of which Rumbashi won. They could not understand why this had not been requested.

Even more damning than the conclusions of this internal investigation were the copies of the witness statements that tied Rumbashi to more than thirty-two murders. We were well on the way to preparing a watertight submission.

Then in November 2006 – just before Augustin and a colleague were to go to Kigali to meet the Rwandan general prosecutor – the Rwandan government broke diplomatic ties with France. Overnight, access was lost to the direct testimony of witnesses still in Rwanda and to the files of the Rwandan government. Without these our efforts became incomplete.

Augustin returned to his firm. And I returned to my position as the UN representative in Myanmar. But two things had changed in me, once and for all. First, I came back with a new sense of purpose, and that purpose was to see justice done for the murdered UN colleagues. From now on I would live and breathe the case of Rumbashi. Secondly, and more importantly, I came back angry. Not the form of anger that burns and consumes, but rather the cold, heartless type. I came back to the UN profoundly despising the system that ran it.

38

Reviving the Rumbashi Case in New York

An extraordinary event in Myanmar in 2007 provided an unexpected opportunity, in a roundabout way, to revive Rumbashi's case. At exactly 12h00 on 22 September, I was stopped at a traffic light in Yangon, caught in one of those phenomenal monsoon downpours. Suddenly, out of the monastery to my right emerged a long line of monks. The eldest monk took the lead, carrying in outstretched arms an upside-down alms bowl. It was a proclamation: the order would no longer accept donations from the authorities.

Over the next few days, the scene was repeated throughout Yangon. Precisely at midday, the monks emerged from their monasteries and, at the same moment, the heavens unleashed torrential rains. The first day traffic stopped. People in the streets knelt in prayer. The days after, the population formed human chains alongside the procession to protect the monks from the wrath of the military.

The Saffron Revolution had been triggered by the military junta's cutting of fuel subsidies, which provoked dramatic price increases and resulted, among other things, in an overnight doubling of bus fares. The people of Myanmar, worn down by the poor management of the economy – the effects of which were compounded by years of international sanctions – were unable to absorb the economic shock. The monks, who depended on alms for their sustenance and were receiving a growing number of orphans in their monastic schools, knew how difficult life was for the majority of the population. They took to the streets to ask that, as they put it, 'the generals stop insulting the people'.

When, after a week or so, the political opposition joined the procession, the military was provided with the justification it needed. It ruled that the act of defiance was actually a political demonstration, and had to be crushed. But even that did not go as planned. When commanded to intervene, the Yangon military commander refused to instruct his troops to attack the monks. Eventually, another military unit had to be brought into Yangon to do the job, and they did it with great efficiency.

During those tense days in the city, I arranged meetings with as many of the junta leaders as I could. I insisted on the need to take the monks' message seriously – the same message the UN had been trying to get across to the military government for the past five years. The people were desperately poor, it was as simple as that. The military leadership listened, or at least the younger officers did.

An important deadline was approaching. On United Nations Day, 24 October, when the UN would be celebrating its anniversary, and the violence would doubtless still be in full swing, I would be expected to read out a set speech from the secretary-general. I requested UN headquarters in New York to include in the speech a specific reference to the situation in Myanmar. Impossible, I was told. It would set a precedent for other countries in turmoil.

I decided instead that I would transmit the secretary-general's message and then follow it with a second speech. The speech that my colleagues and I drafted said, basically, that the UN in Myanmar stood with the monks. Late one evening in the conference room, with a storm raging outside, I presented it to the other representatives of the UN system in Yangon and waited for their reaction. All agreed to stand by the text.

On 24 October, both speeches were read as planned. I write this as if it was an obvious and straightforward undertaking, but it wasn't. I was scared. I tried to rationalize my fear, asking myself whether this was really as tough as telling a Congolese warlord that his actions could land him in an international court. It didn't help. My knees were shaking as I read out the speech.

Naturally, the speech was not well received. The generals informed the secretary-general that I was a persona non grata and had to leave. The authorities in Myanmar would no longer have anything to do with me.

I had not informed the UN in New York beforehand that I was going to read the speech, knowing full well that they would not have sanctioned it. I accepted that I would be severely reprimanded for insubordination. Thinking it better to leave in style rather than to slink away, I sent the speech to the secretary-general's office in New York and copies to all UN staff throughout the world. To my great surprise, the first response I got was a ringing endorsement from one of the most respected high-level UNDP officials, Kathleen Cravero. In her message, also copied to all staff, she explained that this was probably one of the proudest moments of her UN career. She was proud to belong to an organization that had the courage to stand firm on its principles and in defence of the oppressed. Her message basically set the tone of the UN's response.

When I returned to New York, I found myself not fired but feted. Not by all, but at least by the new secretary-general, Ban Ki-moon, which was critical. I determined to use this newly acquired – and undoubtedly short-lived – celebrity to revisit the issue of Rumbashi. When I met with the secretary-general, I responded to his words of congratulation by telling him that, if he had appreciated the position I had taken on his behalf in Myanmar, I had an even better story to share. I managed in a few minutes to highlight the key elements of the Rumbashi case. The secretary-general was clearly not aware of the case. It must have have been considered closed by the time he took office. He appeared shocked. He asked one of his advisors present at the meeting to discuss this further with me and to propose options to deal with the case. I was elated. Action at last, and coming from the very top.

Then began a few months of what seemed like promising exchanges. Gromo, Tony Greig and I worked closely once again. We prepared briefing papers, each tailored to a specific concern that the previous one had raised. We provided copies of the witness statements. We argued the exceptionalism of Rumbashi's position as an individual entrusted with responsibilities derived from the UN Charter. Tony even ranked the solidity of the indictment as one of the strongest he had ever prepared. We did everything we could. But again, to no avail.

Sometime in the month of May, I met again the advisor tasked by the secretary-general to follow up on the case. He explained to me that the secretary-general had been deeply distressed by the case of Rumbashi. It disturbed the secretary-general greatly, he said, that the organization he had known as a beacon of hope during his youth in Korea should have failed so badly. It would never have happened, I was to be assured, on his watch. But what to do now? There seemed to be no possibility of reopening the UN disciplinary procedure. Raising the case of Rumbashi now, at the beginning of the secretary-general's term, would merely embarrass the UN. Why give visibility to an event that he himself would not have let happen? I was told in the nicest possible way that it was time to drop the case. I passed his message on to Gromo. We were disappointed but not devastated, having already trodden the path of defeat many times before.

What had really surprised me, though, was the fatalism of my colleagues in New York. The vast majority seemed to find it admirable that Gromo and I had brought up the case of Rumbashi, but I heard over and over again that these efforts were destined to fail. I found alarming the widespread acceptance among UN staff that the senior management of the United Nations would demonstrate such a lack of commitment to its founding principles. It was a cancer that was being allowed to grow unchecked in the system.

Others within the organization were far less charitable towards Gromo and me. We were accused of being racist. As two white people bringing extraordinary allegations against an African, we were suspect. One unguarded evening, a senior UNDP official went even further. Why are you pursuing Rumbashi, he asked me, when he himself could name at least three or four others who had committed similar acts? Our discussion became heated. Give me the names of the others, I said; I would be happy to go after them too. 'You probably would if they were Africans,' was his response. I told him he could believe what he wanted, but that was not the issue. The real issue for me was that such individuals should not be allowed to work for the UN.

I was still seething that evening. How I hated him, hated his guts. But then the thought struck me: *was I blameless?* Had I done enough? Could I have explained more clearly, detailed more fully, what was at stake? Rwanda was seen as a stain on the UN's reputation, but it was not recognized, as it should have been, as a fundamental failure of the United Nations to pursue its aims. I can't help but feel that the answer to that question is *yes*. But then again, why should it have been necessary for me to do so?

Why was the institution so blind? What was it that made my colleagues ignore so easily any sense of responsibility to uphold the basic values of the organization? To honour the memory of our colleagues killed? Why did no one else feel the same rage?

It pains me to have to admit that in some ways I too probably share responsibility for not enough having been done to secure justice for the UN staff Rumbashi is alleged to have murdered.

39

Kamana Rumbashi and the FDLR

If we had imagined that Kamana Rumbashi's alleged ferocious misdeeds ended here, we were quite wrong. Unbeknownst to all of us, while we were trying to get the UN to reopen the case of Rumbashi's possible involvement in the Rwandan genocide, he was actually very busy elsewhere. Sometime in 2004, Rumbashi joined Hutu extremist militia group the FDLR – the Forces Démocratiques de Libération du Rwanda. In 2007 he was named its executive secretary. While its military wing was based in the Democratic Republic of the Congo, the movement's political leadership was in Europe. Living in Paris, and with the stature of winning a legal case against the UN, Rumbashi became one of the leaders of the movement outside the DRC.

The armed FDLR was established in the DRC after the 1994 Rwandan genocide. It was made up of two branches of Hutu fighters: some five thousand ex-Rwandan ex-military and Interahamwe were based in North Kivu, and more than eleven thousand men based in South Kivu, with many of the officers being old former genocidaires. During Rumbashi's tenure with the FDLR, the two military branches were tasked with the killing of the local populations of eastern DRC to generate humanitarian catastrophes which in turn were leveraged by the political wing of the movement in Europe. A well-orchestrated international media campaign was designed to attempt to secure political concessions, including recognition, from European countries and the United States.

Kamana Rumbashi became the voice of the movement on the airwaves. The fighters on the ground would hear him on the BBC and Voice of America, as he interpreted the conflict and broadcast the objectives of the movement.

Hearing him, fighters in the DRC felt reassured that they had the support of France, Britain and the US. Rumbashi was adept at manipulating the international media. In the aftermath of FDLR operations against innocent men, women and children, he issued press releases, categorically denying any responsibility on the part of the group. At the same time, he engaged in international peace negotiations, shrewdly portraying the FDLR as a movement seeking peace and stability in the Kivus. Sadly, he turned out to be an expert at this.*

In 2009, the FDLR leadership decided to ratchet up its campaign. The new wave of attacks, which started in April, was even more systematic and ruthless. FDLR troops would swoop on a particular village and go from hut to hut, pillaging goods, burning homes, raping women and murdering inhabitants. Whole villages were destroyed. The intention was that the fleeing population would have nothing to return to once the FDLR had passed through.

The first village to be attacked was Mianga. The assault was launched at approximately 14h00 and lasted until the following morning. Close to a

---

* For example, claiming in a 2015 AFP interview, 'We in FDLR condemn all exactions against civilian populations, rapes, killings, abductions, etcetera, etcetera. We still condemn such kind of acts which are unjustified, which are unjust.'

hundred people were killed. A UN patrol in the area a few days later found that heads had been cut off, necks had been broken, skulls crushed, and eyes and ears pierced with knives. Nearby the patrol found the bodies of three women who had been raped multiple times.

The attacks multiplied and the atrocities spiralled. In the village of Busurungi, babies were pounded to death in wooden millet bowls. In a village called Ekingi, sixty civilians were killed and thirty troops from a nearby government base were subjected to prolonged torture, their limbs and private parts cut off while they were still alive.

In Manje in North Kivu, some of the villagers managed to flee, but the FDLR held a number of women in the forest for a week and raped them repeatedly.

In August, two hundred and fifty FDLR fighters attacked a larger village called Malembe, again in North Kivu, where they completely destroyed six hundred houses and savagely murdered three hundred occupants.

And so it went on. Attacks with machetes, bayonets, knives and clubs in the villages of Nyabuluze and Muhungu left eighteen people dead and twenty-seven wounded at first count. Later, more bodies were uncovered, and it was learned that many villagers had been abducted.

All of the areas that suffered ferocious attacks by the FDLR had something in common: they were rich in natural resources – in gold and diamonds, and in coltan, a mineral essential in the production of many electronic devices including mobile phones. These resources were smuggled abroad by the killers through Burundi, Rwanda and Uganda, and yielded a major source of income for the FDLR.

And Kamana Rumbashi, who was alleged to have been involved in the killing of thirty-two people in Rwanda while under the protective mantle of the United Nations, was now the vicious FDLR's representative in Europe.

40

Kamana Rumbashi Is Arrested

It was mid-2010. Gromo was managing a World Bank-funded UN project that aimed at the demobilization of combatants in the eastern DRC.* A great opportunity, the culmination of years of hard work, had arisen. A large group of FDLR fighters had gathered around the village of Minova and signalled their willingness to give themselves up. Gromo had flown in a UN helicopter to an isolated area in the middle of the Kivu jungle. He was excited at the prospect of concluding the rendition of a large number of fighters.

The discussion with the commander of the force went extremely smoothly. The only thing he asked for was to have his rank confirmed and to retire with a pension; for his men, he wanted that those who wished to integrate into the Rwandan army be allowed to so, while the others

---

*   Gromo died a few years ago. As a result, I have not been able to confirm the details of the story he shared with me, of which I took no notes, and which serves as the basis of what follows.

284

who wanted to go home be given permission to do so. Gromo thought it was possible to arrange, and they agreed to remain in radio contact and possibly meet again a few days later.

When Gromo returned to UN headquarters in Goma, he called New York with the exciting news of a potential victory, getting a few hundred FDLR fighters out of the jungle. Two days later, the agreement was reached. The World Bank allocated the funds necessary to the UN for a large-scale regroupment and initial screening operation. An area near the village of Minova was identified. The commander agreed to assemble his men in the coming week.

But the day before he was to fly out to the assembly area, Gromo received another call from the UN in New York. He was told that the operation had to be put on hold. A permanent representative on the Security Council – whom his contact refused to name – insisted that the security guarantees were insufficient. The representative had put forward an additional condition: before the fighters surrendered, the Kigali government must acknowledge the FDLR as a legitimate political party.

When Gromo asked what should be done with the fighters who had already started to collect near Minova, he was told that if they hadn't yet received UN-marked assistance, nothing.

*

Obviously, another series of conversations were taking place in the jungle near Minova. Initially the commander was told to temporarily halt the operation. And then, a week later, he was informed that the negotiations had collapsed and instructed to take his men back into the jungle.

The horror of what happened next is indescribable. It was getting late into the afternoon, and the women had just returned from the fields and forests, with bundles of wood for the fires. The fighters, under a curtain of darkness, positioned themselves around the village. Then began three days and three nights of savage rape and murder. When the FDLR fighters had spent their rage on the villagers, they returned to the jungle more soiled than when they had come out.

A UN position some three kilometres away knew and heard nothing of what was happening. They had no local liaison officers. They did not intervene.

Was Rumbashi involved in this story? Was this the call that, unbeknownst to him, was being monitored by German intelligence? Whatever the case, based on transcripts of such recordings, as well as on various depositions made by Gromo and others, the International Criminal Court prepared an arrest warrant. Finally, on 11 October 2010, Kamana Rumbashi was arrested.

41

Sri Lanka Review Panel

In June 2011, I was asked by the UN secretary-general to conduct an internal review of the UN's actions at the end of the Sri Lankan war, 2008–2009. I would lead a team of three charged with highlighting the dilemmas that the UN had faced in Sri Lanka, and proposing options to deal with such problems in the future.* I was promised unfettered access to all internal documents and, as well, to the unpublished results of an extensive inquiry already undertaken into abuses committed by both the Tamil Tigers and Sri Lankan government forces during the final phase of the conflict. I jumped at the opportunity.

I met the rest of the team – Lena from UNDP and Ben from the Office of the High Commissioner for Human Rights – in New York. We began to comb through the documentation that the preceding team had collected

---

* The details of what I discovered happened in Sri Lanka and the UN's response – or lack of it – is another story. But the parallels with Rwanda are all too glaring.

as well as piles of internal reports and communications. We drew up a long list of people to be interviewed for our inquiry, only to find that a few key senior UN officials designated by their agencies to be interviewed by the panel refused to participate. I called in favours from friends and was finally able to talk to a number of these officials. I discovered that they did not want to be sanctioned by their organization for having contributed to a report that they knew in advance would be damning. It was an extraordinary condemnation of the organization's management culture. So much for unfettered access. So much for the truth. Ultimately a few of the senior UN officials who had initially refused to be interviewed agreed to participate on the understanding that the discussions would be confidential.

The report that the team and I produced was, as predicted, devastating. We confirmed that in the last nine months of the war, as it entered its final stages, some seventy thousand civilians, crowded into an ever-smaller part of the Wanni pocket of northern Sri Lanka, died from sustained artillery shelling, illness and starvation. When the fighting ended, the survivors were forcibly interned in military-run camps outside the conflict area.

The report questioned the limited political involvement of the United Nations. Why had UN member states not formally considered the situation until after the war had ended? Why had UN agencies not provided adequate support to the populations trapped in the pocket? Once the pocket had been overrun, why had the UN allowed the survivors to be forced into internment camps against their free will?

We argued in the report that the UN's failings in Sri Lanka were systemic. There was a sustained reluctance among UN actors to stand up for the rights of the people they were mandated to protect when the body that threatened those rights was the state. The report recommended that the secretary-general should restate the vision of the UN, referring specifically to its charter and to the UN's responsibility towards the peoples of the world.

I was told by one of the secretary-general's advisors that this judgment on the organization was one of the most critical produced. It confronted the UN in the starkest way possible with its internal failings.

Of course, there were some in the United Nations who saw the report as nothing more than a hatchet job. I found myself having to deal with many uncomfortable meetings. In one, my interlocutor maintained that, even had the UN acted as the report prescribed, it would not necessarily have resulted in a different outcome. That was not the issue, I replied, and in any case one could not know the outcome of something that had not been done. But more importantly, the real issue was that the UN had not lived up to its obligations. Worse still, the UN had not lived up to what those who were being killed expected of the organization. It had failed. And it had failed badly.

Unlike the critics, the secretary-general, the same who had congratulated me on being kicked out of Myanmar, took the issue of the systemic failings of the organization seriously. He set up an interdepartmental body tasked with reviewing the recommendations of the report and defining options to implement them. It worked hard and, at the end of its deliberations, the secretary-general issued a statement to all staff.

In it, the secretary-general acknowledged the serious failures of the UN to take appropriate action in the case, most emblematically, of the 1994 Rwandan genocide, but also in Srebrenica in 1995, and in the final stages of armed conflict in Sri Lanka. The secretary-general acknowledged that there were limits to what the UN could do when a government abused its own people, shut out the UN, or when gridlock among states paralysed action. But he insisted that this was no excuse for not doing its utmost to meet its responsibilities – and above all, to adhere to the fundamentals of the United Nations Charter: the organization's commitment to act on behalf of 'we the peoples'; the commitment to reaffirm 'faith in fundamental human rights'; the commitment to establish conditions under which justice and respect for international law could be maintained.

When people faced grave risks, the statement said, they had a right to expect the UN to act – and it was against this benchmark that the UN's performance should be measured.

How incredible those words sounded. I cried as I read them. This was success. When later a plan of action, entitled 'Rights up Front', emerged from the secretary-general's commitment to place the protection of people at the heart of UN strategies and operational activities, I was exultant. This was not just a step forward, but a quantum leap.

42

Hope Unravels

Yes, I was exultant, until I learned of one massive step backwards. Against all expectation, Rumbashi had been released by the International Criminal Court in The Hague. In stunned disbelief, I heard the details of what had happened.

At the start of the hearings, the prosecution team had hit hard. In the opening statement, the prosecutor argued that Rumbashi was the chief propagandist of the FDLR, and as such had been responsible for making political capital out of FDLR crimes. He was accused of covering up for crimes committed by the FDLR, and in the process giving the cutthroat movement a veneer of legitimacy. Even though Rumbashi had not been in the Kivus, but in Paris, he bore direct responsibility for FDLR action on the ground, whether it was the large-scale destruction of property, the willful killing of civilians, or the rape and torture of the innocent. The prosecution concluded that Kamana Rumbashi should be charged with both war crimes and crimes against humanity.

As I listened to these details, I couldn't help but imagine Kamana Rumbashi in the courtroom. In his bespoke suit, his crisp white shirt and his professorial glasses, Rumbashi would have made a good impression. His whole demeanour would have cried out: *What, me? A killer? Never!*

Rumbashi must have thought it impossible that the French government would allow him to be extradited to The Hague, but the extent of the evidence against him seemed incontrovertible. And as the prosecution team detailed the evidence against him – the statements of numerous witnesses, the incriminating materials seized from his house, the communication intercepts by German authorities and the documents assembled by Human Rights Watch – I wondered how much anxiety it produced? How much fear the idea of spending a lengthy future in a miserable cell induced?

But then came the turn of Rumbashi's defence team. They whittled away at the prosecution's arguments. Far from being responsible for any of the attacks attributed to the FDLR, the well-resourced defence team insisted, Rumbashi could at most be blamed only for having shown sympathy for the FDLR's political goals – and that fell entirely within the scope of freedom of association. The prosecution had failed to prove Rumbashi's culpable involvement in a project designed to create a humanitarian catastrophe. It had failed to demonstrate that Rumbashi was intent on harming civilians, or that he had positive knowledge of any criminal intent on the part of the FDLR.

*

And when Kamana Rumbashi heard the pre-trial court decline to confirm the charges against him, he must have let out a long, long sigh of relief.

For me, on the other hand, the news of his release was like a punch in the gut. With gritted teeth, I delved into the reasons for the court's decision.

The records show that the tribunal questioned the strength of the evidence provided by the prosecution on four main points. First, that there was insufficient evidence that attacks on civilians were carried out by the FDLR. Second, where the involvement of the FDLR was proven, there was insufficient evidence to prove that the civilian population was the target of the attack; the deaths of civilians could equally have been collateral damage during operations aimed at the other armed groups, who might have located their troops among the civilian population. Third, the identification of the perpetrators by the victims was largely based on their language and therefore unreliable, since there were many different militias active in the DRC who spoke the language in question. Finally, even if some civilians did perish at the hands of FDLR soldiers, it had not been proven that those killings were authorized by the FDLR leadership. These reservations about the strength of the evidence against Rumbashi led two of the three judges to reach a majority decision that the charges against him should not be confirmed.

However, the presiding judge disagreed. In fact, she disagreed so strongly that she wrote a dissenting opinion stretching to sixty-five pages, which was read aloud in the court.

The presiding judge agreed with her colleagues that the evidence had been in some respects unsatisfactory. She condemned in no uncertain terms the preparation that had gone into the prosecution's case, pointing to significant oversights and mistakes. Errors, internal inconsistencies, omissions and duplications had weakened substantially what otherwise would have been an overwhelming case.

This court, 'meant to be a beacon for litigation in international criminal law ... had a right to expect higher standards', she stated.

The presiding judge concluded that, in spite of shortcomings in the case presented by the prosecution, the evidence, examined in its totality, confirmed the allegations against Kamana Rumbashi. But she had no alternative than to accept the majority decision.

The court adjourned. Kamana Rumbashi became the first individual to be released following indictment by the International Criminal Court.

*

And that is, basically, where this story ends. Kamana Rumbashi lives somewhere in Paris, and I continue to struggle to come to terms with the UN's failure to act.

Gromo Alex

Postscript: *Obsessively Refusing the Triumph of Evil*

Gromo died in 2013, while still in eastern Congo, managing the World Bank reintegration project. I feared initially that he had been poisoned, but it turned out to be cancer. I was asked to make a eulogy at his funeral. I wanted to say that, even though we had not found justice for our murdered colleagues, at least the UN had been forced to confront its internal failings through the evaluation of its (non-) performance in Sri Lanka. But as I wrote, and later uttered, those words, I realized that not enough had been done. It was then that I decided to take time off to write a book about the whole affair.

When I began the project, the world was a slightly saner place. Since then, various referendums and elections have revealed the darker sides of individual self-interest. The result is that I have felt increasingly uneasy at the thought of this story being potentially misunderstood as nothing more than that of a disgruntled former UN employee's attack on an international construct – multilateralism – which, however flawed in its implementation, is still needed.

And then one day, a way around my existential dilemma was suggested to me by a survivor of the genocide with whom I shared one of the earlier drafts of the manuscript. I had wanted to make sure that what I wrote was respectful of what she and others had gone through. To her it was. But the comment of hers that touched me the most was her belief that telling the story of the UN's failure was important, but better still would be to bring the accused to account for his crimes. She was right; she *is* right. Ultimately that has to be the purpose of this effort.

Following up on her suggestion, I got in touch with a lawyer who was supporting the attempt by a collective of survivors to bring cases against twenty-eight alleged genocidaires living in France. Since France is one of the countries that accepts the universality of the Genocide Convention, a case had been opened against Kamana Rumbashi.

Finding a publisher having the necessary courage to take on this project was initially difficult. The manuscript did not fit into accepted genres and addressing the potential liabilities involved was seen as too daunting. I ended up signing an agreement with Unbound. Having read the manuscript, they proposed the production of a mixed-media book, part text and part graphic novel. I thought it was a great idea, and by pure chance I found a fantastic young illustrator, Spike Zephaniah Stephenson.

What particularly appealed to me about the Unbound collaboration was linking such an original product to the social mobilization aspect of crowdfunding. It added an additional dimension to this effort. Thus, the crowdfunding campaign was launched on 7 April 2019 – on the day the genocide started in Rwanda twenty-five years earlier – and remained open for one hundred days, matching the time period that defined the duration of the horrors that engulfed Rwanda. Over the one hundred days, short excerpts of the book and illustrations were released on various social media platforms to convey a sense of how the horrific events unfolded. The amount needed was pledged in under fifty days.

The plan is now for a significant percentage of the revenues from the book (and the excess amounts raised through the crowdfunding campaign) to be given to the ongoing efforts in French courts to hold to account those living in France accused of having participated in the 1994 Rwandan genocide.

*

But what is it I am pursuing? What form of justice? Does the case in France even have a chance of actually being heard? After all, many witnesses have died, some continue to be intimidated, and others just want to move on. And what of the United Nations?

Rwanda itself is moving on and this became evident in the course of a visit I made to Kigali in April 2019. I had been invited by the Rwandan government to attend the twenty-fifth anniversary commemoration of the genocide against the Tutsis (as it is now officially called). I seized the opportunity offered, as I wanted to try to contact the surviving members of the families of killed UN colleagues.

What struck me about the commemoration was the youthful spirit that imbued it. It was much less a remembrance of a horrifically painful past than something much more forward-looking, with a celebration of what had been learned and achieved. More than 60 per cent of the Rwandan population is less than twenty-five years old, and close to 75 per cent are under thirty. Thus, the majority of the current Rwandan population has not lived through the horrific events of those hundred days.

And those family members of UN colleagues killed gave a similar message. While deeply appreciative of the fact that a former UN official would continue to seek justice for their loved ones, they were very sceptical of its success. They offered to help me, but it felt as if they had already come to terms with the tragedy and injustices they had suffered.

And the United Nations in all of this? Ultimately, the lessons from Sri Lanka were not internalized. Less than ten years later the exact same systemic deficiencies led to UN inaction in Myanmar. And in 2019 another internal investigation was conducted to review the UN's failure in the case of the Rohingya crisis, and the exact same conclusions were drawn. Clearly, there is still much work that needs to be done.

And this fact makes me angry, very angry. I cannot accept that those serving an institution created to uphold a higher ideal should refuse to understand the consequences of their inaction – the lives lost, the hopes shattered. Why don't they act, damn it? Are they too comfortable in their positions of supposed responsibility? Is that it? Is that how evil triumphs?

So, why this book? I return to Father Vjeko. It wants to serve as 'a torch in the middle of the darkness' that will inspire you to continue the fight, the fight against indifference, the fight for justice. It is essential to keep alive the hope that tomorrow can and will be better!

Acknowledgements

Writing this story has been a journey in itself. I discovered along the way that some of the certitudes I once held about my motivations and their consequences were not necessarily those I believed them to be. Doors were opened in my mind that then necessitated professional support, support to deal with what was contained behind them. I was forced to acknowledge how much more than I could have ever imagined my decisions and actions – however noble I had thought them to be – had hurt those I most loved. I cannot undo what has been done, nor erase the pain that I have caused. But I can apologize, and I do so from the bottom of my heart.

As mentioned at the outset, while this story is grounded in actual events, slight liberties have been taken in recounting some of what happened: time scales condensed on occasion and minor events merged for purposes of pace; certain events dramatized, though the essence unchanged; and when necessary names altered to protect the privacy of individuals.

In terms of acknowledgements, were this to have been an autobiography, there would be many I would have liked to recognize. But it is not, so I will limit myself to acknowledging the support I received in writing this tale. Michelle Spring was of remarkable support in transforming at time drudged UNese into more gripping prose. I am indebted to Lizzie Kaye for her imagination and support in turning this project into a mixed medium product. In that regard, I cannot express enough my admiration and respect for Spike and his work. It has been an extraordinary honour to have gotten to know Spike and to have worked with him. I am of course also grateful to Unbound, and specifically Katy Guest, for believing this project was worth supporting. Anna Simpson very ably guided me through the complicated process, and I am very grateful.

I can't honestly conclude these acknowledgements without mentioning my three sons – Arthur, Oliver and Victor. Their profound kindness and their love are among the things I treasure the most in my life. And of course, my wife, Jeannette. I wouldn't be here telling this story were it not for your love and support. You are an extraordinary partner, and I am eternally grateful for that day in Bujumbura, at the funeral of the twelve Burundian soldiers killed by a suicide bomber in Mogadishu, when we met again.

References

- Raymond Debelle, Diagnostic study of the Forces Démocratiques de Libération du Rwanda – a contextual description of the historical, political, and military dimensions of the FDLR, 1 October 2012.
- Rakiya Omaar, consultant to the Rwanda Demobilization and Reintegration Commission, 'The leadership of Rwandan armed groups abroad with a focus on the FDLR and RUD/URUNANA', December 2008.
- Nasra Hassan, 'An Arsenal of Believers: Talking to the "human bombs"', *New Yorker*, 19 November 2001.
- David Belton, *When the Hills Ask for Your Blood: A Personal Story of Genocide and Rwanda*, Doubleday, 2014.
- International Criminal Court document no. IIC-01/04-01/10, The Case of the Prosecutor V. Callixte Mbarushimana, 16 December 2011.
- Administrative Tribunal: Judgement No. 1192 – Case No. 1287, Mbarushimana Against the Secretary-General of the United Nations.
- 'The Review of the Handling of Callixte Mbarushimana's Alleged Complicity in the Genocide of Rwanda in 1994', Confidential Mission Report, UNDP New York, 12 November 2004.

- The series of papers arguing the need for the UN to investigate the allegations against the former UN official Callixte Mbarushimana.
- Fourteen witness statements collected by the investigators of the International Criminal Tribunal for Rwanda.
- Witness Statement, International Criminal Tribunal for the Prosecution of Persons Responsible for Genocide and Other Serious Violations of International Humanitarian Law Committed in the Territory of Rwanda, Between 1 January 1994 and 31 December 1994, UN Secretariat, New York, 8 and 12 September 1995.
- Report of the Secretary-General's Internal Review Panel of the United Nations Action in Sri Lanka.
- International Criminal Court document no. IIC-01/04-01/10, dated 16 December 2011.
- Secretary-General's message: 'Renewing our commitment to the peoples and purposes of the United Nations', 1 November 2013.

Bibliography

Rwanda-related Books

African Rights, *The Cycle of Conflict: The Democratic Republic of Congo – Which Way Out in the Kivus?*, African Rights, 2000

Belton, David, *When the Hills Ask for Your Blood: A Personal Story of Genocide and Rwanda*, Doubleday, 2014

Berry, John, and Pott Berry, Carol (eds), *Genocide in Rwanda: A Collective Memory*, Howard University Press, 1999

Dallaire, Roméo, *Shake Hands with The Devil: The Failure of Humanity in Rwanda*, Arrow Books, 2005

Des Forges, Alison, *Leave None to Tell the Story: Genocide in Rwanda*, Human Rights Watch, 1999

Johnson, Dominic; Schlindwein, Simone; and Schmolze, Bianca, *Les FDLR, histoire d'une milice rwandaise: des forêts du Kivu aux tribunaux de l'Allemagne*, Version française du livre original *Tatort Kongo – Prozess in Deutschland*, publié par Ch.Links Verlag, Berlin, Allemagne, 2019

Malagardis, Maria, *Sur la piste des tueurs rwandais*, Flammarion, 2012

Melvern, Linda, *A People Betrayed: The Role of the West in Rwanda's Genocide*, Zed Books, 2009

Prunier, Gérard, *The Rwanda Crisis: History of a Genocide*, Hurst & Company, 1995

Richburg, Keith, *Out of America: A Black Man Confronts Africa*, Basic Books, 1997

Rittner, Carol; Roth, John K.; and Whitworth, Wendy (eds), *Genocide in Rwanda: Complicity of the Churches?*, Paragon House, 2004

Saint-Exupéry, Patrick de, *Complices de l'Inavouable – La France au Rwanda*, Editions Les Arènes, 2009

Holocaust-related Books

Anonymous, *A Woman in Berlin*, Virago, 2005

Arendt, Hannah, *Eichmann in Jerusalem: A Report on the Banality of Evil*, Faber & Faber, 1963

Browning, Christopher, *Ordinary Men: Reserve Police Battalion 101 and the Final Solution in Poland*, Penguin Books, 2001

El-Hai, Jack, *The Nazi and the Psychiatrist: Hermann Goring, Dr Douglas M. Kelley, and a Fatal Meeting of Minds at the End of WWI*, Public Affairs, 2014

Hilberg, Raul, *The Destruction of the European Jews*, Holmes & Meier, 1985

Hilberg, Raul, *Perpetrators Victims Bystanders – The Jewish Catastrophe 1933–1945*, Aaron Asher Books, 1992

Sereny, Gitta, *Into That Darkness: An Examination of Conscience*, Pan Books, 1977

Notes

[1] Figure based on calculations by Gérard Prunier (*The Rwanda Crisis: History of a Genocide*) and Alison Des Forges (*Leave None to Tell the Story*). Subsequent estimates of deaths over ten-day periods are also based in large part on the same sources.

[2] Melvern, Linda, *A People Betrayed: The Role of the West in Rwanda's Genocide*, Zed Books, 2009, p. 152.

[3] All of the Security Council sections of Part Four benefited from the excellent piece written by Karel Kovanda, 'The Czech Republic on the UN Security Council: The Rwandan Genocide', *Genocide Studies and Prevention: An International Journal*: Vol. 5: Iss. 2: Article 7(2010).

[4] Based on the findings of the Belgian 'Parliamentary Commission of Inquiry Regarding the Events in Rwanda' (Belgian Senate Session of 1997–1998), a number of related articles, and discussions with UN military observers during the genocide.

5   Frank Smyth, 'French Guns, Rwandan Blood', *New York Times*, 14 April 1994.

6   I am indebted to discussions with Nasra Hassan at the time and her article, 'An Arsenal of Believers: Talking to the "human bombs"', *New Yorker*, 19 November 2001.

7   Raul Hilberg, *The Destruction of the European Jews*, Holmes & Meier, 1985, p. 245.

8   I am indebted to David Belton for the last quote in Father Vjeko's story. It captures so well a fundamental truth. The original version of the quote can be found on page 256 of *When the Hills Ask for Your Blood: A Personal Story of Genocide and Rwanda*.

Unbound is the world's first crowdfunding publisher, established in 2011.

We believe that wonderful things can happen when you clear a path for people who share a passion. That's why we've built a platform that brings together readers and authors to crowdfund books they believe in – and give fresh ideas that don't fit the traditional mould the chance they deserve.

This book is in your hands because readers made it possible. Everyone who pledged their support is listed below. Join them by visiting unbound.com and supporting a book today.

Super friends
Jacques Bandelier
Andreas Indregard and Nevena Pejic
Lili and Robert Levy
Nang San Hom Maung
Eugene Park

Supporters
Erik Aerts
Sally Ager-Harris
Shahzada Ahmad
Mohammed Ahmed
Gauthier Alain
Brittany Alex
Jeffrey Alex
Joel Alex
Matthew Alex
William Alex
Homayoun Alizadeh
Ashley Allen

Dea Andersen
Georges-Marc André
Antoine
Catherine Baber
Guy Patrick Banim
Yuval Bar-Zemer
Muriel Barras
Peter Bartu
Oliver Behn
Julie & Brian Belanger Williams
John Benson
Alban Biaussat
Jakub Bijak
Lisa Sara Bird
Georgina Blair
Julia Blaski
Chris Bleers
Peter Bouckaert
Yves Bourny
Genevieve Boutin
Mark Bowden

Edith Bowles
Susanne Josefine Brezina
Richard Bridle
Tania Brisby
Andrea Broggi
Beth Brundage Murphy
Fiona Burton
Mary Callahan
Vittorio Cammarota
Alastair Campbell
Julien Camugli
Margaret Carey
John P Carr
Antonella Caruso
Jorge Castilla
Joao Tomas Castro Melo
Alexandra Cerquone
Frank Chalk
Charles Choel
Lance Clark
Samuel Clendon
Christopher Collingridge
Yanthe Cornelissen
Kathleen Cravero-Kristoffersson
Sophie d'Andigné
Sophie Da Câmara Gomes
Jessica Davey
Emmanuelle de Foy
Guillaume De Luxembourg
Manuel de Rivera
Patrick de Saint-Exupery
Alexandra de Sousa
Luc de Waegh
Anki Dellnas
Cigdem Demirel
Tobias Denskus
Saurea Didry-Stancioff
Benjamin Dix
Mark Donoghue
Brigitte Doppler

Drawing Booth
Olivier Dubois
Claudia Duran Miranda
Sebastian Einsiedel
Brioney Euden
Geraint Evans
Patrick Evans
Catalina Fang
The Farnsworth and Shepel Family
Claire Felicie
Carla Ferstman
Andreas Fickers
Mary Flaherty
Laura Forest
Marc-Andre Franche
François
Polina Frolova
Rory Geoghegan
Karina Gerlach
Andrew Gilmour
Karsten Gjefle
Gold Dust
Susan Golombok
Marte Graff Jenssen
Stephen Gray
Frank Gruber
Katy Guest
Edouard Guillaud
Bertrand Guillemot
Antoine Haarman
Claudine Haenni
David Haeri
Mariann Ruud Hagen
Timothy Hancock
Richard Hands
Christopher Harland
Arzu Hatakoy
Anthony Heath
Zunetta Herbert
Dennis Hesseling

Richard Hill
Ben Holmes
Richard Horsey
Amanda Howland
Matt Huggins
C Hurd
Eiko Ikegaya
Bertrand Jacob
Jacques
Clare James
Mike James
Janani Jananayagam
Isobelle Jaques
Trond Jensen
Pat Johnson
Ron & Sandy Johnson
Stephen Johnson
Wouter Jurgens and Stephanie
    Bleeker
Andres Kabel
Walter Kaelin
Marcia Kammitsi
Tim Karr
Michel Noureddine Kassa
Friedrich Katschnig
Zachary Kaufman
Jay Kay
Valérie Kaye
Amy Keitzer Wallace
Susanne Kempel
Dan Kieran
Kees Kingma
Jenty Kirsch-Wood
Stephanie Kleine-Ahlbrandt
Stella Kloth
Knight of Words
Ingrid Koeck
Iryna Koval
Helene Kreysa
Mit Lahiri

Phil Lancaster
Laure
Philippe Lazzarini
Amra Lee
Emilia Leese
Rodney Lelah
Michael Lidauer
Biswajit Kumar Lima
Verena Linneweber
Aurélien LLorca
Kayleigh Long
Vince Losacco
Seve Loudon & Tori Griffiths
Michael Luffingham
Jose Miguel Vicente Luna
Jessica Lutz
Matthew Maguire
Jemilah Mahmood
Sarah Maitland-Jones
Ben Majekodunmi
Susana Malcorra
Suranga Mallawa
Steve Marshall
Elaine Martel
Martijn & Camila
Harriet Martin
Ian Martin
Dania Marzouki
Emma Mawdsley
Alexander Mayer-Rieckh
Marc Mazairac
Jerry McCann
Roisin McCarthy
Yvonne Carol McCombie
Megan McCormick
Bairbre Meade
Sandra Melone
Alessandra Menegon
Claire Messina
Leslie Miller-Bernal

John Mitchinson
Ingeborg Moa
Tracey Mohabir
Alastair Monk
Isabel Montgomery
Beth Moorsmith
Adrian Morrice
James O Morrice
Edward Mortimer
Nikolas Myint
Thant Myint-U
Lucia Nass
Carlo Navato
Polly Newall
Gary Nicol
Lous Nieuwenhof
Norah Niland
For Noah & Liam, nextgen 2 fight injustice
Peter Nordstrom
MP Nunan
Lee O'Brien
Thomas O'Neill
Stephen O'Malley
Poppy Ogier
Emily Oliver
Simona Opitz - Becker
Martin Orton
Yuko Osawa
Knut Ostby
Michael Payne
Julie Pereira
Charles Petrie
Cordelia Petrie
Fabienne Petrie
Lydwine Petrie
Nicholas Petrie
Wilfrid Petrie
Arthur Petrie & Pauline Raffaitin
Cynthia Petrigh

Joana Pierre Michel
Cedric Piralla
Philippe Poggianti
Justin Pollard
Isabell Poppelbaum
Renate Pors
Miriam Price
Suzy Price
Nick Pyle
Pascale Raffaitin
Jose Ravano
Moira Reddick
Joe Redston
Edward Rees
Janet Reibstein
John Renninger
Deb Roberts
Natalie Roberts
Kate Rodde
Gert Rosenthal
Iris Sao Siri Rupa
Einar Rystad
Laura Sandys
Tullio Santini
Aafke Schaapherder
Jonas Schier
Tim Paul Schroeder
Rachel Scott
Eric Sevrin
Ivan D. Shalev
Karen Shaw
Jake Sherman
Richard Siegler
Lena Sinha-Connolly
Marielouise & Rick Slettenhaar
Alan Smith
Rob K. Smith
Nigel Snoad
Lili Soh
Ashley South

Peter Spadafora
Michelle Spring
Morgan Staden
Wendy Staden
Emily Starling
Aksel Steen-Nilsen
Ginny Stein
Tony Stern
Christine Stones
Arber Stublla
Floor Swart
Julie M. Jacobsen Takahashi
Lex Takkenberg
Kari Tapiola
Heather Taylor-Nicholson
Annabel Taylor-Ross
Godert Tegelberg
Robert Templer
Frank Thomson
Cheyenne Thornton
Marina Throne-Holst
Liv Torres
Etienne Tremblay-Champagne
Darejan Tsurtsumia
Mike Turner
Koen Uitdehaag
Marijke Uitdehaag
Heli Uusikyla
Gerhard van 't Land

Laetitia van den Assum
Alexander van Geen
Eugène van Kemenade
Anne Vincent
Henriette von Kaltenborn
Selina Walker
Victoria Walker
Gareth Wall
Andrew Wallis
Kim Wallis
Joanna Warecka
Katy Webley
Ingo Wiederhofer
Elias Wieland
Pim Wientjes
Catherine Williamson
Keeley Wilson
Thin Lei Win
Yoma Winder
Bart Woelders
Jenni Wolfson
Leonard Wong
Andrea Woodhouse
Mari Yamashita
Simon Yazgi
Kirsten Young
Michele Young
Robin Young
Alexander Yushev